Why Do You Need This New Edition?

If you're wondering why you should buy this new edition of *Mosaics*, here are 8 good reasons!

1. **Brief Presentation:** If you've ever asked "why do we need a 700-page book when we only use half of it?" then *Mosaics: Reading and Writing Sentences* 4/e is for you! This new streamlined edition is a book you will use in its entirety.

2. **Key Skills and Application:** *Mosaics* teaches the key grammar skills common to all good academic writing, helping students apply the techniques and skills to their own writing now and for the rest of their lives.

3. **Straightforward:** *Mosaics* offers pure and succinct instruction, critical discussion, and clear-cut practice to enhance grammar skills.

4. **Grammar and Usage:** *Mosaics: Reading and Writing Sentences* 4/e encourages you to discover the many advantages that good grammar can bring to your writing. The book presents sentence basics and grammar usage in a very accessible, down-to-earth style that enables you to comprehend the various elements of grammar usage.

5. **Total Systematic Integration of MWL:** Pearson's MyWritingLab (www.mywritinglab.com) is now integrated <u>into the content rather than just into the format</u> of every chapter of the new edition. Starting with Chapter 1, references to MWL, or MWL Notes, are "teacher talk" that is directed to the students, giving them options for more instruction and practice along with tips on how to succeed with a particular skill or process.

6. **Strategic Instruction:** The "MyWriting Lab" prompts appear at strategic points within a given chapter, enabling students to truly benefit from the use of this dynamic online product.

7. **Learning Process & MWL:** The "MyWriting Lab" prompts consist of general directions that talk and walk students through the process of bringing MWL instruction and practice into the classroom and into the learning process.

8. **Transferability:** The exercises in this book all progress through the same cycle of identifying a grammar concept, applying your understanding of it to a piece of writing, and then using it in your own writing, enabling you to transfer these vital skills to your assignments in all your college courses.

PEARSON

If practice makes perfect, imagine what *better* practice can do...

MyWritingLab is an online learning system that provides better writing practice through progressive exercises. These exercises move students from literal comprehension to critical application to demonstration of their ability to write properly. With this better practice model, students develop the skills needed to become better writers!

When asked if they agreed with the following statements, here are how students responded:

97%
The MyWritingLab Student-user Satisfaction Level

"MyWritingLab helped me to improve my writing." **89%**

"MyWritingLab was fairly easy to use." **90%**

"MyWritingLab helped make me feel more confident about my writing ability." **83%**

"MyWritingLab helped me to better prepare for my next writing course." **86%**

"MyWritingLab helped me get a better grade." **82%**

"I wish I had a program like MyWritingLab in some of my other courses." **78%**

"I would recommend my instructor continue using MyWritingLab." **85%**

Student Success Story

"The first few weeks of my English class, my grades were at approximately 78%. Then I was introduced to MyWritingLab. I couldn't believe the increase in my test scores. My test scores had jumped from that low score of 78 all the way up to 100% (and every now and then a 99)."

—Exetta Windfield, *College of the Sequoias* (MyWritingLab student user)

TO PURCHASE AN ACCESS CODE, GO TO
WWW.MYWRITINGLAB.COM

Fourth Edition

MOSAICS

READING AND WRITING SENTENCES

Fourth Edition

MOSAICS
READING AND WRITING SENTENCES

KIM FLACHMANN
California State University, Bakersfield

Prentice Hall
Boston   Columbus   Indianapolis   New York   San Francisco   Upper Saddle River
Amsterdam   Cape Town   Dubai   London   Madrid   Milan   Munich   Paris   Montréal   Toronto
Delhi   Mexico City   São Paulo   Sydney   Hong Kong   Seoul   Singapore   Taipei   Tokyo

Senior Acquisitions Editor: *Matthew Wright*
Editorial Assistant: *Samantha Neary*
Managing Editor: *Linda Mihatov Behrens*
Associate Managing Editor: *Bayani*
   Mendoza de Leon
Manufacturing Buyer: *Mary Ann Gloriande*
Marketing Director: *Megan Galvin*
Marketing Manager: *Tom DeMarco*

Media Editor: *Stefanie Liebman*
Senior Supplements Editor: *Donna Campion*
Art Director: *Anne Bonanno Nieglos*
Text Permission Specialist: *Wesley Hall*
Project Coordination, Text Design, and Electronic
   Page Makeup: *Integra*
Cover Designer: *Ximena Tamvakopoulos*
Cover Image: *mihau/iStockphoto*

Library of Congress Cataloging-in-Publication Data

Flachmann, Kim.
  [Mosaics, focusing on sentences in context]
  Mosaics : reading and writing sentences/Kim Flachmann.—4th ed.
     p. cm.—87 (Mosaics)
  Includes index.
  ISBN-13: 978-0-205-82435-9
  ISBN-10: 0-205-82435-8
  1. English language—Sentences—Problems, exercises, etc.
  2. English language—Rhetoric—Problems, exercises, etc.   I. Title.   II. Series.
PE1441.F48 2011
808'.042076—dc22

                                             2010049887

For
Laura

1 2 3 4 5 6 7 8 9 10—DOC—14 13 12 11

Prentice Hall
is an imprint of

www.pearsonhighered.com

ISBN-13: 978-0-205-82435-9
ISBN-10:   0-205-82435-8

BRIEF CONTENTS

CONTENTS

PREFACE

Experience tells us that students have the best chance of succeeding in college if they learn how to respond productively to the varying academic demands made on them throughout the curriculum. One extremely important part of this process is being able to analyze ideas and respond critically in standard written English. *Mosaics: Reading and Writing Sentences* is the first in a series of four books that teach the basic skills essential to all good academic writing. This series illustrates how the companion skills of reading and writing are parts of a larger, interrelated process that moves back and forth through the tasks of prereading and reading, prewriting and writing, and revising and editing. This particular book focuses on how the conventions of grammar and usage work as an integral part of this process.

OVERALL GOAL

Ultimately, each book in the *Mosaics* series portrays writing as a way of thinking and processing information. One by one, these books encourage students to discover how the "mosaics" of their own reading and writing processes work together to form a coherent whole. By demonstrating the interrelationship among thinking, reading, and writing on progressively more complex levels, these books promise to help prepare students for success in college throughout the curriculum.

THE *MOSAICS* SERIES

The four books of the *Mosaics* series each have a different emphasis: *Reading and Writing Sentences*, *Reading and Writing Paragraphs*, *Reading and Writing Essays*, and *The Mosaics Reader*. As the titles imply, the first book highlights grammar, usage, and sentence structure; the second paragraph development; the third the composition of essays; and the fourth reading selections.

This entire four-book series is based on the following fundamental assumptions:

- Students build confidence in their ability to read and write by reading and writing.
- Students learn best from discovery and experimentation rather than from instruction and abstract discussions.
- Students profit from studying both professional and student writing.
- Students need to discover their personal reading and writing processes.
- Students learn both individually and collaboratively.
- Students benefit most from assignments that actually integrate reading and writing.
- Students learn how to revise by following clear guidelines.
- Students learn grammar and usage rules by editing their own writing.
- Students must be able to transfer their writing skills to all their college courses.
- Students must think critically/analytically to succeed in college.

UNIQUE FEATURES OF THIS BOOK

Several other unique and exciting features define this book.

It connects reading and writing in creative ways throughout the book.

- Each chapter starts with a self-test for students to diagnose their strengths and weaknesses in a particular area.
- Each chapter looks at a specific grammar element from different perspectives.
- Several Review Boxes are provided in each chapter for easy reference.
- The exercises in each chapter move students systematically from identifying a rule to filling in the blank to writing their own sentences.
- Each chapter ends with a peer-editing and a self-editing exercise.
- The book offers logs for students to keep track of their own grammar and spelling errors.

The innovative lessons of Pearson's MyWritingLab (www.MyWritingLab.com) are strategically integrated into the content of every chapter in the book:

- MyWritingLab Hints appear at strategic points within each chapter, thereby enabling students to truly benefit from the use of this dynamic online product.

- The MyWritingLab Hints consist of general directions that walk students through the process of bringing MWL instruction and practice into the classroom and into the learning process.
- The Chapter Reviews in the grammar handbook now start with MWL notes.
- An "insert" for students about how to use MWL with *Mosaics: Reading and Writing Sentences* is included in this edition.
- Full instructor directions for teaching with MWL and integrating it into class and/or individual work are provided in the accompanying *Instructor's Resource Manual.*

The series provides three comprehensive Instructor's Resource Manuals:

Especially designed by the author, the IRMs for the first three books in the series provide explanations of key rhetorical theories; ideas for the first day of class; sample syllabi; additional practices, activities, quizzes, and teaching tips for each chapter; grading rubrics for each rhetorical mode; appendixes for graphing student progress; and a list of sources for further reading. The manual for *Mosaics: Reading and Writing Sentences* also features detailed information on how instructors can fully integrate MWL into their curriculum.

HOW THIS BOOK WORKS

Mosaics: Reading and Writing Sentences teaches students how to read and write critically. For flexibility and easy reference, this book has three main features:

The Handbook is a complete grammar/usage guide, including exercises that cover eight units: The Basics, Sentences, Verbs, Pronouns, Modifiers, Punctuation, Mechanics, and Choosing the Right Word. Each chapter starts with a self-test based on student writing so students can determine their strengths and weaknesses in that area. The chapters provide at least three types of practice after each grammar concept, moving the students systematically from identifying a usage rule to filling in the blanks to writing their own sentences. Each chapter ends with a practical editing workshop that asks students to use the skills they just learned to edit another student's writing and then their own writing.

Unit Tests—including practice with single sentences and paragraphs—are offered at the end of each unit.

The Appendixes will help students keep track of their progress in grammar and spelling. References to these appendixes are interspersed throughout the book so that students know when to use them as they study the concepts in each chapter:

- Appendix 1: Error Log
- Appendix 2: Spelling Log

ACKNOWLEDGMENTS

I want to acknowledge the support, encouragement, and sound advice of several people who have helped me through the development of the *Mosaics* series. First, Pearson Higher Education has provided guidance and inspiration for this project through the enduring wisdom of Craig Campanella, previous senior acquisitions editor of developmental English, and Matt Wright, current senior acquisitions editor; the foresight and prudence of Joe Opiela, editor-in-chief; the creative inspiration of Thomas DeMarco, senior marketing manager; the unparalleled support of Jessica Kupetz, assistant editor; the exceptional organizational skills of Bayani Mendoza de Leon, production manager; the insight and vision of Marta Tomins and Harriett Prentiss, development editors; the care and wisdom of Debbie Meyer, production editor; the hard work and patience of Wesley Hall, permissions editor; the flawless organization of Samantha Neary, editorial assistant for developmental English; the brilliant leadership of Roth Wilkofsky, President of Humanities and Social Sciences. Also, this book would not be a reality without the insightful persistence of Phil Miller, publisher for modern languages.

I want to give very special thanks to Cheryl Smith, my constant source of inspiration in her role as consultant and advisor for the duration of this project. I am also grateful to Rebecca Hewett, Valerie Turner, and Li'i Pearl for their discipline and hard work on the *Instructor's Resource Manuals* for each of the books in the series. In addition, I want to thank Crystal Huddleston, Zandree Stidham, Brooke Hughes, and Anne Elrod for their expertise and assistance. Finally, I am very appreciative to Lauren Martinez and Annalisa Townsend for their special work on this edition and to Brooke Hughes and Randi Brummett for their valuable expertise integrating MyWritingLab into this text.

In addition, I am especially grateful to the following reviewers who have guided me through the development and revision of this book: Lisa Berman, Miami-Dade Community College; Patrick Haas, Glendale Community College; Jeanne Campanelli, American River College; Dianne Gregory, Cape Cod Community College; Clara Wilson-Cook, Southern University at New Orleans; Thomas Beery, Lima Technical College; Jean Petrolle, Columbia College; David Cratty, Cuyahoga Community College;

Allison Travis, Butte State College; Suellen Meyer, Meramec Community College; Jill Lahnstein, Cape Fear Community College; Stanley Coberly, West Virginia State University at Parkersville; Jamie Moore, Scottsdale Community College; Nancy Hellner, Mesa Community College; Ruth Hatcher, Washtenaw Community College; Thurmond Whatley, Aiken Technical College; W. David Hall, Columbus State Community College; Marilyn Coffee, Fort Hays State University; Valerie Russell, Valencia Community College; Elizabeth McCall, Gaston College; Sara Safdie, Bellevue Community College; Garrett Flagg, Fayetteville Technical Community College; Irene Gilliam, Tallahassee Community College; and Patricia M. Shade, Merced College.

Finally, I owe a tremendous personal debt to the people who have lived with this project for the last fifteen years; they are my closest companions and my best advisers: Michael, Christopher, and Laura Flachmann. I also want to thank one of my newest consultants to the project, Abby Flachmann. To Michael, I owe additional thanks for the valuable support and feedback he has given me through the entire process of creating and revising this series.

Kim Flachmann

PEARSON
mywritinglab

If practice makes perfect, imagine what *better* practice can do . . .

MyWritingLab is an online learning system that provides better writing practice through progressive exercises. These exercises move students from literal comprehension to critical application to demonstration of their ability to write properly. With this better practice model, students develop the skills needed to become better writers!

When asked if they agreed with the following statements, students responded favorably.

97%
The MyWritingLab Student-user Satisfaction Level

"MyWritingLab helped me to improve my writing." **89%**

"MyWritingLab was fairly easy to use." **90%**

"MyWritingLab helped make me feel more confident about my writing ability." **83%**

"MyWritingLab helped me to better prepare for my next writing course." **86%**

"MyWritingLab helped me get a better grade." **82%**

"I wish I had a program like MyWritingLab in some of my other courses." **78%**

"I would recommend my instructor continue using MyWritingLab." **85%**

Student Success Story

"The first few weeks of my English class, my grades were at approximately 78%. Then I was introduced to MyWritingLab. I couldn't believe the increase in my test scores. My test scores had jumped from that low score of 78 all the way up to 100% (and every now and then a 99)."

—Exetta Windfield, *College of the Sequoias* (MyWritingLab student user)

If your book did not come with an access code, you may purchase an access code at www.mywritinglab.com

Registering for MyWritingLab™...

It is easy to get started! Simply follow these steps to get into your MyWritingLab course.

1) **Find Your Access Code** (it is either packaged with your textbook, or you purchased it separately). You will need this access code and your course ID to join your MyWritingLab course. Your instructor has your course ID number, so make sure you have that before logging in.

2) **Click on "Students"** under "Register or Buy Access." Here you will be prompted to enter your access code, enter your e-mail address, and choose your own login name and password. After you register, you can **login under "Returning Users"** to use your new login name and password every time you go back into MyWritingLab.

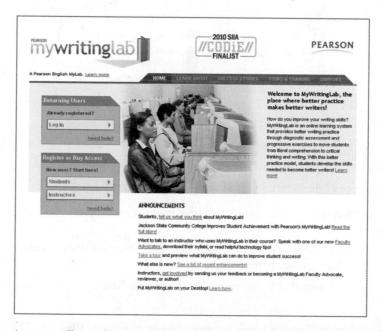

After logging in, you will see all the ways MyWritingLab can help you become a better writer.

The Homepage . . .

Here is your MyWritingLab HomePage.
You get a bird's eye view of where you are in your course every time you log in.

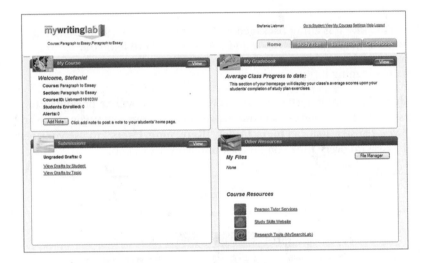

Your **Course** box shows your class details.

Your **Study Plan** box shows what you last completed and what is next on your **To Do** list.

Your **Gradebook** box shows you a snapshot of how you are doing in the class.

Your **Other Resources** box supplies you with amazing tools such as:

- **Pearson Tutor Services**—click here to see how you can get help on your papers by qualified tutors . . . before handing them in!

- **Research Navigator**—click here to see how this resembles your library with access to online journals for research paper assignments.

- **Study Skills**—extra help that includes tips and quizzes on how to improve your study skills

Now, let's start practicing to become better writers. Click on the Study Plan tab. This is where you will do all your course work.

The Study Plan ...

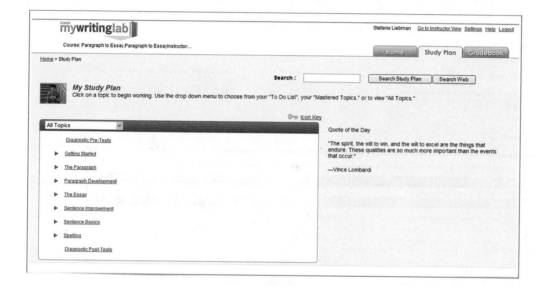

MyWritingLab provides you with a simple Study Plan of the writing skills that you need to master. You start from the top of the list and work your way down. You can start with the Diagnostic Pre-Tests.

The Diagnostic Pre-Tests contain five exercises on each of the grammar, punctuation, and usage topics. You can achieve mastery of the topic in the Diagnostic Pre-Test by getting four of five or five of five correct within each topic.

After completing the Diagnostic Pre-Test, you can return to your Study Plan and enter any of the topics you have yet to master.

Watch, Recall, Apply, Write . . .

Here is an example of a MyWritinglab Activity set that you will see once you enter into a topic. Take the time to briefly read the introductory paragraph, and then watch the engaging video clip by clicking on "Watch: Tense."

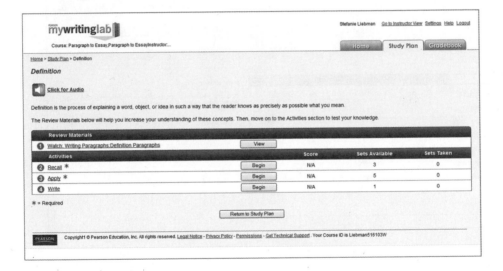

The video clip provides you with a helpful review.
Now you are ready to start the exercises. There are three types:

- Recall—activities that help you *recall* the rules of grammar
- Apply—activities that help you *apply* these rules to brief paragraphs or essays
- Write—activities that ask you to demonstrate these rules of grammar in your own writing

PEARSON
mywritinglab

Helping Students Succeed . . .

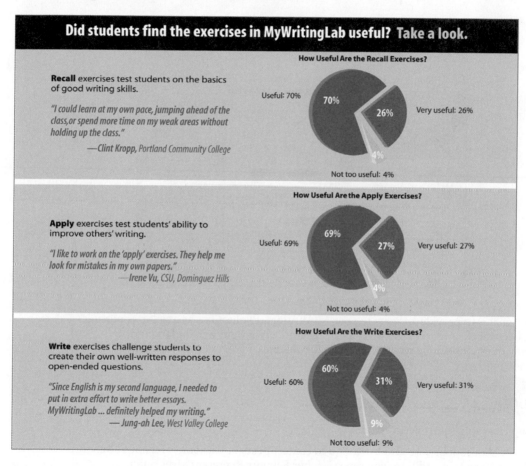

Did students find the exercises in MyWritingLab useful? Take a look.

How Useful Are the Recall Exercises?

Recall exercises test students on the basics of good writing skills.

"I could learn at my own pace, jumping ahead of the class, or spend more time on my weak areas without holding up the class."

—*Clint Kropp, Portland Community College*

Useful: 70% 70% 26% Very useful: 26% 4% Not too useful: 4%

How Useful Are the Apply Exercises?

Apply exercises test students' ability to improve others' writing.

"I like to work on the 'apply' exercises. They help me look for mistakes in my own papers."

—*Irene Vu, CSU, Dominguez Hills*

Useful: 69% 69% 27% Very useful: 27% 4% Not too useful: 4%

How Useful Are the Write Exercises?

Write exercises challenge students to create their own well-written responses to open-ended questions.

"Since English is my second language, I needed to put in extra effort to write better essays. MyWritingLab ... definitely helped my writing."

—*Jung-ah Lee, West Valley College*

Useful: 60% 60% 31% Very useful: 31% 9% Not too useful: 9%

Students just like you are finding MyWritingLab's Recall, Apply, and Write exercises useful in their learning.

Here to Help You ...

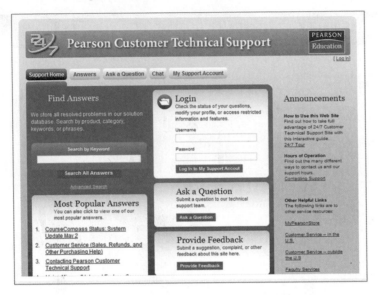

Our goal is to provide answers to your MyWritingLab questions as quickly as possible and deliver the highest level of support. By visiting **www.mywritinglab.com/help.html**, many questions can be resolved in just a few minutes. Here you will find help on the following:

- System Requirements
- How to Register for MyWritingLab
- How to Use MyWritingLab

For student support, we also invite you to contact Pearson Customer Technical Support (shown above). In addition, you can reach our Support Representatives online at **http://247.pearsoned.com**. Here you can do the following:

- Search Frequently Asked Questions about MyWritingLab
- E-mail a Question to Our Support Team
- Chat with a Support Representative

MOSAICS

Fourth Edition

READING AND WRITING SENTENCES

The Basics

This handbook uses very little terminology. But sometimes talking about the language and the way it works is difficult without a shared understanding of certain basic grammar terms. For that reason, your instructor may ask you to study parts of this introduction to review basic grammar—parts of speech, phrases, and clauses. You might also use this introduction for reference.

This section has two chapters:

Chapter 1: Parts of Speech
Chapter 2: Phrases and Clauses

Parts of Speech

Read the following paragraph, written by a student, and label two of each part of speech listed below.

verbs (v)	pronouns (pro)	adverbs (adv)	conjunctions (conj)
nouns (n)	adjectives (adj)	prepositions (prep)	interjections (int)

The personality trait that I like best about myself is my healthy sense of humor. No matter how bad a situation is, I can usually say something funny to everyone. When Toby's ancient car was stolen, I told him it was a piece of junk anyway, and I felt sorry for the foolish person who stole it. Man, we laughed so hard, imagining the car thief stalled on the side of the road somewhere in town. Oh, there are some things that I don't ever joke about, like death and diseases. A person would be extremely insensitive to joke about those situations.

Every sentence is made up of a variety of words that play different roles. Each word, like each part of a coordinated outfit, serves a distinct function. These functions fall into eight categories:

1. Verbs
2. Nouns
3. Pronouns
4. Adjectives
5. Adverbs
6. Prepositions

7. Conjunctions

8. Interjections

Some words, such as *is*, can function in only one way—in this case, as a verb. Other words, however, can serve as different parts of speech depending on how they are used in a sentence. For example, look at the different ways the word *paint* can be used:

Verb: We **paint** our house every five years.
             (*Paint* is a verb here, telling what we do.)

Noun: The **paint** needs two days to dry.
             (*Paint* functions as a noun here, telling what needs two days to dry.)

Adjective: My dog knocked over the **paint** can.
                (*Paint* is an adjective here, modifying the noun *can*.)

Understanding Parts of Speech

To learn more about parts of speech, go to MyWritingLab.com, and watch the video called **Introduction: Parts of Speech, Phrases, and Clauses.** Then, return to this chapter, which will go into more detail about parts of speech and give you opportunities to practice using them. Finally, you will apply your understanding of parts of speech to your own writing.

Student Comment:
"After being out of school for over 20 years, I forgot a lot about writing—especially grammar. The **Parts of Speech** topic helped me brush up on what I had forgotten."

VERBS

The **verb** is the most important word in a sentence because every other word depends on it in some way. Verbs tell what's going on in the sentence.

There are three types of verbs: action, linking, and helping. An **action verb** tells what someone or something is doing. A **linking verb** tells what someone or something is, feels, or looks like. Sometimes an action or linking verb has **helping verbs**—words that add information, such as when an action is taking place. A **complete verb** consists of an action or linking verb and all the helping verbs.

Action: The boy **hiked** up the hill.

Action: Jeremy **watches** the birds.

Linking: Myra **looks** lonely.

Linking: I **was** happy to be chosen.

Helping:	They **will be** leaving when the job is finished.
Helping:	Jennifer **has been** taking piano lessons.
Complete Verb:	They **will be leaving** when the job is finished.
Complete Verb:	Jennifer **has been taking** piano lessons.

Reviewing Verbs

Define each of the following types of verbs, and give an example of each.

Action: _____

_____

Linking: _____

_____

Helping: _____

_____

What is a complete verb? Give an example with your definition.

_____

_____

PRACTICE 1: Identifying

A. In each of the following sentences, identify the underlined verbs as action (A), linking (L), or helping (H).

1. _____ The baby <u>is</u> asleep.

2. _____ We <u>have</u> looked for the best deal.

3. _____ The outfielder <u>saw</u> the ball coming toward him.

4. _____ Most college students <u>want</u> lower tuition.

5. _____ Geoffrey <u>should have</u> paid for my dinner.

6. _____ The orchestra <u>played</u> music by Bach.

7. _____ He <u>looks</u> happy today.

8. _____ Every Sunday, we <u>give</u> money to charity.

9. _____ This <u>seems</u> like the best choice.

10. _____ Marci <u>had been</u> swimming for an hour.

B. Underline the complete verbs in the following sentences. Some sentences have more than one verb.

1. I feed my fish every morning.

2. The banker forgot his money.

3. My favorite restaurant is Steak 'n Shake.

4. This instructor seems strict.

5. I was planning a party this weekend.

6. Janelle feels ignored.

7. My friends had been dancing all night.

8. Mario wished for a new car.

9. Tiffany has five dollars.

10. The lady walked to the bench and sat down.

PRACTICE 2: Completing Fill in each blank in the following paragraph with a complete verb.

Yesterday I (1) _____ to the radio when the disc jockey (2) _____ a new contest. He (3) _____ a music question and said he (4) _____ the tenth caller. I immediately (5) _____ the telephone and (6) _____ for the DJ to answer. The phone (7) _____ several times, and it (8) _____ like I was waiting forever. When he finally (9) _____ my call, I (10) _____ $50 and tickets to an upcoming concert.

PRACTICE 3: Writing Your Own

A. Write a sentence of your own for each of the following verbs.

1. were growing _____

2. ran _____

3. looks _____

4. had been singing _____

5. draw _____

B. Write five sentences of your own, and underline all the verbs. Remember that sentences can have more than one verb.

_____

_____

_____

_____

_____

NOUNS

People often think of **nouns** as "naming words" because they identify—or name—people (*teacher, Jimmy, brother, clerk*), places (*town, lake, Phoenix*), or things (*flower, car, desk, pants*). Nouns also name ideas (*freedom, liberty*), qualities (*honesty, kindness*), emotions (*sadness, happiness*), and actions (*competition, agreement*). A **common noun** names something general (*singer, hill, water, theater*). A **proper noun** names something specific (*Britney Spears, Grand Canyon, Sprite, McDonald's*).

Hint: To test whether a word is a noun, try putting *a*, *an*, or *the* in front of it:

    Nouns: a dog, an apple, the courage

    NOT Nouns: a silly, an under, the sing

This test does not work with proper nouns:

    NOT   a Jeffrey or the Washington

Reviewing Nouns

What is a noun?

_____

_____

What is the difference between a common noun and a proper noun? Give an example of each.

Common noun: _____

_____

Proper noun: _____

_____

PRACTICE 4: Identifying

A. In each of the following sentences, identify the underlined nouns as common (C) or proper (P).

1. _____ There are many tourists at <u>Niagara Falls</u>.

2. _____ My last <u>girlfriend</u> was a model for Calvin Klein.

3. _____ This is the last gas station before we get to <u>Tulsa</u>.

4. _____ Give me a <u>dollar</u> for lunch.

5. _____ Is Elizabeth ready for her big <u>date</u>?

6. _____ I can't find my pencil from <u>Disneyland</u>.

7. _____ Jack is having a <u>hamburger</u> for dinner.

8. _____ While I was at the office, I met <u>Michael Jordan</u>.

9. _____ Can you take me to <u>school</u> today?

10. _____ The <u>Beale Library</u> is closed for remodeling.

B. Underline the nouns in the following sentences. Some sentences have more than one noun.

1. We will be going to San Francisco next week.

2. My coin collection is very important to me.

3. Travis is my nephew.

4. George is going to see a movie this afternoon.

5. *Lost* was a very popular TV series.

6. I am tired of this hot weather.

7. My grandma makes the best cookies.

8. The basketball player has broken several records.

9. Steve is writing an essay about *Gulliver's Travels* by Jonathan Swift.

10. Melissa grew up in New York City.

PRACTICE 5: Completing Fill in each blank in the following paragraph with a noun.

In the month of (1) _____, I had two vacations planned. The first was a short visit to (2) _____, and the other was a five-day cruise in (3) _____. I had to travel by (4) _____ to get to both places, and I was excited about the (5) _____. My younger (6) _____ was going with me on the first trip, and we hadn't been getting along very well. To make sure there was (7) _____ between us, I brought along some old (8) _____ from our younger days. My mom also gave me (9) _____ that brought back lots of funny memories. By the end of our trip, we had become so close that we vowed to be (10) _____ forever!

PRACTICE 6: Writing Your Own

A. Write a sentence of your own for each of the following nouns.

1. pastor _____

2. Sea World _____

3. strength _____

4. audience _____

5. actions _____

B. Write five sentences of your own, and underline all the nouns. Remember that sentences can have more than one noun.

_____

_____

_____

_____

_____

PRONOUNS

Pronouns can do anything nouns can do. In fact, **pronouns** can take the place of nouns. Without pronouns, you would find yourself repeating nouns and producing boring sentences. Compare the following sentences, for example:

Matt rode **Matt's** bike to **Matt's** house because **Matt** was late for dinner.

Matt rode **his** bike to **his** house because **he** was late for dinner.

There are many different types of pronouns, but you only need to focus on the following four types for now.

Most Common Pronouns

Personal (refer to people or things)

Singular:	*First Person:*	*I, me, my, mine*
	Second Person:	*you, your, yours*
	Third Person:	*he, she, it, him, her, hers, his, its*
Plural:	*First Person:*	*we, us, our, ours*
	Second Person:	*you, your, yours*
	Third Person:	*they, them, their, theirs*

Demonstrative (point out someone or something)

Singular:	*this, that*
Plural:	*these, those*

Relative (introduce a dependent clause)

who, whom, whose, which, that

Indefinite (refer to someone or something general, not specific)

Singular: *another, anybody, anyone, anything, each, either, everybody, everyone, everything, little, much, neither, nobody, none, no one, nothing, one, other, somebody, someone, something*

Plural: *both, few, many, others, several*

Either Singular or Plural: *all, any, more, most, some*

Hint: When any of these words are used with nouns, they become adjectives instead of pronouns.

Adjective: My brother wants to borrow **some money.**

Pronoun: My brother wants to borrow **some.**

Adjective: The dog wants **that bone.**

Pronoun: The dog wants **that.**

Reviewing Pronouns

What is a pronoun?

Define the four most common types of pronouns, and give two examples of each.

Personal: _____

Demonstrative: _____

Relative: _____

Indefinite: _____

PRACTICE 7: Identifying

A. In each of the following sentences, identify the underlined pronouns as personal (P), relative (R), demonstrative (D), or indefinite (I).

1. _____ This drink is <u>his</u>.

2. _____ <u>It</u> doesn't matter what you wear to the game.

3. _____ I think the person <u>who</u> broke the lamp should pay for it.

4. _____ Tiffany gave me <u>that</u> for my birthday.

5. _____ If <u>anyone</u> could do a better job, please tell me.

6. _____ Jackie is taking <u>her</u> to the doctor.

7. _____ <u>These</u> are my favorite shoes.

8. _____ There is <u>something</u> I have to tell you.

9. _____ I hope <u>that</u> we can meet at the movie.

10. _____ I am donating <u>both</u> to the thrift store.

B. Underline the pronouns in the following sentences. Some sentences have more than one pronoun.

1. Some of us are not happy with the results.

2. These are not the right answers.

3. I think they are being honest with us.

4. Nobody wants to do the work.

5. Is that the dress I loaned you?

6. If you would just study, everything would be easier for you.

7. It is not my fault that Steve broke his arm.

8. Kari knows whose job that is.

9. Those were the best appetizers at the party.

10. My sister believes in that theory.

PRACTICE 8: Completing In the following paragraph, replace the nouns in parentheses with pronouns.

   Anne bought (1) _____ (Anne's) cat when Anne was 12. It was a kitten at the time, and (2) _____ (Anne) couldn't resist its cute face. When (3) _____ (Anne's) friends saw the cat, (4) _____ (Anne's friends) told (5) _____ (Anne) to name (6) _____ (the cat) Marble because (7) _____ (the cat) was so colorful. Anne decided to name the cat Spunky instead because (8) _____ (the cat) had lots of energy. Now Anne is going away to college and (9) _____ (Anne's) cat is going with (10) _____ (Anne).

PRACTICE 9: Writing Your Own

A. Write a sentence of your own for each of the following pronouns.

   1. anybody _____

   2. those _____

   3. who _____

   4. both _____

   5. we _____

B. Write five sentences of your own, and underline the pronouns. Remember that sentences can have more than one pronoun.

   _____

   _____

   _____

   _____

   _____

ADJECTIVES

Adjectives modify—or describe—nouns or pronouns. Adjectives generally make sentences clear and vivid.

Without Adjectives:　He took candy, a camera, and a backpack to the amusement park.

With Adjectives:　He took **licorice** candy, a **digital** camera, and a **blue** backpack to the amusement park.

Reviewing Adjectives

What is an adjective?

_____

Give three examples of adjectives.

_____

PRACTICE 10: Identifying

A. For each of the following sentences, if the underlined word is an adjective, write Adj in the blank.

1. _____ That was an <u>ugly</u> dog.

2. _____ My father is a <u>generous</u> man.

3. _____ Stan tried to <u>scare</u> Jessica.

4. _____ The <u>new</u> student has been very helpful.

5. _____ I met a <u>boy</u> in the library today.

6. _____ The <u>rich</u> man is giving his estate to charity.

7. _____ His <u>proud</u> smile was beautiful.

8. _____ Put the <u>cup</u> in the dishwasher.

9. _____ I need a <u>cold</u> drink.

10. _____ Jeremy's <u>computer</u> has a virus.

B. Underline the adjectives in the following sentences. Some sentences have more than one adjective.

1. The curly hair is full of thick knots.

2. Linda plays concert piano in front of large audiences.

3. The longest novel I have ever read is *Bleak House* by Charles Dickens.

4. I need a good parking place today.

5. It was a cold day in November when we won the big football game.

6. That cheese pizza looks like a great meal.

7. The baby's loud cry is giving me a headache.

8. I need a cup of strong coffee to stay awake.

9. Kevin has to mow the long grass in the backyard.

10. Renee uses a black ballpoint pen to sign her checks.

PRACTICE 11: Completing Fill in each blank in the following paragraph with an adjective.

Last summer, my brother and I drove to a (1) _____ city in Texas. I have some (2) _____ relatives who live there, and they wanted us to visit. We stayed for a (3) _____ week and talked about (4) _____ things. I took lots of (5) _____ pictures also, because I didn't know when we would be back to see them again. All in all, it was a (6) _____ visit. We enjoyed our (7) _____ conversations, and we learned about our family's (8) _____ history. I promised to write often, and they were (9) _____ to see us leave. On the way home, we felt a little more (10) _____ about our relatives and ourselves.

PRACTICE 12: Writing Your Own

A. Write a sentence of your own for each of the following adjectives.

1. pretty _____

2. heavy _____

3. small _____

4. fourth _____

5. loud _____

B. Write five sentences of your own, and underline all of the adjectives. Remember that sentences can have more than one adjective.

_____

_____

_____

_____

_____

ADVERBS

Adverbs modify or describe adjectives, verbs, and other adverbs. They do *not* modify nouns. Adverbs also answer the following questions:

How?	thoughtfully, kindly, briefly, quietly
When?	soon, tomorrow, late, now
Where?	inside, somewhere, everywhere, there
How often?	daily, always, annually, rarely
To what extent?	generally, specifically, exactly, very

Hint: Notice that adverbs often end in *-ly*. That might help you recognize them.

Reviewing Adverbs

What is an adverb?

_____

What are the five questions that adverbs answer?

_____   _____   _____

_____   _____

Give one example of an adverb that answers each question.

_____

PRACTICE 13: Identifying

A. For each of the following sentences, if the underlined word is an adverb, write Adv in the blank.

   1. _____ He <u>kindly</u> waited for me at the corner.

   2. _____ Jan spoke <u>softly</u>, and I couldn't hear her.

3. _____ He was <u>outside</u> when I called her.

4. _____ Henry can <u>hop</u> on one leg.

5. _____ That was <u>very</u> thoughtful of you.

6. _____ Pam was <u>much</u> appreciated for her hard work.

7. _____ The <u>power</u> bill is higher this month than last.

8. _____ Peggy's <u>son</u> is a sweet boy.

9. _____ Meet me <u>tomorrow</u> in the lobby.

10. _____ I read it <u>quickly</u>, so I don't remember what it said.

B. Underline the adverbs in the following sentences. Some sentences have more than one adverb.

1. I surely won't be at that party.

2. They almost collided in the hall.

3. Tammy will come by today to wash the car.

4. This is the very last time you will make that mistake.

5. Don't drive too fast.

6. This was quite a good movie.

7. Jennifer quickly ran to the bus stop.

8. Are you absolutely sure you can be here?

9. I suddenly realized that I forgot my homework.

10. We went to the meetings monthly.

PRACTICE 14: Completing Fill in each blank in the following paragraph with an adverb.

When the grocery store in our small town (1) _____ closed, several people were out of work. It was a (2) _____ sad situation for many people. One family, the Johnsons, (3) _____ found a solution. They opened a new grocery store with more (4) _____ priced items. They also

(5) _____ employed people from the first store, and they
(6) _____ donated food items for families that were
(7) _____ struggling. The town was (8) _____
grateful for their generous help. The Johnsons were
(9) _____ awarded a key to the city at a big dinner held in
their honor. I know the Johnsons never planned to get so much
recognition, but they (10) _____ deserved it.

PRACTICE 15: Writing Your Own

A. Write a sentence of your own for each of the following adverbs.

   1. often _____

   2. rarely _____

   3. softly _____

   4. too _____

   5. yesterday _____

B. Write five sentences of your own, and underline all of the adverbs.
   Remember that sentences can have more than one adverb.

   _____

   _____

   _____

   _____

   _____

PREPOSITIONS

   Prepositions indicate relationships among the ideas in a sentence.
Something is *up, down, next to, behind, around, near,* or *under* something else. A preposition is always followed by a noun or a pronoun
called the **object of the preposition**. Together, they form a **prepositional phrase**.

Preposition	+	Object	=	Prepositional Phrase
beside		the water	=	beside the water
at		the meeting	=	at the meeting

Here is a list of some common prepositions.

Common Prepositions

about	beside	into	since
above	between	like	through
across	beyond	near	throughout
after	by	next to	to
against	despite	of	toward
among	down	off	under
around	during	on	until
as	except	on top of	up
at	for	out	upon
before	from	out of	up to
behind	in	outside	with
below	in front of	over	within
beneath	inside	past	without

Hint: *To* + a verb (as in *to go, to come, to feel*) is not a prepositional phrase. It is a verb phrase, which we will discuss later in this unit.

Reviewing Prepositions

What is a preposition?

_____

Give two examples of prepositions:

_____   _____

What is a prepositional phrase?

_____

Give two examples of prepositional phrases:

_____   _____

PRACTICE 16: Identifying

A. For each of the following sentences, if the underlined word is a preposition, write P in the blank.

1. _____ The most important papers are <u>on</u> the top.

2. _____ My cousins live <u>around</u> the corner.

3. _____ The fisherman went <u>over</u> his limit of trout.

4. _____ I am hanging a <u>poster</u> of Ben Affleck in my room.

5. _____ Don't walk <u>behind</u> that building at night.

6. _____ Julie went <u>through</u> the neighborhood with fliers.

7. _____ I have been writing in my <u>diary</u> since I was eight years old.

8. _____ The museum is <u>near</u> the community center.

9. _____ Turn off the <u>radio</u> while I'm studying.

10. _____ Paul flew his plane <u>above</u> the clouds.

B. Underline the prepositions in the following sentences. Some sentences have more than one preposition.

1. Before getting out of the car, he noticed a lady in a white hat.

2. The house is on the hill at the end of the windy road.

3. The best hotels in San Diego are beside the ocean.

4. My new computer is in a box by my desk.

5. During the dance, I leaned against the table, and it fell.

6. One of the twins has a birthmark under her knee.

7. The cookie jar is sitting on top of the refrigerator.

8. We forgot about the balloons the car.

9. My slip is hanging below my skirt.

10. Iris walked through the mall with Becky.

PRACTICE 17: Completing Fill in each blank in the following paragraph with a preposition.

Miguel has been walking (1) _____ campus all day, trying to sell tickets to a car wash. He walked (2) _____ me this morning and asked me to buy one. He said he was raising money (3) _____ the chess club because the club members are going (4) _____ Disney World (5) _____

Florida. I don't know how much money they need, but
(6) _____ the time of our conversation, they had only $50.
The chess club is usually very disorganized and is always
(7) _____ money. This year, it has a new president, who
went (8) _____ the club's books and found a way to pay its
bills. Miguel was the vice president, but he quit because he didn't want
to be (9) _____ so much pressure. I think he just wants to
graduate (10) _____ next year and needs more time for
studying.

PRACTICE 18: Writing Your Own

A. Write a sentence of your own for each of the following prepositions.

1. below _____

2. with _____

3. around _____

4. between _____

5. toward _____

B. Write five sentences of your own, and underline the prepositions.
Remember that sentences can have more than one preposition.

_____

_____

_____

_____

_____

CONJUNCTIONS

Conjunctions connect groups of words. Without conjunctions, most of
our writing would be choppy and boring. The two types of conjunctions are
easy to remember because their names state their purpose: *Coordinating
conjunctions* link equal ideas, and *subordinating conjunctions* make one idea
subordinate to—or dependent on—another.

Coordinating conjunctions connect parts of a sentence that are of equal
importance or weight. Each part of the sentence is an **independent clause,**

a group of words with a subject and verb that can stand alone as a sentence (see pages 32–33). There are only seven coordinating conjunctions:

Coordinating Conjunctions

and, but, or, nor, for, so, yet

Coordinating:	Isaac wanted to see a movie, **and** I wanted to go to dinner.
Coordinating:	I enjoy listening to music, **but** I don't know how to play any instruments.

Subordinating conjunctions join two ideas by making one dependent on the other. The idea introduced by the subordinating conjunction becomes a **dependent clause**, a group of words with a subject and a verb that cannot stand alone as a sentence (see page 9). The other part of the sentence is an independent clause.

	Dependent Clause
Subordinating:	She will stay **until** the baby falls asleep.

	Dependent Clause
Subordinating:	**Unless** I am busy, you are welcome to come visit.

Common Subordinating Conjunctions

after	because	since	until
although	before	so	when
as	even if	so that	whenever
as if	even though	than	where
as long as	how	that	wherever
as soon as	if	though	whether
as though	in order that	unless	while

Reviewing Conjunctions

What is a coordinating conjunction?

_____

_____

Name the seven coordinating conjunctions.

_____   _____   _____

_____   _____   _____

_____

What is a subordinating conjunction?

_____

_____

Write a sentence using a subordinating conjunction.

_____

_____

PRACTICE 19: Identifying

A. In each of the following sentences, identify the underlined conjunction as coordinating (C) or subordinating (S).

1. _____ Polly wanted to be here, <u>yet</u> she had prior commitments.

2. _____ <u>Before</u> you go, sign the guest book.

3. _____ I didn't make cookies, <u>though</u> I knew you would be hungry.

4. _____ <u>As if</u> he could read my mind, he brought me flowers.

5. _____ Henry is allergic to chocolate, <u>so</u> he can't eat that cake.

6. _____ Richard will do that part, <u>unless</u> he gets too busy.

7. _____ <u>While</u> I was waiting, I read an article on computers.

8. _____ <u>Although</u> she's never been there, Cara said Hawaii is beautiful.

9. _____ Dean is a lawyer, <u>and</u> he's working on a big tobacco case.

10. _____ I can make a sandwich, <u>or</u> I can call for pizza.

B. Underline the conjunctions in the following sentences.

1. We all want to go, but there are only ten tickets left.

2. As long as you're watching him, the baby can play outside.

3. I had a good time, yet I never did see my friends there.

4. When you were at the store, I worked on my essay.

5. I know it's going to be hot today, for the forecast predicted mid-90s.

6. Although it's only June, stores are selling Halloween costumes.

7. We can begin the meeting as soon as Peter arrives.

8. Stephanie will buy the donuts even though she lost her job.

9. I made a special card for Amber, so I hope you will sign it.

10. Whenever you come to town, you should call me.

PRACTICE 20: Completing Fill in each blank in the following paragraph with a conjunction.

　　Cooking is not fun for me, (1) _____ I have been learning alot about it. (2) _____ I usually make my girl-friend do the cooking, last night it was my turn. I planned to make a pasta dish, (3) _____ I forgot a couple of things at the store, (4) _____ I decided to make chef salads instead. (5) _____ I was doing the cooking, my girlfriend was surf-ing on the Internet in the back room. (6) _____ she wasn't paying attention to me, she didn't notice how many times I licked my fingers or dropped things on the floor. I think the salads were just fine, (7) _____ I did notice a cat hair had somehow landed in mine. (8) _____ there was anything strange in my girl-friend's salad, she didn't bring it to my attention. I think she was just glad to have the night off, (9) _____ the next time I have to cook, I will get take-out. (10) _____ I've heard that cooking is an expression of love, I still think it is too much work.

PRACTICE 21: Writing Your Own

A. Write a sentence of your own for each of the following conjunctions.

1. but _____

2. until _____

3. so _____

4. wherever _____

5. as long as _____

B. Write five sentences of your own, and underline the conjunctions. Remember that sentences can have more than one conjunction.

_____

_____

_____

_____

_____

INTERJECTIONS

Interjections are words that express strong emotion, surprise, or disappointment. An interjection is usually followed by an exclamation point or a comma.

Interjection: **Hey!** You're standing on my foot.

Interjection: **Wow,** that was scary!

Other common interjections include *aha, alas, great, hallelujah, neat, oh, oops, ouch, well, whoa, yeah,* and *yippee.*

Reviewing Interjections

What is an interjection?

_____

_____

Write a sentence using an interjection.

_____

_____

PRACTICE 22: Identifying

A. For each of the following sentences, if the underlined word is an interjection, write I in the blank.

1. _____ <u>Ouch</u>, I hit my finger!

2. _____ <u>No</u>! That's the wrong house.

3. _____ <u>Oops</u>, I didn't mean to say that.

4. _____ <u>Thank you</u> for taking me home.

5. _____ I can't believe you made it! <u>Wow</u>!

6. _____ <u>Yes</u>! I got an A on that paper.

7. _____ <u>Please</u> take me to the dance.

8. _____ <u>Can</u> you hand me the salt?

9. _____ The car didn't run out of gas. <u>Thank goodness</u>!

10. _____ <u>Well</u>, I think I can find time.

B. Underline the interjections in the following sentences.

1. My goodness! That was a terrible storm.

2. The boys' team, alas, has beaten the girls' team again.

3. Yeah! We are going to the semifinals!

4. Wow, do you know how much that costs?

5. My mom is paying my tuition! Hallelujah!

6. Man, this is a steep hill.

7. Oh, guess who's having another baby!

8. Hooray! We won a new car.

9. That was a great save! Neat!

10. Hey! Am I the only one who knows how to take out the trash around here?

PRACTICE 23: Completing Fill in each blank in the following paragraph with an interjection.

(1) _____, we were almost late for the plane! (2) _____! We thought it was departing at 11:00 a.m., but our tickets actually said 9:30 a.m. (3) _____, I can't believe we were that careless. Fortunately, we left for the airport two hours early because we were going to buy lunch there. (4) _____! During the drive, I looked at the ticket and, (5) _____, it said 9:30 a.m. in bold. I can't believe I didn't see it before. (6) _____! We ran and ran through the terminal, and when we got to the gate, they told us there were only two seats left. (7) _____! (8) _____, there were only two of us traveling that day. We found our seats on the plane, and (9) _____, was it stuffy! At least we made it to Denver on time. (10) _____!

PRACTICE 24: Writing Your Own

A. Write a sentence of your own for each of the following interjections.

1. yikes _____

2. wow _____

3. yeah _____

4. ouch _____

5. mercy _____

B. Write five sentences of your own, and underline the interjections.

_____

_____

_____

_____

_____

CHAPTER REVIEW

Reviewing Parts of Speech

This video goes over many different parts of speech in great detail, which is particularly helpful if you need a quick grammar review.

To review this material before you complete the Review Practices, watch the **Parts of Speech, Phrases, and Clauses** video at **MyWritingLab.com** one more time. This time, keep the video open as you complete the rest of the practices in this chapter. For best results, do the **MyWritingLab** exercises online as well as the Chapter Review practices in the book.

REVIEW PRACTICE 1: Identifying Use the following abbreviations to label the underlined words in these sentences.

verb (v)   pronoun (pro)   adverb (adv)   conjunction (conj)

noun (n)   adjective (adj)   preposition (prep)   interjection (int)

1. <u>Wow</u>, <u>I</u> can't believe how much <u>those</u> shoes <u>cost</u>!

2. <u>Yesterday</u>, Marisol <u>went</u> <u>to</u> the St. Louis Rams football <u>game</u>.

3. Sammi wanted the <u>newly</u> built house, <u>but</u> he couldn't afford the monthly <u>payments</u>.

4. Whatever class Irulan <u>is taking</u> this semester, she <u>reviews</u> her notes and studies <u>in</u> the <u>library</u> every night.

5. The most <u>unique</u> car <u>of</u> the 1980s was <u>probably</u> the Delorian.

6. <u>Gee</u>, I didn't know that <u>tomorrow</u> <u>we</u> were having our <u>history</u> test.

7. Zora wants to <u>get</u> a job, so she can <u>pay</u> the bill <u>for</u> her college tuition.

8. Lacie <u>forgot</u> to pay her telephone bill <u>and</u> received a notice from <u>them</u> about <u>late</u> charges.

9. <u>Although</u> I needed to take a math class, <u>I</u> was told by my <u>adviser</u> to take history instead.

10. Last winter was <u>warm</u> and sunny, <u>so</u> it was hard to get into the Christmas <u>mood</u>.

 **Practicing Parts of Speech**

Now complete the **Recall** activity for **Parts of Speech, Phrases, and Clauses** at MyWritingLab.com. If you're having a difficult time with a question, open up the video in the lower right-hand corner for some help.

REVIEW PRACTICE 2: Completing Fill in each blank in the following paragraph with an appropriate word, as indicated.

The most expensive trip I ever took was to (1) _____ (noun) with my best friend, Alex. Halfway through our trip, the car began to make a (2) _____ (adjective) sound. After a (3) _____ (adjective) time, we decided to stop at a car repair shop. The mechanic (4) _____(verb) that I needed a new muffler and a new exhaust pipe. I asked him how much the esti-mate would be (4) _____ (preposition) him to fix the car, and he replied it would cost over $2,500. (5)_____ (interjection), we couldn't believe how much the estimate was! I bought the car for $1,200, (6) _____ (conjunction) I really didn't want to spend that much to fix it. Still, we needed a way to get back home so I (7) _____ (adverb) told the mechanic to start work on the car. Seven hours later, (8) _____ (pronoun) began to drive home. As we drove into my driveway, smoke began coming out of the (10) _____ (noun), and I realized that I had been swindled out of $2,500.

Practicing Parts of Speech

Next, complete the **Apply** activity for **Parts of Speech, Phrases, and Clauses** at **MyWritingLab.com.** Pay close attention to the directions, and click only on what you're asked to.

REVIEW PRACTICE 3: **Writing Your Own** Write your own paragraph about your favorite pet. What did you name it? What kind of animal was it?

Practicing Parts of Speech

For more practice, complete the **Write** activity for **Parts of Speech, Phrases, and Clauses** at **MyWritingLab.com.** Make sure to pay close attention to the use of phrases and clauses.

EDITING THE STUDENT WRITING

Return to the student paragraph at the beginning of this chapter, and do the following activities.

Individual Activity Review your labels in the student paragraph. Did you find two of each part of speech?

Collaborative Activity Team up with a partner, and check your work by listing the parts of speech in columns.

EDITING YOUR OWN WRITING

Exchange paragraphs from Review Practice 3 with a classmate, and do the following:

1. Circle any words that are used incorrectly.

2. Underline any words that don't make sense.

Then return the paragraph to its writer, and use the information in this chapter to edit your own paragraph. Record your errors on the Error Log in Appendix 1.

Phrases and Clauses

READING PHRASES AND CLAUSES

Underline the phrases and put the clauses in brackets in the following sentences written by a student.

I was surprised how quickly I completed my writing assignment on my cousin's computer. I had been using one of the computers at the library, and it kept erasing my work. With a fresh start on my cousin's computer, I found that the words were just falling out of my head naturally. I didn't have to spend time trying to find lost paragraphs or recreating sections of my composition. I have to get a computer of my own, but I just changed part-time jobs and need to get settled again before I can make any major purchases. The life of a college student can be complex sometimes.

Phrases and clauses are two more basic units of grammar that you must understand to be proficient in sentence structure. Along with parts of speech, they make up the complete arsenal you need to produce your best writing.

Understanding Phrases and Clauses

For more information about phrases and clauses, go to **MyWritingLab. com,** and view the video called **Introduction: Parts of Speech, Phrases, and Clauses.** Then, return to this chapter, which will go into more detail about phrases and clauses and give you opportunities to practice them. Finally, you will apply your understanding of phrases and clauses to your own writing.

Student Comment:
"From a combination of **MyWritingLab** and **Mosaics**, I now understand that seeing the difference between phrases and clauses is essential for writing correct sentences.

PHRASES

A **phrase** is a group of words that function together as a unit. Phrases cannot stand alone, however, because they are missing a subject, a verb, or both.

Phrases: the new reality TV show, my best friend (missing verbs)

Phrases: had been working, can jump (missing subjects)

Phrases: without any money, near the bank (missing both)

Phrases: helping other people, to be listening (missing subjects)

Notice that all these groups of words are missing a subject, a verb, or both.

> ### Reviewing Phrases
>
> *What is a phrase?*
>
> _____
>
> _____
>
> *Give two examples of phrases.*
>
> _____
>
> _____

PRACTICE 1: Identifying

A. In each of the following sentences, identify the underlined phrase as missing a subject (S), missing a verb (V), or missing both (B).

1. _____ <u>A new car</u> is parked in my driveway.

2. _____ James is transferring <u>to a new college</u>.

3. _____ Mabel and Sarah <u>should have been exercising</u> instead of sleeping.

4. _____ <u>A very high ladder</u> was leaning against the wall.

5. _____ We wanted to swim <u>under the bridge</u>.

6. _____ Rachel asked <u>for directions</u> when she was lost.

7. _____ We became friends <u>in this dorm room</u>.

8. _____ I don't know how to find a pet <u>with a good personality</u>.

9. _____ <u>The bald plumber</u> stopped to get some milk on his way home.

10. _____ All of us <u>were willing</u> to help her with her math homework.

B. Underline the phrases in each sentence. Every sentence has more than one phrase.

   1. The Harris family will be vacationing in the mountains for two weeks

   2. Driving home from school, Jack remembered about his wallet on his dresser.

   3. During the blackout, no one could find the candles.

   4. We should have been paying more attention to the time.

   5. Tired and exhausted, Maria was thankful when her shift ended.

   6. The car sped down the street despite the speed limit signs.

   7. Pam and Cecilia have been best friends since they were in elementary school.

   8. It was foolish to lie to the instructor.

   9. Kevin and I talked for hours sitting underneath the stars.

   10. I would have accepted that job offer.

PRACTICE 2: Completing Fill in each blank in the following paragraph with an appropriate phrase to complete the sentence.

Ever since Sam applied for vacation time at (1) _____, he found that he was very excited about (2) _____. As he walked (3) _____, he heard that his roommate, Tony, also got (4) _____. Sam learned that (5) _____ were coming for a surprise visit and (6) _____ in their apartment. Even though Sam had tried hard to get ahead (7) _____, he knew he was going to have to (8) _____ in order to keep up with his classes. In only three hours, he got most of his homework done (9) _____. Now he has to (10) _____. His friends were arriving today.

PRACTICE 3: Writing Your Own

A. Write a sentence of your own for each of the following phrases.

   1. tapes, CDs, and videotapes _____

   2. around town _____

3. should have been ready _____

4. the man sitting in the front row _____

5. to qualify for the Olympics _____

B. Write five sentences of your own, and underline all the phrases.

_____

_____

_____

_____

_____

CLAUSES

Like phrases, **clauses** are groups of words. But unlike phrases, a clause always contains a subject and a verb. There are two types of clauses: *independent* and *dependent*.

An **independent clause** contains a subject and a verb and can stand alone and make sense by itself. Every complete sentence must have at least one independent clause.

Independent Clause: Tracy loved to watch sunrises.

Now look at the following group of words. It is a clause because it contains a subject and a verb. But it is a **dependent clause** because it is introduced by a word that makes it dependent, *because*.

Dependent Clause: **Because** Tracy loved to watch sunrises.

This clause cannot stand alone. It must be connected to an independent clause to make sense. Here is one way to complete the dependent clause and form a complete sentence.

          Dependent   **Independent**

Because Tracy loved to watch sunrises, she always woke up early.

Hint: Subordinating conjunctions (such as *since, although, because, while*) and relative pronouns (*who, whom, whose, which, that*) make clauses dependent. (For more information on subordinating conjunctions, see page 20, and on relative pronouns, see page 9.)

Reviewing Clauses

For a group of words to be a clause, it must have a _____
and a _____

What is an independent clause?

_____

_____

What is a dependent clause?

_____

_____

Name the two kinds of words that can begin a dependent clause.

_____   _____

Name five subordinating conjunctions.

_____   _____   _____

_____   _____

Name the five relative pronouns.

_____   _____   _____

_____   _____

PRACTICE 4: Identifying

A. Identify the following clauses as either independent (I) or dependent (D).

1. _____ Karen was late for class.

2. _____ Because her car wouldn't start.

3. _____ What I really don't know.

4. _____ The Grand Canyon is one of the Seven Wonders of the World.

5. _____ I only buy name-brand clothes.

6. _____ When Walt visited me last month.

7. _____ Tirana wears beautiful clothes and is self-confident.

8. _____ Although Angela bought a new computer.

9. _____ The next-door neighbor is ready to go overseas.

10. _____ When they are first born.

B. Underline the clauses in the following sentences, and label them independent (I) or dependent (D). Some sentences have more than one clause.

1. Dawn started playing soccer when she was six years old.

2. His plans had been changed, and he didn't mind.

3. Even though Martin liked roller coasters, he didn't want to try the new one.

4. All of my relatives want to stay forever when they visit me.

5. My brothers and sisters created a company, but they got help from our mom and dad.

6. The coach put the girl back in the game after she rested.

7. Children's books have great pictures in them.

8. The number of homeless people in the United States is growing.

9. Alternative rock music is for people who like a heavy beat.

10. I saw Margaret running on the track that is across from the dorms.

PRACTICE 5: Completing Make the following dependent clauses into independent clauses by crossing out the subordinating word (either a subordinating conjunction or a relative pronoun).

1. Before I got into the car.

2. The waiter who made $50 in tips every night.

3. Each one of the beautiful gardens that contained fresh herbs and flowers.

4. While my brother stayed in Salem, Oregon, and I lived off the Puget Sound in Washington State.

5. When you can earn a living.

6. After they were ten years old.

7. The shark that lingered near the boat.

8. Although he bought a Chevy Tahoe.

9. Since I passed my final exam.

10. The party that got out of control.

PRACTICE 6: Writing Your Own

A. Add a dependent clause to the following independent clauses.

   1. The cat is sleeping on the sofa.

   _____

   2. My brother borrowed my computer.

   _____

   3. This test covers five chapters in our textbook.

   _____

   4. I can't come over until after lunch.

   _____

   5. The box is filled with candy.

   _____

B. Write five independent clauses. Then add at least one dependent clause to each independent clause.

_____

_____

_____

_____

CHAPTER REVIEW

You might have seen this video in the previous chapter, but focus this time on phrases and clauses. Review parts of speech if necessary.

Reviewing Phrases and Clauses

To review this material before you complete the Review Practices, watch the **Introduction: Parts of Speech, Phrases, and Clauses** video at **MyWritingLab.com** one more time. This time, keep the video open as you complete the rest of the practices in this chapter. For best results, do the **MyWritingLab** exercises online as well as the Chapter Review practices in the book.

REVIEW PRACTICE 1: Identifying Underline the phrases and put the clauses in brackets in each of the following sentences.

1. [She wants to buy her books] before the first day of classes.

2. [When you leave], [I'll tell you the best route].

3. [I want to talk to him] [when he gets back from his errands].

4. [Why do you think] [they were late]?

5. [While they rested], [Sheila and I exercised].

6. [Tad wanted to date Samantha], [but she is dating Reggie].

7. [I can't reach that shelf] [unless I get a stool].

8. After dress rehearsal, [the cast felt very good about their opening the next day].

9. [I was excited to learn] [that hang-gliding is lots of fun].

10. [When you leave the party], [I will be waiting for you].

Practicing Phrases and Clauses

Now complete the **Recall** activity for **Introduction: Parts of Speech, Phrases, and Clauses** at MyWritingLab.com. If you're having a difficult time with a question, open up the video in the lower right-hand corner for some help.

REVIEW PRACTICE 2: Completing Fill in each blank in the following paragraph with an appropriate phrase or clause, as indicated.

The most expensive trip I ever took was to (1) _____ (phrase) with my best friend, Alex. Halfway through our trip, the car began to make a (2) _____ (phrase). After (3) _____ (clause), we decided to stop at a car repair shop. The mechanic explained (4) _____ (phrase) that I needed a new muffler and a new exhaust pipe. I asked him how much the estimate would be (4) _____ (phrase), and he replied it would cost over $2,500. We were (5) _____ (phrase) because we couldn't believe how much the estimate was! I bought the car for $1,200, (6) _____ (clause). Still, we needed a way to get back home so I told the mechanic (7) _____ (phrase) on the car. Seven hours later, (8)_____ (clause). As we drove into my driveway, smoke began coming (10)_____ (phrase), and I realized that I had been swindled out of $2,500.

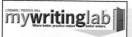
Practicing Phrases and Clauses

For more practice, complete the **Write** activity for **Introduction: Parts of Speech, Phrases, and Clauses** at **MyWritingLab.com.** Make sure to pay close attention to the use of phrases and clauses.

REVIEW PRACTICE 3: Writing Your Own Write your own paragraph about your favorite pet. What did you name it? What kind of animal was it?

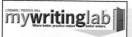
Practicing Phrases and Clauses

Next, complete the **Apply** activity for **Introduction: Parts of Speech, Phrases, and Clauses** at **MyWritingLab.com.** Pay close attention to the directions, and click only on what you're asked to.

EDITING THE STUDENT WRITING

Return to the student paragraph at the beginning of this chapter, and do the following activities.

Individual Activity   Review your marks on the student paragraph. Were you able to separate the phrases from the clauses?

Collaborative Activity   Team up with a partner, and check your work by listing the phrases and clauses in two columns.

EDITING YOUR OWN WRITING

Exchange paragraphs from Review Practice 3 with a classmate, and do the following:

1. Underline any phrases that do not read smoothly.

2. Put an X in the margin where you find a dependent clause that is not connected to an independent clause.

Then return the paragraph to its writer, and use the information in this chapter to edit your own paragraph. Record your errors on the Error Log in Appendix 1.

UNIT QUIZZES

Here are some exercises that test your understanding of all the material in this unit: Parts of Speech, Phrases, and Clauses.

Unit Quiz 1 Identifying

Read the following paragraph, written by a student, and label two of each part of speech listed below.

verbs (v)   pronouns (pro)   adverbs (adv)   conjunctions (conj)

nouns (n)   adjectives (adj)   prepositions (prep)   interjections (int)

[I love my soccer days]. Since high school, [I've had to reduce the amount of time] [I spend playing soccer] [so I can fulfill my other obligations in college]. But [I miss the fun and the competition of the game]. [Even though I am no longer on a team], [I now dedicate Saturday morning to soccer at the community center]. [I run across all sorts of people there]. [I never know] [who will make up our teams], [but we all have a great time]. [I get exercise, a surge of energy, and lots of satisfaction.] [Then, I fill my week with classes, homework, and a part-time job] [so I can spend another Saturday morning on the soccer field].

Unit Quiz 2 Identifying

Underline the phrases, and put the clauses in brackets in the paragraph above.

UNIT WRITING ASSIGNMENTS

1. Find a picture, and explain what is going on in it. Use your imagination to fill in the details.

2. Describe the atmosphere of the classroom in your English class. Who sets the pace of the instruction in the class? What is the chemistry in the class? How does it compare to other classes? What is your opinion of the classroom atmosphere?

3. You have been asked by your college newspaper to contribute to an article on study habits. Explain your daily routine for this publication.

Sentences

Complete sentences are one of the staples of good writing. But sometimes our thoughts pour out of our heads faster than we can get them all down. As a result, we write sentences that need to be corrected in the editing stage. This is a natural part of writing. Always get your ideas down first, and edit your sentences later.

To help you start editing your writing, we will focus on the following sentence elements:

Subjects and Verbs

READING FOR SUBJECTS AND VERBS

Read the following paragraph, written by a student, and underline the subjects once and complete verbs twice.

When I was in sixth grade, I came home from school one day to fire engines in front of my house. Smoke was pouring out of the kitchen window. There was a police car, and I could see my mom and my dog sitting in the back of the car. My mom was holding one hand over her mouth and was petting the dog with her other hand. I ran to my mom as if I was moving in slow motion. It seemed like it took forever to get to the police car. Finally, she put her arms around me and told me that things would be all right. My family and I will never forget that day.

A sentence has a message to communicate, but for that message to be meaningful, it must have a subject and a verb. The subject is the topic of the sentence, what the sentence is about. The verb is the sentence's motor. It moves the message forward to its destination. Without these two parts, the sentence is not complete.

Understanding Subjects and Verbs

To find out more about this topic, go to **MyWritingLab.com,** and watch the video on **Subjects and Verbs.** Then, return to this chapter, which will go into more detail about these elements and give you opportunities to practice them. Finally, you will apply your understanding of subjects and verbs to your own writing.

Student Comment:
"The program lets me go back and look at a topic again if I feel like I didn't get it. With lectures, there's no rewind button."

SUBJECTS

To be complete, every sentence must have a subject. The **subject** tells who or what the sentence is about.

Subject

The **students**   study for their tests.

Computers   solve many problems.

Compound Subjects

When two or more separate words tell what the sentence is about, the sentence has a **compound subject**.

Compound Subject: **Dogs** and **cats** are fun to play with.

Compound Subject: The **cars** and **trucks** were on display.

Hint: Note that *and* is not part of the compound subject.

Unstated Subjects

Sometimes a subject does not actually appear in a sentence but is understood. This occurs in commands and requests. The understood subject is always *you*, meaning either someone specific or anyone in general.

Command: Move away from the fire.

Unstated Subject: **(You)** move away from the fire.

Request: Help me open the jar, please.

Unstated Subject: **(You)** help me open the jar, please.

Subjects and Prepositional Phrases

The subject of a sentence cannot be part of a prepositional phrase. A **prepositional phrase** is a group of words that begins with a **preposition**, a word such as *in, on, under, after,* or *from.* Here are some examples of prepositional phrases:

in the street	**next to** the wall	**on** the bus	**before** lunch
under the water	**with** Brad	**behind** the car	**instead of** you
after work	**into** the boat	**around** the mess	**across** the alley
from the left	**during** the storm	**for** the children	**at** the intersection

(See page 17 for a more complete list of prepositions.)

If you are looking for the subject of a sentence, first cross out all the prepositional phrases. Then figure out what the sentence is about.

~~During the flood~~, the **men** and **women** helped block the water.

The **phone** ~~around the corner~~ was working fine.

Some ~~of the water~~ leaked ~~into our boat~~.

Reviewing Subjects

What is a subject?

_____

_____

What is a compound subject?

_____

_____

What is an unstated subject?

_____

_____

How can you find the subject of a sentence?

_____

_____

PRACTICE 1: Identifying and Correcting

A. Put an X next to the sentence if the underlined portion is not a subject. Cross out the prepositional phrases first.

1. _____ The <u>dogs</u> ate their food.

2. _____ Good musicians practice <u>every day</u>.

3. _____ Manuel was a talented <u>baseball player</u>.

4. _____ After June, <u>I</u> will take a vacation.

5. _____ <u>Every month</u>, Ioana gets money from her parents.

6. _____ The <u>television</u> blared all night.

7. _____ The fountain in the plaza was built <u>by my uncle</u>.

8. _____ <u>Shawna</u> wants an interview with you in the near future.

9. _____ <u>Money</u> doesn't grow on trees.

10. _____ I am <u>applying</u> for a new job.

B. Correct the errors in Practice 1A by underlining the correct subjects.

PRACTICE 2: Completing Fill in each blank in the following sentences with a subject that is not a person's name.

1. _____ took a trip to Hawaii last summer.

2. _____ is a beautiful place in the winter.

3. _____ has been working out every day.

4. _____ is in the shoe department.

5. _____ just finished her medical residency.

6. _____ and _____ have been best friends since kindergarten.

7. Under the umbrella, _____ was staying nice and dry.

8. _____ has a black belt in karate.

9. In two days, _____ will have earned all of his tuition money.

10. Sometimes _____ makes me laugh at myself.

PRACTICE 3: Writing Your Own Write a sentence of your own using each of the following nouns as a subject.

1. shirt _____

2. teacher _____

3. courage _____

4. award _____

5. computer _____

VERBS

To be complete, a sentence must have a verb as well as a subject. A **verb** tells what the subject is doing or what is happening.

Verb

The students **study** for their tests.
Computers **solve** many problems.

Action Verbs

An **action verb** tells what a subject is doing. Some examples of action verbs are *skip*, *ski*, *stare*, *flip*, *breathe*, *remember*, *restate*, *sigh*, *cry*, *decrease*, *write*, and *pant*.

Action Verb: The lobsters **scurry** across the ocean floor.

Action Verb: The car **swerved** out of the way.

Linking Verbs

A **linking verb** connects the subject to other words in the sentence that say something about it. Linking verbs are also called **state-of-being verbs** because they do not show action. Rather, they say that something "is" a particular way. The most common linking verb is *be* (*am*, *are*, *is*, *was*, *were*).

Linking Verb: The water **is** in the gutter.

Linking Verb: I **am** worried about the presentation.

Other common linking verbs are *remain*, *act*, *look*, *grow*, and *seem*.

Linking Verb: The woman **remained** concerned about her clothes.

Linking Verb: Firefighters **act** proud.

Linking Verb: The cliff **looks** tall.

Linking Verb: The stream **grew** wide.

Linking Verb: Children **seem** happy about going to Six Flags Magic Mountain.

Some words, such as *smell* and *taste*, can be either action verbs or linking verbs.

Action Verb: I **smell** flowers.

Linking Verb: This house **smells** like flowers.

Action Verb: She **tasted** the soup.

Linking Verb: It **tasted** too salty.

Compound Verbs

Just as a verb can have more than one subject, some subjects can have more than one verb. These are called **compound verbs**.

Compound Verb: She **skips** and **hops** over the cracks in the sidewalk.

Compound Verb: He **laughs** when he's happy and **cries** when he's sad.

Hint: A sentence can have both a compound subject and a compound verb.

     s   s   v   v

Men and **women avoided** the crowds and **dashed** to their cars.

Helping Verbs

Often the **main verb** (the action verb or linking verb) in a sentence needs help to convey its meaning. **Helping verbs** add information, such as when an action took place. The **complete verb** consists of a main verb and all its helping verbs.

Complete Verb: The snow <u>**will be**</u> gone tomorrow.

Complete Verb: You <u>**might**</u> fall in the ditch.

Complete Verb: We <u>**should have**</u> fixed the faucet.

Complete Verb: City workers <u>**have**</u> checked the stoplights.

Complete Verb: The repair technician <u>**will be**</u> coming to fix the problem.

Complete Verb: You <u>**should**</u> not go outside today.

Hint: Note that *not* isn't part of the helping verb. Similarly, *never, always, only, just,* and *still* are never part of the verb.

Complete Verb: I <u>**have**</u> always **liked** hot weather.

The most common helping verbs are

be, am, is, are, was, were
have, has, had
do, did

Other common helping verbs are

may, might
can, could
will, would
should, used to, ought to

Reviewing Verbs

What is a verb?

_____

_____

What is the difference between action and linking verbs?

_____

_____

Give an example of a compound verb.

_____

_____

Give an example of a helping verb.

_____

_____

What is the difference between a subject and a verb?

_____

_____

PRACTICE 4: Identifying and Correcting

A. Put an X next to the sentence if the underlined portion is not a verb.

1. _____ I <u>gave</u> you my best advice.

2. _____ Gwyneth wrote a <u>paper</u> about *The Tempest*.

3. _____ Next year, I <u>will take</u> piano lessons.

4. _____ Jill just filed her <u>income taxes</u>.

5. _____ The child jumped <u>into the pool</u>.

6. _____ Water <u>is</u> better for you than soft drinks.

7. _____ My father <u>walked</u> to the car and <u>opened</u> the door.

8. _____ Edgar's car is <u>definitely</u> totaled.

9. _____ Doctors and lawyers often have big <u>houses</u>.

10. _____ Abby <u>does</u> not <u>want</u> that cookie.

B. Correct the errors in Practice 4A by underlining the correct verbs.

PRACTICE 5: Completing Fill in each blank in the following sentences with a verb that makes sense. Avoid using *is*, *are*, *was*, and *were* by themselves.

1. The doctor _____ my forehead.

2. My grandmother _____ me a check for my birthday.

3. We always _____ bottled water on camping trips.

4. They _____ happy soon.

5. My friend _____ jigsaw puzzles.

6. Sometimes college _____ solutions to difficult problems.

7. Most of the time, my uncle _____ the dishes.

8. I _____ n't _____ to leave.

9. We _____ a midnight flight to Las Vegas.

10. I _____ often _____ magazines in bed.

PRACTICE 6: Writing Your Own Write a sentence for each of the following verbs, and label the verb as either action or linking.

1. grow _____

2. should have been asking _____

3. appears _____

4. will pay _____

5. has gone _____

CHAPTER REVIEW

You can save your work in the Write activity and come back to it later.

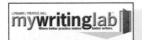

Reviewing Subjects and Verbs

To review this material before you complete the Review Practices, watch the **Subjects and Verbs** video at **MyWritingLab.com** one more time. This time, keep the video open as you complete the rest of the practices in this chapter. For best results, do the **MyWritingLab** exercises online as well as the Chapter Review practices in the book.

REVIEW PRACTICE 1: Identifying Underline the subjects once and the verbs twice in each of the following sentences. Cross out the prepositional phrases first.

1. The dogs barked at the door.

2. My neighbor has tropical fish.

3. We watched "Dancing with the Stars" last night.

4. Rocky swam in the lake.

5. Janine and Wallis went to the movies.

6. I ran to the car and unlocked the door.

7. You have been driving all night.

8. Marny is not feeling well today.

9. The TV is fuzzy.

10. They will never see her again.

Practicing Subjects and Verbs

Now complete the **Recall** activity for **Subjects and Verbs** at **MyWritingLab.com.** Remember to read the answers carefully because many of them look similar.

REVIEW PRACTICE 2: Correcting List any subjects and verbs you didn't identify correctly in Review Practice 1.

Practicing Subjects and Verbs

Next, complete the **Apply** activity for **Subjects and Verbs** at **MyWritingLab.com.** If you're stuck, you can go to the lower right-hand corner and open up the video again, or you can click on the hint button.

REVIEW PRACTICE 3: Writing Your Own Write your own paragraph about your favorite pastime. What does it entail? Why do you like it?

Practicing Subjects and Verbs

For more practice, complete the **Write** activity for **Subjects and Verbs** at **MyWritingLab.com.** Make sure to pay close attention to subjects and verbs in your paragraph.

EDITING THE STUDENT WRITING

Return to the student paragraph at the beginning of this chapter, and do the following activities.

Individual Activity   Review your underlining in the student paragraph. Did you find all the subjects and their verbs? There are 13 subjects and 15 verbs.

Collaborative Activity   Team up with a partner, and check your work by listing the subjects and their verbs in two columns.

EDITING YOUR OWN WRITING

Exchange paragraphs from Review Practice 3 with a classmate, and do the following:

1. Circle the subjects of each sentence.

2. Underline the verbs.

Then return the paragraph to its writer, and edit any sentences in your own paragraph that do not have both a subject and a verb. Record your errors on the Error Log in Appendix 1.

Fragments

The following paragraph, written by a student, contains fragments and complete sentences. Read the paragraph, and underline the subjects once and complete verbs twice.

Our downtown center was just renovated. It has bricks down the center of the street. And lights on the trees all year long. A beautiful sight. I never thought that I would enjoy downtown so much. Every building is also being replastered and repainted. So that the buildings stay in good shape. The bars are now reopening. Downtown is attracting new people. And bringing in a lot of money.

One of the most common errors in college writing is the fragment. A fragment is a piece of a sentence that is punctuated as a complete sentence. But it does not express a complete thought. Once you learn how to identify fragments, you can avoid them in your writing.

ABOUT FRAGMENTS

A complete sentence must have both a subject and a verb. If one or both are missing or if the subject and verb are introduced by a dependent word, you have only part of a sentence, a **fragment.** Even if it begins with a capital letter and ends with a period, it cannot stand alone and must be corrected in your writing. The five most common types of fragments are explained in this chapter.

Type 1: Afterthought Fragments
He works at the garage. **And the bank.**

Type 2: *-ing* Fragments
Breaking the sidewalk. The oak tree is large and strong.

Type 3: *to* **Fragments**
Some people have moved. **To live in the heart of town.**

Type 4: Dependent-Clause Fragments
Because there are no malls here. We go to another city to shop.

Type 5: Relative-Clause Fragments
The hardware store is on the corner. **Which is a good location.**

Understanding Fragments

To help you understand this sentence error, go to **MyWritingLab.com,** and watch the video on **Fragments.** Then, return to this chapter, which will go into more detail about these errors and give you opportunities to practice correcting them. Finally, you will apply your understanding of fragments to your own writing.

Once you have identified a fragment, you have two options for correcting it. You can connect the fragment to the sentence before or after it, or you can make the fragment into an independent clause.

Correction 1:   *Connect the fragment to the sentence before or after it.*

Correction 2:   *Make the fragment into an independent clause:*
          (a) add the missing subject and/or verb, or
          (b) drop the subordinating word before the fragment.

We will discuss these corrections for each type of fragment.

Reviewing Fragments

What is a sentence fragment?

_____

_____

What are the five types of fragments?

_____   _____

_____   _____

_____

What are the two ways to correct a fragment?

1. _____

2. _____

IDENTIFYING AND CORRECTING FRAGMENTS

The rest of this chapter discusses the five types of fragments and the corrections for each type.

Type 1: Afterthought Fragments

Afterthought fragments occur when you add an idea to a sentence but don't punctuate it correctly.

Fragment: He works at the garage. **And the bank.**

The phrase *And the bank* is punctuated and capitalized as a complete sentence. Because this group of words lacks a verb, however, it is a fragment.

Correction 1:   *Connect the fragment to the sentence before or after it.*
Example: He works at the garage **and the bank.**

Correction 2:   *Make the fragment into an independent clause.*
Example: He works at the garage. **He also works at the bank.**

The first correction connects the fragment to the sentence before it. The second correction makes the fragment an independent clause with its own subject and verb.

Reviewing Afterthought Fragments

What is an afterthought fragment?

_____

_____

Give an example of an afterthought fragment.

_____

_____

What are the two ways to correct an afterthought fragment?

1. _____

_____

2. _____

_____

PRACTICE 1: Identifying and Correcting

A. Underline the afterthought fragments in each of the following sentences.

1. I applied for a credit card. But was turned down.

2. Tim looked into the room and saw his keys. On the end table. He was very frustrated.

3. Sharla is sleeping in class today because she stayed up late. With her homework.

4. Spring is my favorite time of year because flowers are growing. And blooming.

5. Carlene turned in her paper by the deadline. But received a poor grade.

6. Jerome ate pizza. With anchovies on it. His breath smelled disgusting.

7. Juana sits next to me. In class. And tries to copy my homework.

8. The best books I ever read are *Gulliver's Travels*. And *Lord of the Flies*. *The Slave Dancer* is good too.

9. The boy bumped his head. On the bedpost. And cried loudly until his mother heard him.

10. My air conditioner isn't working. Or blowing out any cold air.

B. Correct the afterthought fragments in Practice 1A by rewriting them, using both correction methods.

PRACTICE 2: Completing Underline the afterthought fragments in the following paragraph. Rewrite the paragraph, correcting the fragments.

The best day of my life was July 5, 2004. A Monday. My sister helped me move into my new apartment. On the east side of town. I loved living with my parents, but I felt it was time to move on. When I found this apartment, I knew it was perfect. And just my style. The apartment has a big living room and kitchen. But only one tiny bedroom. While we were moving my stuff, my sister said she was jealous. She had no job. And couldn't move out on her own yet. I almost felt sorry for her. Then I remembered how nice it was to have my own place. And stopped worrying about her.

PRACTICE 3: Writing Your Own Write five afterthought fragments of your own, or record five from your papers. Correct these fragments using both correction methods.

1. _____

2. _____

3. _____

4. _____

5. _____

Type 2: *-ing* Fragments

Words that end in *-ing* are forms of verbs that cannot be the main verbs in their sentences. For an *-ing* word to function as a verb, it must have a helping verb with it (*be*, *do*, or *have*; see page 46).

Fragment: **Breaking the sidewalk.** The oak tree is large and strong.

Breaking is not a verb in this sentence because it has no helping verb. Also, this group of words is a fragment because it has no subject.

Correction 1:   *Connect the fragment to the sentence before or after it.*
Example: **Breaking the sidewalk,** the oak tree is large and strong.

Correction 2:   *Make the fragment into an independent clause.*
Example: **The oak tree is breaking the sidewalk.** The oak tree is large and strong.

Hint: When you connect an *-ing* fragment to a sentence, insert a comma between the two sentence parts. You should insert the comma whether the *-ing* part comes at the beginning or the end of the sentence.

The oak tree is large and strong, **breaking the sidewalk.**
Breaking the sidewalk, the oak tree is large and strong.

Reviewing *-ing* Fragments

How can you tell if an -ing word is part of a fragment or is a main verb?

_____

_____

Give an example of an -ing fragment.

_____

_____

What are the two ways to correct an -ing fragment?

1. _____

   _____

2. _____

   _____

What kind of punctuation should you use when you join an -ing fragment to another sentence?

_____

_____

PRACTICE 4: Identifying and Correcting

A. Underline the *-ing* fragments in each of the following sentences.

   1. Driving to the store. I wore my seat belt.

   2. The boy is coloring. Breaking the crayons in half.

   3. Sleeping in the corner. The cat is curled into a ball.

   4. Something has leaked on the floor. Making a big mess.

   5. I hear soft music in the background. Setting the tone of the movie.

   6. Eating a large pastrami sandwich. Nick got a stomach ache.

   7. When this term is over, I'm going home. Starting my big vacation.

   8. Reading at night. Travis fell asleep on his books.

   9. The last time we went to that restaurant, we were unhappy. Waiting 20 minutes for drink refills.

   10. Playing in the swimming pool all afternoon. I got a sunburn.

B. Correct the –*ing* fragments in Practice 4A by rewriting them, using both correction methods. Remember to insert a comma when using correction 1.

PRACTICE 5: Completing Underline the -*ing* fragments in the following paragraph. Rewrite the paragraph, correcting the fragments. Remember to insert a comma when using correction 1.

When my brother joined the Navy, he was very excited. Wanting to travel around the world and meet new people. The reality was not so entertaining. He did get to travel, but he wasn't always stationed in exotic places. Lying on the beach or visiting famous landmarks. He also had a pretty boring job. Washing jet planes. Working the grave-yard shift. When he was in high school, he was quite rebellious. Making bad choices in friends. He was often in trouble for breaking his curfew and staying out too late. Overall, the Navy was good for him. Forcing him to grow up. Though it wasn't the paid vacation that he expected, it did give him the taste of responsibility that he needed.

PRACTICE 6: Writing Your Own Write five -*ing* fragments of your own, or record five from your papers. Correct these fragments, using both correction methods.

1. _____

2. _____

3. _____

4. _____

5. _____

Type 3: *to* Fragments

When *to* is added to a verb (*to see, to hop, to skip, to jump*), the combination cannot be a main verb in its sentence. As a result, this group of words is often involved in a fragment.

Fragment: Some people have moved. **To live in the heart of town.**

Because *to* + a verb cannot function as the main verb of its sentence, *to live in the heart of town* is a fragment as it is punctuated here.

Correction 1:	*Connect the fragment to the sentence before or after it.*
Example:	Some people have moved **to live in the heart of town.**
Correction 2:	*Make the fragment into an independent clause.*
Example:	Some people have moved. **They live in the heart of town.**

Hint: A *to* fragment can also occur at the beginning of a sentence. In this case, insert a comma between the two sentence parts when correcting the fragment.

To live in the heart of town, some people have moved.

Reviewing *to* Fragments

What does a to *fragment consist of?*

_____

Give an example of a to *fragment.*

_____

What are the two ways to correct a to *fragment?*

1. _____

_____

2. _____

_____

PRACTICE 7: Identifying and Correcting

A. Underline the *to* fragments in each of the following sentences.

1. My neighbors drive an expensive car. To look like they are rich.

2. Harry is going with me. To help me buy a car. He is a good negotiator.

3. Breanne makes her own clothes. To save money.

4. To be more prepared for the test. I will devote my weekend to studying.

5. To grow tomatoes in your backyard. You need a big garden area.

6. This is the last time we will call you. To ask you for a donation.

7. To finish wallpapering the living room. My wife will take tomorrow off work.

8. This morning I got up at 5 a.m. To jog around the block before I got in the shower.

9. Mira was getting her nails done. To be in a wedding on Saturday.

10. Put your feet up and relax. To watch this movie with me.

B. Correct the *to* fragments in Practice 7A by rewriting them, using both correction methods.

PRACTICE 8: Completing Underline the *to* fragments in the following paragraph. Rewrite the paragraph, correcting the fragments. Rearrange the sentences, if necessary. Remember to insert a comma when you add the *to* fragment to the beginning of a sentence.

My parents are finally putting in a swimming pool. To keep us from bothering the neighbors. We have been telling them for years that we need a pool, but they always complained about money. To avoid the discussion. Last weekend, my dad learned from a friend about a company that installs swimming pools at a reasonable price. We were so happy. To finally get a pool of our own. The contractor said it would take six to eight weeks. To finish the pool. In the meantime, our back fence has been pulled down. To make room for the big backhoe. It is exciting for my brother and me. To watch the construction. We can't wait to go swimming in our own backyard.

PRACTICE 9: Writing Your Own Write five *to* fragments of your own, or record five from your papers. Correct these fragments, using both correction methods.

1. _____

2. _____

3. _____

4. _____

5. _____

Type 4: Dependent-Clause Fragments

A group of words that begins with a **subordinating conjunction** (see the list that follows) is called a **dependent clause** and cannot stand alone. Even though it has a subject and a verb, it is a fragment because it depends on an independent clause to complete its meaning. An **independent clause** is a group of words with a subject and a verb that can stand alone. (See pages 32–35 for help with clauses.)

Here is a list of some commonly used subordinating conjunctions that create dependent clauses.

Subordinating Conjunctions

after	because	since	until
although	before	so	when
as	even if	so that	whenever
as if	even though	than	where
as long as	how	that	wherever
as soon as	If	though	whether
as though	in order that	unless	while

Fragment: **Because there are no malls here.** We go to another city to shop.

This sentence has a subject and a verb, but it is introduced by a subordinating conjunction, *because*. As a result, this sentence is a dependent clause and cannot stand alone.

Correction 1:   *Connect the fragment to the sentence before or after it.*
Example: **Because there are no malls here,** we go to another city to shop.

Correction 2:   *Make the fragment into an independent clause.*
Example: ~~Because~~ **There are no malls here.** We go to another city to shop.

Hint: If the dependent clause comes first, put a comma between the two parts of the sentence. If the dependent clause comes second, the comma is not necessary.

Because there are no malls here, we go to another city to shop.

We go to another city to shop **because there are no malls here.**

Reviewing Dependent-Clause Fragments

What is a dependent-clause fragment?

_____

What type of conjunction makes a clause dependent?

_____

What is an independent clause?

_____

Give an example of a dependent-clause fragment.

_____

What are the two ways to correct a dependent-clause fragment?

1. _____

_____

2. _____

_____

PRACTICE 10: Identifying and Correcting

A. Underline the dependent-clause fragments in each of the following sentences.

1. While my daughter slept. I finished her scrapbook.

2. Although my brother is in my Spanish class. He will not help me with homework.

3. This winter will be very cold. Since this summer was not as warm as usual.

4. Jared will practice basketball every day. Even if he doesn't make the team.

5. As soon as Maury gets here. I'm going home.

6. Nelly can do the video portion of the project. Unless you have a better idea.

7. Before the sun comes up tomorrow. We will be driving through New Mexico.

8. The Dixie Chicks sang "There's Your Trouble." When they gave a concert in our town.

9. My computer speakers went out. While I was listening to a radio show on the Internet.

10. As long as I am in charge. This is the way we should organize the club.

B. Correct the dependent-clause fragments in Practice 10A by rewriting them, using both correction methods.

PRACTICE 11: Completing Underline the dependent-clause fragments in the following paragraph. Rewrite the paragraph, correcting the fragments. When you use correction 1, remember to add a comma if the dependent clause comes first.

> While I was driving through my hometown. I noticed the ice-cream parlor where I used to work. During my high school years, the parlor was a popular hangout. Even though the ice cream was a little overpriced. The owners were Sam and Billy, who let my friends come by to visit with me. Whenever I had to work weekends. Before it was an ice-cream parlor. The building was used as a bank. Everyone in the town was glad to have the parlor instead. So that teenagers had somewhere safe to spend time. Sam and Billy were the best bosses I could have asked for. Although the pay was not very good. I will never forget that job. Because I learned so much about myself.

PRACTICE 12: Writing Your Own Write five dependent-clause fragments of your own, or record five from your papers. Correct these fragments, using both correction methods.

1. _____

2. _____

3. _____

4. _____

5. _____

Type 5: Relative-Clause Fragments

A **relative clause** is a dependent clause that begins with a relative pronoun: *who, whom, whose, which,* or *that.* When a relative clause is punctuated as a sentence, the result is a fragment.

Fragment: The hardware store is on the corner. **Which is a good location.**

Which is a good location is a clause fragment that begins with the relative pronoun *which*. This word automatically makes the words that follow it a dependent clause, so they cannot stand alone as a sentence.

Correction 1:   *Connect the fragment to the sentence before or after it.*
Example: The hardware store is on the corner, **which is a good
                  location.**

Correction 2:   *Make the fragment into an independent clause.*
Example: The hardware store is on the corner. **It is a good location.**

Reviewing Relative-Clause Fragments

How is a relative-clause fragment different from a dependent-clause fragment?

_____

_____

Give an example of a relative-clause fragment.

_____

_____

What are the two ways to correct a relative-clause fragment?

1. _____

2. _____

PRACTICE 13: Identifying and Correcting

A. Underline the relative-clause fragments in the following sentences.

1. The company president is Mr. Liu. Who always sits with my family at church.

2. My brother is taking the class. That is taught by Dr. Roberts.

3. Those are the neighbors. Whose dogs run loose in the streets.

4. I am taking a trip to Poughkeepsie. Which is in New York.

5. Maureen talked to the woman. Whose car is for sale.

6. You are the one. Whom the committee selected.

7. I just quit smoking. Which was the hardest thing I've ever done.

8. This afternoon, I have a meeting with the dean. Who is in charge of admissions.

9. Dennis works at the restaurant. That is on Elm Street.

10. Laila is going on a date with Jack. Whom she met at the coffeehouse.

B. Correct the relative-clause fragments in Practice 13A by rewriting them, using both correction methods.

PRACTICE 14: Completing Underline the relative-clause fragments in the following paragraph. Rewrite the paragraph, correcting the fragments.

Last year, I celebrated Independence Day with Christine. Whom I met through work. She had a dinner party at her house. Which is on the corner of Fourth Street and Harker Avenue. Christine invited several other people as well. Who brought fireworks and sparklers. The food was great, the company was nice, and the fireworks were entertaining. I met one guy at the party, who drove a beautiful 1965 Mustang. That was fully restored. He was friendly and attractive, but he had a girlfriend. Whose father happened to be the city's mayor. This year, Christine is having another party, and I hope to go.

PRACTICE 15: Writing Your Own Write five relative-clause fragments of your own, or record five from your papers. Correct these fragments, using both correction methods.

1. _____

2. _____

3. _____

4. _____

5. _____

CHAPTER REVIEW

Reviewing Fragments

If you get stuck on the Grammar Apply tasks, click "Hint" to receive helpful information about the exercise.

To review this material before you complete the Review Practices, watch the **Fragments** video at **MyWritingLab.com** one more time. This time, keep the video open as you complete the rest of the practices in this chapter. For best results, do the **MyWritingLab** exercises online as well as the Chapter Review practices in the book.

REVIEW PRACTICE 1: Identifying Underline the fragments in each of the following sentences.

1. I went to the grocery store. To buy a pound of hamburger.

2. Trying to get the best seats. We arrived at the concert early.

3. Since there was nothing we could do. We decided to go home.

4. Yesterday I spoke with my grandfather. Who is also my best friend.

5. Mrs. Robinson teaches history. And economics.

6. While I was walking to the mailbox. I tripped on my untied shoelaces.

7. Janie got her navel pierced. Thinking that would make her happy.

8. To find the best price on computers. We searched the Internet.

9. The small boy played with the heavy door. And pinched his fingers.

10. We invested in the alarm system. That also comes with a paging service.

 **Practicing Fragments**

Now complete the **Recall** activity for **Fragments** at **MyWritingLab.com**. Remember to read the answers carefully because many of them look similar.

REVIEW PRACTICE 2: Correcting Correct the fragments in Review Practice 1 by rewriting each incorrect sentence. Use the methods that you learned in this chapter.

 **Practicing Fragments**

Next, complete the **Apply** activity for **Fragments** at **MyWritingLab.com**. Pay close attention to the directions and click only on what you're asked to.

REVIEW PRACTICE 3: Writing Your Own Write a paragraph about your favorite restaurant. Where is this restaurant? What does it specialize in? Why do you like it? What is your favorite meal?

Practicing Fragments

For more practice, complete the **Write** activity for **Fragments** at
MyWritingLab.com. Pay close attention to which sentences might be
potential sentence fragments.

EDITING THE STUDENT WRITING

Return to the student paragraph at the beginning of this chapter, and do
the following activities.

Individual Activity   Review your underlining in the student paragraph. Did you find all the subjects and verbs? There are eight subjects and nine verbs. Now put brackets around the four fragments in
the paragraph.

Collaborative Activity   Team up with a partner, and use what
you have learned in this chapter to correct these errors using both
correction methods. Rewrite the paragraph with your corrections.

EDITING YOUR OWN WRITING

Exchange paragraphs from Review Practice 3 with a classmate, and do
the following:

1. Put brackets around any fragments you find.

2. Identify the types of fragments you find.

Then return the paper to its writer, and use the information in this chapter
to correct any fragments in your own paragraph. Record your errors on the
Error Log in Appendix 1.

Fused Sentences and Comma Splices

The following student paragraph contains fused sentences, comma splices, and correct sentences. Read the paragraph, and underline each of the independent clauses. See Chapter 2 if you need to review independent clauses.

My imagination has saved my life several times I call on it to get me out of binds all the time. When I am depressed, it finds a way to take me away from the problem that is bothering me. My mom would call this activity day-dreaming, I call it self-defense. Usually, I just start drifting in my mind away from the trouble at hand. I remember one time in my first few weeks of college, I got a paper back in English class with a low grade. To keep myself from crying, I started to drift. I took a journey up into my childhood tree house I stayed up there in my mind for a long time, playing with old toys and talking to my childhood friends. I don't know what happened in class that day, I had a great time remembering.

When we cram two separate statements into a single sentence without correct punctuation, we create **fused sentences** and **comma splices**. These run-together sentences generally distort our message and cause problems for our readers. In this chapter, you will learn how to identify and avoid these errors in your writing.

IDENTIFYING FUSED SENTENCES AND COMMA SPLICES

Whereas a fragment is a piece of a sentence, **fused sentences** and **comma splices** are made up of two sentences written as one. In both cases, the first sentence runs into the next without the proper punctuation between the two.

Fused Sentence: The movie ended I went home.

Comma Splice: The movie ended, I went home.

Both of these sentences incorrectly join two independent clauses. The difference between them is one comma.

Student Comment:
"The videos are great! I finally get comma splices!"

 **Understanding Fused Sentences and Comma Splices**

To learn more about these sentence errors, go to **MyWritingLab.com,** and view the video on **Run-Ons.** Then, return to this chapter, which will go into more detail about these errors and give you opportunities to practice correcting them. Finally, you will apply your understanding of fused sentences and comma splices to your own writing.

A **fused sentence** is two sentences "fused" or jammed together without any punctuation. Look at these examples:

Fused Sentence: I was lying on the sofa I had just eaten lunch.

This example consists of two independent clauses with no punctuation between them:

1. I was lying on the sofa.

2. I had just eaten lunch.

Fused Sentence: I began to think about my brother I felt good.

This example also consists of two independent clauses with no punctuation between them:

1. I began to think about my brother.

2. I felt good.

Like a fused sentence, a **comma splice** incorrectly joins two independent clauses. However, a comma splice puts a comma between the two independent clauses. The only difference between a fused sentence and a comma splice is the comma. Look at the following examples:

Comma Splice: I was lying on the sofa, I had just eaten lunch.

Comma Splice: I began to think about my brother, I felt good.

Both of these sentences consist of two independent clauses. But a comma is not the proper punctuation to separate these two clauses.

> **Reviewing Fused Sentences and Comma Splices**
>
> *What are the two types of run-together sentences?*
>
> _____   _____
>
> *What is the difference between them?*
>
> _____
>
> _____

PRACTICE 1: Identifying Identify each of the following sentences as either fused (F) or comma splice (CS). Put a slash between the independent clauses that are not joined correctly.

1. _____ Devon wanted to join the swim team he had been practicing all summer.

2. _____ The car stalled in the middle of the road, two men helped push it out of traffic.

3. _____ I don't know why you weren't there, I'm sure you had a good excuse.

4. _____ Henrietta ran quickly to the phone she didn't want to miss the call.

5. _____ Summer is coming, the children are ready for a vacation from school.

6. _____ The team practiced for the tournament, it was three weeks away.

7. _____ The book is on the table it is collecting dust.

8. _____ Journals are on the third floor of the library the copy machines are there too.

9. _____ I like to see movies during my free time the last movie I saw was *Shrek*.

10. _____ Kimber is getting married in August, she has already found her wedding dress.

PRACTICE 2: Identifying Label each run-together sentence in the following paragraph as either fused (F) or comma splice (CS).

(1) _____ My girlfriend and I rented a movie last night it was *Proof of Life.* (2) _____ We ordered a pizza and put on the show, within 15 minutes I was falling asleep. (3) _____ I guess I stayed up too late the night before, there was a big test in my math class. Boy, was I embarrassed when I couldn't stay awake! (4) _____ My girlfriend nudged me about five times, trying to wake me up I just couldn't keep my eyes open. (5) _____ Finally, she gave up and let me sleep, just as the movie was ending, I woke up.

PRACTICE 3: Writing Your Own Find five run-together sentences in your writing or in another student's writing, and record them here.

1. _____

2. _____

3. _____

4. _____

5. _____

CORRECTING FUSED SENTENCES AND COMMA SPLICES

You have four different options for correcting your run-together sentences.

1. *Separate the two sentences with a period, and capitalize the next word.*

2. *Separate the two sentences with a comma, and add a coordinating conjunction (and, but, for, nor, or, so, or yet).*

3. *Change one of the sentences into a dependent clause with a subordinating conjunction (such as if, because, since, after, or when) or a relative pronoun (who, whom, whose, which, or that).*

4. *Separate the two sentences with a semicolon.*

Correction 1: Use a Period

Separate the two sentences with a period, and capitalize the next word.

I was lying on the sofa. **I** had just eaten lunch.

I began to think about my brother. **I** felt good.

PRACTICE 4: Correcting Correct the run-together sentences in Practice 1 by rewriting them, using correction 1.

1. _____
2. _____
3. _____
4. _____
5. _____
6. _____
7. _____
8. _____
9. _____
10. _____

PRACTICE 5: Correcting Correct the run-together sentences in Practice 2 by rewriting the paragraph, using correction 1.

_____

_____

_____

_____

_____

PRACTICE 6: Writing Your Own Correct the five run-together sentences from Practice 3 by rewriting them, using correction 1.

1. _____
2. _____
3. _____
4. _____
5. _____

Correction 2: Use a Coordinating Conjunction

Separate the two sentences with a comma, and add a coordinating conjunction (and, but, for, nor, or, so, *or* yet).

I was lying on the sofa, **for** I had just eaten lunch.

I began to think about my brother, **so** I felt good.

PRACTICE 7: Correcting Correct the run-together sentences in Practice 1 by rewriting them, using correction 2.

1. _____
2. _____
3. _____
4. _____
5. _____
6. _____
7. _____
8. _____
9. _____
10. _____

PRACTICE 8: Correcting Correct the run-together sentences in Practice 2 by rewriting the paragraph, using correction 2.

_____

_____

_____

_____

_____

PRACTICE 9: Writing Your Own Correct the five run-together sentences from Practice 3 by rewriting them, using correction 2.

1. _____
2. _____
3. _____
4. _____
5. _____

Correction 3: Create a Dependent Clause

Change one of the sentences into a dependent clause with a subordinating conjunction (such as if, because, since, after, or when) or a relative pronoun (who, whom, whose, which, or that).

I was lying on the sofa **because** I had just eaten lunch.

Whenever I began to think about my brother, I felt good.

For a list of subordinating conjunctions, see page 20.

Hint: If you put the dependent clause at the beginning of the sentence, add a comma between the two sentence parts.

Because I had just eaten lunch, I was lying on the sofa.

PRACTICE 10: Correcting Correct the run-together sentences in Practice 1 by rewriting them, using correction 3.

1. _____
2. _____
3. _____
4. _____
5. _____
6. _____
7. _____
8. _____
9. _____
10. _____

PRACTICE 11: Correcting Correct the run-together sentences in Practice 2 by rewriting the paragraph, using correction 3.

_____

_____

_____

_____

_____

PRACTICE 12: Writing Your Own Correct the five run-together sentences from Practice 3 by rewriting them, using correction 3.

1. _____
2. _____
3. _____

4. _____

5. _____

Correction 4: Use a Semicolon

Separate the two sentences with a semicolon.

I was lying on the sofa; I had just eaten lunch.

I began to think about my brother; I felt good.

You can also use a **transition,** a word or an expression that indicates how the two parts of the sentence are related, with a semicolon. A transition often makes the sentence smoother. It is preceded by a semicolon and followed by a comma.

I was lying on the sofa; **in fact,** I had just eaten lunch.

I began to think about my brother; **consequently,** I felt good.

Here are some transitions commonly used with semicolons.

Transitions Used with a Semicolon Before and a Comma After

also	for instance	in fact	of course
consequently	furthermore	instead	otherwise
finally	however	meanwhile	similarly
for example	in contrast	nevertheless	therefore

PRACTICE 13: Correcting Correct the run-together sentences in Practice 1 by rewriting them, using correction 4.

1. _____

2. _____

3. _____

4. _____

5. _____

6. _____

7. _____

8. _____

9. _____

10. _____

PRACTICE 14: Correcting Correct the run-together sentences in Practice 2 by rewriting the paragraph, using correction 4.

_____

_____

_____

_____

_____

PRACTICE 15: Writing Your Own Correct the five run-together sentences from Practice 3 by rewriting them, using correction 4.

1. _____

2. _____

3. _____

4. _____

5. _____

Reviewing Methods of Correcting Fused Sentences and Comma Splices

What are the four ways to correct a fused sentence or comma splice?

1. _____

_____

2. _____

_____

3. _____

_____

4. _____

_____

Why is correcting fused sentences and comma splices important?

_____

_____

CHAPTER REVIEW

Reviewing Fused Sentences and Comma Splices

To review this material before you complete the Review Practices, watch the **Run-Ons** video at **MyWritingLab.com** one more time. This time, keep the video open as you complete the rest of the practices in this chapter. For best results, do the **MyWritingLab** exercises online as well as the Chapter Review practices in the book.

REVIEW PRACTICE 1: Identifying Put slashes between the following run-together sentences.

1. My brother wants to go with us we'd better let him, or he'll feel bad.

2. The printer is jammed again that's the second time this month.

3. I hope you remembered to pay the water bill I think it's past due.

4. Tracy left the party last night, she was crying.

5. My memory is failing I can't remember anything anymore.

6. Lend me three dollars, I need to bring cookies to the class party.

7. Simon sits next to me in class, he always takes great notes.

8. The airbag inflated during the accident it broke the driver's nose.

9. My favorite shoes are my white Nike sneakers I wear them every day.

10. If you want to go, you should ask, I can't read your mind.

Practicing Fused Sentences and Comma Splices

Now complete the **Recall** activity for **Run-Ons** at **MyWritingLab.com**. If you're having a difficult time with a question, open up the video in the lower right-hand corner for some help.

REVIEW PRACTICE 2: Completing Correct the run-together sentences in Review Practice 1 by rewriting each incorrect sentence. Use the methods you learned in this chapter.

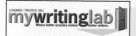 **Practicing Fused Sentences and Comma Splices**

Next, complete the **Apply** activity for **Run-Ons** at MyWritingLab.com. If you're stuck, you can click on the hint button.

REVIEW PRACTICE 3: Writing Your Own Write a paragraph about a first in your life (for example, your first date, your first pizza, your first job).

 **Practicing Fused Sentences and Comma Splices**

For more practice, complete the **Write** activity for **Run-Ons** at **MyWritingLab.com.** Pay close attention to which sentences are fused sentences and which are comma splices.

EDITING THE STUDENT WRITING

Return to the student paragraph at the beginning of this chapter, and do the following activities.

Individual Activity Review your underlining in the student paragraph. Did you find the 13 independent clauses? Now, put slashes between the clauses in the run-together sentences (two fused sentences and three comma splices).

Collaborative Activity Team up with a partner, and use what you have learned in this chapter to correct these errors using all four correction methods. Rewrite the paragraph with your corrections.

EDITING YOUR OWN WRITING

Exchange paragraphs from Review Practice 3 with another student, and do the following:

1. Put brackets around any sentences that have more than one independent clause.

2. Circle the words that connect these clauses.

Then return the paper to its writer, and use the information in this chapter to correct any run-together sentences in your own paragraph. Record your errors on the Error Log in Appendix 1.

UNIT QUIZZES

Here are some exercises that test your understanding of all the material in this unit: Subjects and Verbs, Fragments, Fused Sentences, and Comma Splices.

Unit Quiz 1 Identifying

Underline the subjects once and the verbs twice in the following sentences. Cross out the prepositional phrases first. Then put the fragments in brackets ([ ]), and put a slash (/) between the run-together sentences.

1. Cats and dogs are often treated as children. And part of the family.

2. Carmen was at the public pool, she was meeting Toby there.

3. Hoping it will increase in value. Many people collect old money.

4. When the flowers are in bloom in spring. My grandmother's garden is spectacular.

5. Driving up to Diamond Lake at midnight was a hard task I almost fell asleep at the wheel.

6. Thomas was a fabulous tutor, the university lost him when he became a teacher at Stockdale High.

7. Computers save us a lot of time, they are a good way to organize bills.

8. I went through the old chest. Hoping to find something from my high school days.

9. My mother lives in Sacramento I'm visiting her this weekend.

10. The lawyers were convinced of the jury's decision. After bribing a corrupt juror.

11. The air-pressure gauge was broken she almost panicked underwater when she realized her problem.

12. We visited the Broken Heart. A pub in rural England.

13. To get a better grade. Shelby studied all weekend.

14. If you get a chance, I would like to ask you some questions I have a big decision to make.

15. I didn't get enough sleep last night, now I can't think clearly.

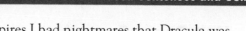

16. I was reading a book about vampires I had nightmares that Dracula was chasing me.

17. People are afraid of the ocean. Because they think that sharks will attack them.

18. Sitting peacefully watching the sunset. She was able to clear her mind.

19. Please carry my books for me, my arm is about to break.

20. During the afternoon that I skipped class. I missed two quizzes and an in-class essay.

Unit Quiz 2 Correcting

Correct the fragments and run-together sentences in Unit Quiz 1 by rewriting each incorrect sentence.

Unit Quiz 3 Identifying

In the following paragraph, cross out the prepositional phrases first. Underline the subjects once and the complete verbs twice. Then put the fragments in brackets ([ ]), and put a slash (/) between the run-together sentences.

Eating fast food is not the healthiest way to go, but it sure is the cheapest. And the best. Places now serve 49-cent tacos, others serve 59-cent hamburgers. Fast-food corporations have ensured that families of four can eat out for less than $10. Which is very cheap. This is appealing to many families then they fall into the fast-food trap. Eating out all the time. Once people become accustomed to eating out cheaply, it's hard to return to making home-cooked meals. Sometimes this can lead to poor health problems often people gain weight. Eating fast food can also cause families to become strangers, they usually don't sit down long enough to talk about what is going on in their lives. Which is very sad. People should take the time to slow down at least once a month. To eat a meal together at home. That way, families can remain connected they will always have one night together. Therefore, families should not get used to eating fast food, then they will never learn good eating habits. They become fast-food junkies for life they will lose valuable time with their family members. Hardly worth it.

Unit Quiz 4 Correcting

Correct the fragments and run-together sentences in Unit Quiz 3 by rewriting the paragraph.

UNIT WRITING ASSIGNMENTS

1. What do you like most about social networking? What do you like least? Analyze your reactions to this form of socializing.

2. You have been asked to write a short statement for your English class about a fairly radical change you just made in your life or in your behavior. What did you change? Why did you make this particular change? Explain this adjustment in detail.

3. You have been asked by a friend to recommend a place for her to travel. What is your recommendation? Why do you recommend this place?

Verbs

Verbs can do just about anything we ask them to do. Because they have so many forms, they can play lots of different roles in a sentence: The bells *ring* on the hour; voices *rang* through the air; we could hear the clock *ringing* miles away. As you can see from these examples, even small changes, like a single letter, mean something; as a result, verbs make communication more interesting and accurate. But using verbs correctly takes concentration and effort on your part.

In this unit, we will discuss the following aspects of verbs and verb use:

Regular and Irregular Verbs

READING FOR REGULAR AND IRREGULAR VERBS

The following paragraph, written by a student, contains correct and incorrect verb usage. Read the paragraph, and underline the 28 complete verbs.

Last year, I walk to the old shed at the edge of my grandmother's backyard. I was determined to either fix the eyesore or tore it down. I begun looking through the old boxes that were inside, and I founded a package of letters. I set down and read them. They was love letters dating back to the early 1900s. The writing was flowery and hard to read, but I eventually begin to make out the words. I set as the sun raised high in the sky. I sat as the sun descended and the moon rose. The letters were from a man whom I had never heard of. He poured his soul out to my grandmother. And then suddenly the letters stop. To this day, I often lay down to go to sleep and wonders about that man. Who was he? What happen to him? Why did my grandmother never mention him? I finally decide to leave the shed standing. I couldn't bear to tear down such a memory.

All verbs are either regular or irregular. **Regular verbs** form the past tense and past participle by adding *-d* or *-ed* to the present tense. If a verb does not form its past tense and past participle this way, it is called an **irregular verb**.

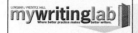 **Understanding Regular and Irregular Verbs**

To improve your understanding of verbs, go to **MyWritingLab.com,** and view the video on **Regular and Irregular Verbs.** Then, return to this chapter, which will go into more detail about verbs and give you opportunities to practice them. Finally, you will apply your understanding of regular and irregular verbs to your own writing.

REGULAR VERBS

Here are the principal parts (present, past, and past participle forms) of some regular verbs. They are **regular verbs** because their past tense and past participle end in *-d* or *-ed*. The past participle is the verb form often used with helping verbs like *have, has,* or *had*.

Some Regular Verbs

PRESENT TENSE	PAST TENSE	PAST PARTICIPLE (USED WITH HELPING WORDS LIKE *HAVE, HAS, HAD*)
listen	listen**ed**	listen**ed**
look	look**ed**	look**ed**
receive	receiv**ed**	receiv**ed**
paint	paint**ed**	paint**ed**
call	call**ed**	call**ed**

The different forms of a verb tell when something happened—in the *present* (I *walk*) or in the *past* (I *walked*, I *have walked*, I *had walked*).

Reviewing Regular Verbs

What is a regular verb?

_____

_____

Identify three forms of a regular verb.

_____   _____

_____

PRACTICE 1: Identifying and Correcting

A. Put an X next to the incorrect verb forms in the following chart.

Present Tense	Past Tense	Past Participle
1. ____ kicked	____ kicked	____ kicked
2. ____ jump	____ jumpt	____ jumped
3. ____ cook	____ cooked	____ cooken
4. ____ bake	____ baken	____ baked
5. ____ mailed	——— mailed	____ mailed
6. ——— played	____ played	____ played
7. ____ watch	____ watched	____ watchen
8. ____ answer	____ answered	____ answerd
9. ____ clean	____ cleant	____ cleaned
10. ____ typed	____ typed	____ typed

B. List the correct form of each of the incorrect verb forms in Practice 1A.

PRACTICE 2: Completing Fill in each blank in the following sentences with a regular verb that makes sense.

1. We _____ to the orchestra.

2. I _____ in that play.

3. Natalie, _____ some flowers out of the garden.

4. They _____ until they cried.

5. I _____ at sad movies.

6. Johnny did _____ for help.

7. The books must have _____ by themselves.

8. The horse _____ over the hedge.

9. The team members have _____ their suitcases to the train station.

10. The workers _____ the wheelbarrow with dirt.

PRACTICE 3: Writing Your Own Write a sentence of your own for each of the following verbs.

1. place _____

2. moan _____

3. has tasted _____

4. lift _____

5. have gained _____

IRREGULAR VERBS

Irregular verbs do not form their past tense and past participle with -*d* or -*ed*. That is why they are irregular. Some follow certain patterns (*sing, sang, sung; ring, rang, rung; drink, drank, drunk; shrink, shrank, shrunk*). But the only sure way to know the forms of an irregular verb is to spend time learning them. As you write, you can check a dictionary or the following list.

Irregular Verbs

PRESENT	PAST	PAST PARTICIPLE (USED WITH HELPING WORDS LIKE *HAVE, HAS, HAD*)
am	was	been
are	were	been
be	was	been
bear	bore	borne, born
beat	beat	beaten
begin	began	begun
bend	bent	bent
bid	bid	bid
bind	bound	bound
bite	bit	bitten
blow	blew	blown
break	broke	broken
bring	brought (not *brang*)	brought (not *brung*)
build	built	built

(continued)

Irregular Verbs

PRESENT	PAST	PAST PARTICIPLE (USED WITH HELPING WORDS LIKE *HAVE, HAS, HAD*)
burst	*burst* (not *bursted*)	*burst*
buy	*bought*	*bought*
choose	*chose*	*chosen*
come	*came*	*come*
cost	*cost* (not *costed*)	*cost*
cut	*cut*	*cut*
deal	*dealt*	*dealt*
do	*did* (not *done*)	*done*
draw	*drew*	*drawn*
drink	*drank*	*drunk*
drive	*drove*	*driven*
eat	*ate*	*eaten*
fall	*fell*	*fallen*
feed	*fed*	*fed*
feel	*felt*	*felt*
fight	*fought*	*fought*
find	*found*	*found*
flee	*fled*	*fled*
fly	*flew*	*flown*
forget	*forgot*	*forgotten*
forgive	*forgave*	*forgiven*
freeze	*froze*	*frozen*
get	*got*	*got, gotten*
go	*went*	*gone*
grow	*grew*	*grown*
hang[1] (a picture)	*hung*	*hung*
has	*had*	*had*
have	*had*	*had*

hear	heard	heard
hide	hid	hidden
hurt	hurt (not *hurted*)	hurt
is	was	been
know	knew	known
lay	laid	laid
lead	led	led
leave	left	left
lend	lent	lent
lie[2]	lay	lain
lose	lost	lost
meet	met	met
pay	paid	paid
prove	proved	proved, proven
put	put	put
read [rēēd]	read [rĕd]	read [rĕd]
ride	rode	ridden
ring	rang	rung
rise	rose	risen
run	ran	run
say	said	said
see	saw (not *seen*)	seen
set	set	set
shake	shook	shaken
shine[3] (a light)	shone	shone
shrink	shrank	shrunk
sing	sang	sung
sink	sank	sunk
sit	sat	sat
sleep	slept	slept
speak	spoke	spoken
spend	spent	spent

(continued)

Irregular Verbs

PRESENT	PAST	PAST PARTICIPLE (USED WITH HELPING WORDS LIKE *HAVE, HAS, HAD*)
spread	spread	spread
spring	sprang (not *sprung*)	sprung
stand	stood	stood
steal	stole	stolen
stick	stuck	stuck
stink	stank (not *stunk*)	stunk
strike	struck	struck, stricken
strive	strove	striven, strived
swear	swore	sworn
sweep	swept	swept
swell	swelled	swelled, swollen
swim	swam	swum
swing	swung	swung
take	took	taken
teach	taught	taught
tear	tore	torn
tell	told	told
think	thought	thought
throw	threw	thrown
understand	understood	understood
wake	woke	woken
wear	wore	worn
weave	wove	woven
win	won	won
wring	wrung	wrung
write	wrote	written

1. *Hang* meaning "execute by hanging" is regular: *hang, hanged, hanged.*
2. *Lie* meaning "tell a lie" is regular: *lie, lied, lied.*
3. *Shine* meaning "brighten by polishing" is regular: *shine, shined, shined.*

Reviewing Irregular Verbs

What is the difference between regular and irregular verbs?

_____

_____

What is the best way to learn how irregular verbs form their past tense and past participle?

_____

_____

PRACTICE 4: Identifying and Correcting

A. Put an X next to the incorrect verb forms in the following chart.

Present Tense	Past Tense	Past Participle
1. —— shake	—— shooked	—— shaken
2. —— bound	—— bound	—— bound
3. —— am	—— was	—— was
4. —— feed	—— fed	—— feded
5. —— choose	—— chosen	—— chosen
6. —— deal	—— dealed	—— dealt
7. —— pay	—— payed	—— paid
8. —— ring	—— rang	—— rang
9. —— understood	—— understood	—— understood
10. —— get	—— gotten	—— gotten

B. List the correct form of each of the incorrect verb forms in Practice 4A.

PRACTICE 5: Completing Fill in each blank in the following sentences with an irregular verb that makes sense.

1. We didn't _____ the problem.

2. We had _____ that book before.

3. Every few months, a cable station _____ a James Bond movie marathon.

4. The storm _____ away our garage.

5. Many people _____ their luggage.

6. My foot _____ after I twisted it.

7. My sister will not _____ anything but bottled water.

8. The old man _____ us fishing.

9. Kenneth and Brian _____ Sarah and Jenny to the movies last Friday.

10. My dogs have _____ time in a kennel.

PRACTICE 6: Writing Your Own Write a sentence of your own for each of the following irregular verbs.

1. draw _____

2. spread _____

3. fight _____

4. swear _____

5. lay _____

USING *LIE/LAY* AND *SIT/SET* CORRECTLY

Two pairs of verbs are often used incorrectly—*lie/lay* and *sit/set*.

Lie/Lay

	Present Tense	Past Tense	Past Participle
lie (recline or lie down)	lie	lay	(have, has, had) lain
lay (put or place down)	lay	laid	(have, has, had) laid

The verb *lay* always takes an object. You must lay something down:

Lay down *what?*
Lay down *your books.*

Sit/Set

	Present Tense	Past Tense	Past Participle
sit (get into a seated position)	sit	sat	(have, has, had) sat
set (put or place down)	set	set	(have, has, had) set

Like the verb *lay*, the verb *set* must always have an object. You must set something down:

Set *what?*
Set *the presents* over here.

Reviewing *Lie/Lay* and *Sit/Set*

What do lie *and* lay *mean?*

_____

_____

What are the principal parts of lie *and* lay?

_____

_____

What do sit *and* set *mean?*

_____

_____

What are the principal parts of sit *and* set?

_____

_____

Which of these verbs always take an object?

_____

_____

PRACTICE 7: Identifying and Correcting

A. Put an X next to the sentence if the underlined verb is incorrect.

1. _____ <u>Lie</u> those heavy crates on the ground.

2. _____ I <u>laid</u> back and relaxed while the hairdresser washed my hair.

3. _____ You had <u>sat</u> on a cactus.

4. _____ We had <u>set</u> down in the cool grass.

5. _____ You have <u>lain</u> around the house all day.

6. _____ Please <u>set</u> beside me during the movie.

7. _____ The workers have <u>lay</u> down the concrete.

8. _____ I had <u>sat</u> my purse on the kitchen table.

9. _____ When I'm stressed, I <u>lay</u> on my bed to relax.

10. _____ Will you <u>sit</u> those books on the counter?

B. Correct the verb errors in Practice 7A by rewriting each incorrect sentence.

PRACTICE 8: Completing Fill in each blank in the following sentences with a form of *lie/lay* or *sit/set* that makes sense.

1. You have _____ your new suit in a puddle of grape juice.

2. I had _____ the hot iron down for only a minute, but it burned my shirt anyway.

3. Sara _____ down in the warm sun and fell asleep.

4. How long did you _____ in the dentist's office?

5. That lazy, overfed cat _____ in the window seat all day and night.

6. Mischa gently _____ the antique artifact on the table.

7. Please _____ on the inside so I can have the outside seat.

8. "_____ still while I remove these bandages," said the doctor.

9. Last month we were on vacation, so the newspapers piled up and _____ in the sun for a week.

10. Ouch! I just _____ on a tack.

PRACTICE 9: Writing Your Own Write a sentence of your own for each of the following phrases.

1. you just sat _____

2. José had lain _____

3. Mary Ann has set her _____

4. lay out your clothes _____

5. set that _____

CHAPTER REVIEW

Reviewing Regular and Irregular Verbs

To review this material before you complete the Review Practices, watch the **Regular and Irregular Verbs** video at **MyWritingLab.com** one more time. This time, keep the video open as you complete the rest of the practices in this chapter. For best results, do the **MyWritingLab** exercises online as well as the Chapter Review practices in the book.

Did you know that spelling counts in the Apply section?

REVIEW PRACTICE 1: Identifying Underline the incorrect verb forms in each of the following sentences.

1. We drived in the car all night long.

2. He lays down right after he gets home from school.

3. I called you last night, but the phone just ringed.

4. Peter was very supportive, and he said he feeled my pain.

5. Elsa filt up the gas tank yesterday, but it's already empty.

6. The air conditioner broked yesterday.

7. He standed in my front yard and sang to me.

8. When I asked the question, the teacher acted like she never heared me.

9. After Jerry divorced Ruth, she never forgived him.

10. I sat the fork in the sink.

Practicing Regular and Irregular Verbs

Now complete the **Recall** activity for **Regular and Irregular Verbs** at **MyWritingLab.com.** Remember to read the answers carefully because many of them look similar.

REVIEW PRACTICE 2: Correcting Correct the verb errors in Review Practice 1 by rewriting each incorrect sentence.

Practicing Regular and Irregular Verbs

Next, complete the **Apply** activity for **Regular and Irregular Verbs** at **MyWritingLab.com.** Remember that spelling counts.

REVIEW PRACTICE 3: Writing Your Own Write a paragraph explaining how active or inactive you are in life. What are the reasons for the choices you have made regarding your level of daily activity?

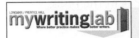

Practicing Regular and Irregular Verbs

For more practice, complete the **Write** activity for **Regular and Irregular Verbs** at **MyWritingLab.com.** Pay close attention to which verbs need to be changed because they are irregular.

EDITING THE STUDENT WRITING

Return to the student paragraph at the beginning of this chapter, and do the following activities.

Individual Activity   Review your underlining. Did you find the 28 complete verbs? Next, place an X above the 14 verb errors.

Collaborative Activity   Team up with a partner, and use what you have learned in this chapter to correct these errors. Rewrite the paragraph with your corrections.

EDITING YOUR OWN WRITING

Exchange paragraphs from Review Practice 3 with another student, and do the following.

1. Circle any verb forms that are not correct.

2. Suggest a correction for these incorrect forms.

Then return the paper to its writer, and use the information in this chapter to correct the verb forms in your own paragraph. Record your errors on the Error Log in Appendix 1.

Verb Tense

The following student paragraph contains correct and incorrect verb usage. Read the paragraph, and underline each of the 23 complete verbs.

My unique pastime, ice-skating, is something that is not really popular in all parts of the country, but no matter where I be, I always find an ice rink. I been skating my entire life. In fact, I am skating before I will walk. It is a very freeing activity. I just get on the ice and set my spirit free. I will skate for a half-hour and feel like I have been relaxing for a week. I forget all the pressures of being a student, and I remember what it is like to be a kid again when I skated alongside my boyfriend. Sometimes, I does competitions. So far, I have beat all of my opponents. To most of my friends and family, skating is a strange way to relieve stress, especially since I has a 30-minute drive to the ice rink. But I don't mind. This December, I will have skated in my spare time for 20 years.

When we hear the word *verb*, we often think of action. We also know that action occurs in time. We are naturally interested in whether something happened today or yesterday or if it will happen sometime in the future. The time of an action is indicated by the **tense** of a verb, specifically in the ending of a verb or in a helping verb. This chapter discusses the most common errors in using verb tense.

 **Understanding Verb Tense**

To find out more about this subject, go to **MyWritingLab.com,** and view the video on **Verb Tense.** Then, return to this chapter, which will go into more detail about tense and give you opportunities to practice it. Finally, you will apply your understanding of verb tense to your own writing.

PRESENT TENSE

One of the most common errors in college writing is reversing the present-tense endings—adding an *-s* where none is needed and omitting the *-s* where it is required. This error causes problems in subject-verb agreement. Make sure you understand this mistake, and then proofread carefully to avoid it in your writing.

Present Tense

Singular		Plural	
INCORRECT	CORRECT	INCORRECT	CORRECT
NOT *I laughs*	*I **laugh***	**NOT** *we laughs*	*we **laugh***
NOT *you laughs*	*you **laugh***	**NOT** *you laughs*	*you **laugh***
NOT *he, she, it laugh*	*he, she, it **laughs***	**NOT** *they laughs*	*they **laugh***

You also need to be able to spot these same errors in sentences.

Incorrect	Correct
The black cat **climb** the tree.	The black cat **climbs** the tree.
My brother **love** chocolate.	My brother **loves** chocolate.
You **speaks** beautifully.	You **speak** beautifully.
They **sings** in the choir.	They **sing** in the choir.

Reviewing Present-Tense Errors

What is the most common error in using the present tense?

_____

_____

How can you prevent this error?

_____

_____

PRACTICE 1: Identifying and Correcting

A. Put an X next to the sentence if the underlined verb is incorrect.

1. _____ Claude <u>walk</u> his dog in the park every day.

2. _____ They <u>hopes</u> for a miracle.

3. _____ A rabbit's tail <u>bring</u> good luck.

4. _____ The flowers <u>smells</u> nice.

5. _____ The river <u>swell</u> in the spring.

6. _____ My grandparents <u>visit</u> us often.

7. _____ The sun <u>dries</u> grapes into raisins.

8. _____ All the books <u>belongs</u> to the library.

9. _____ Our family <u>travel</u> out of the country every year.

10. _____ You <u>need</u> to be more careful.

B. Correct the verb errors in Practice 1A by rewriting each incorrect sentence.

PRACTICE 2: Completing Fill in each blank in the following sentences with a present-tense verb that makes sense.

1. Every spring, they _____ under the stars.

2. I _____ it when you smile.

3. The pots and pans _____ to be cleaned.

4. The professionals _____ the problem.

5. She _____ whenever he walks by.

6. Will you _____ me a song?

7. This season's new comedies _____ hilarious.

8. Martha _____ once a week.

9. Many people _____ in the supernatural.

10. This jasmine _____ only at night.

PRACTICE 3: Writing Your Own Write a sentence of your own for each of the following present-tense verbs.

1. graduate _____

2. wastes _____

3. improve _____

4. arrests _____

5. operate _____

PAST TENSE

Just as we know that a verb is in the present tense by its ending, we can tell that a verb is in the past tense by its ending. Regular verbs form the past tense by adding *-d* or *-ed*. But some writers forget the ending when they are writing the past tense. Understanding this problem and then proofreading carefully will help you catch this error.

Past Tense

Singular		Plural	
INCORRECT	CORRECT	INCORRECT	CORRECT
NOT *I call*	*I* ***called***	**NOT** *we call*	*we* ***called***
NOT *you call*	*you* ***called***	**NOT** *you call*	*you* ***called***
NOT *he, she, it call*	*he, she, it* ***called***	**NOT** *they call*	*they* ***called***

You also need to be able to spot these same errors in sentences.

Incorrect	Correct
Janet yell the cheer.	**Janet yelled** the cheer.
He **wander** through the store.	He **wandered** through the store.
Those girls talk too loudly.	**Those girls talked** too loudly.
Yes, **we want** to win the game.	Yes, **we wanted** to win the game.

Reviewing Past-Tense Errors

What is the most common sentence error made with the past tense?

_____

How can you prevent this error?

_____

PRACTICE 4: Identifying and Correcting

A. Put an X next to the sentence if the underlined past-tense verb is incorrect.

1. _____ Waldo <u>plans</u> the wedding a year ago.

2. _____ They <u>worked</u> very hard on the project.

3. _____ The witches <u>came</u> out on All Hallow's Eve.

4. _____ I <u>burn</u> the meal for tonight's supper.

5. _____ The teacher <u>helps</u> me with this paper yesterday.

6. _____ The neighbor's stereo <u>blares</u> last night.

7. _____ The flag <u>waved</u> in the wind.

8. _____ The politician <u>speaks</u> at the banquet yesterday.

9. _____ Last summer, we <u>drive</u> to Yosemite.

10. _____ Hey! You <u>drink</u> my Pepsi.

B. Correct the verb errors in Practice 4A by rewriting each incorrect sentence.

PRACTICE 5: Completing Fill in each blank in the following sentences with a past-tense verb that makes sense.

1. The baby _____ loudly.

2. The basket weavers _____ many beautiful designs.

3. The meal _____ appetizing.

4. You _____ the wrong question.

5. The Salingers _____ until morning.

6. The firecrackers _____ high in the sky.

7. It _____ me.

8. Oh no! The cat _____ a mouse.

9. These gates _____ only once a year.

10. The thieves _____ into the school.

PRACTICE 6: Writing Your Own Write a sentence of your own for each of the following past-tense verbs.

1. regretted _____

2. swore _____

3. crashed _____

4. wrote _____

5. jumped _____

USING HELPING WORDS WITH PAST PARTICIPLES

Helping words are used with the past participle form, *not* with the past-tense form. It is incorrect to use a helping verb (such as *is, was, were, have, has,* or *had*) with the past tense. Make sure you understand how to use helping words with past participles, and then proofread your written work to avoid making these errors.

Incorrect	Correct
They **have drove** to town.	They **have driven** to town.
She **has shook** the shake.	She **has shaken** the shake.
I **have wrote** a book.	I **have written** a book.
We **had took** the test early.	We **had taken** the test early.

Reviewing Errors with Helping Words and Past Participles

What is the most common sentence error made with past participles?

_____

_____

How can you prevent this error?

_____

_____

PRACTICE 7: Identifying and Correcting

A. Put an X next to the sentence if the underlined verb is incorrect.

1. _____ They <u>had ridden</u> all the rides.

2. _____ We <u>have grew</u> a garden.

3. _____ My chair <u>had broken</u> before I sat in it.

4. _____ The jeans <u>have tore</u> at the knees.

5. _____ Poor Tom! He <u>has spent</u> all his money.

6. _____ He <u>has drew</u> the pictures in black and white.

7. _____ The children <u>have forgot</u> their coats and gloves.

8. _____ We <u>had begun</u> to see daylight.

9. _____ The ice <u>has froze</u> the fish solid.

10. _____ He <u>has forgave</u> your mean comments.

B. Correct the verb errors in Practice 7A by rewriting each incorrect sentence.

PRACTICE 8: Completing Fill in each blank in the following sentences with a correct past-participle verb that makes sense.

1. The pictures have _____ off the wall.

2. The worker has _____ a break.

3. The attendant has _____ our tickets.

4. The dealer had _____ me a bad hand.

5. Cassidy had _____ her nose all morning.

6. The teacher has _____ the boy many times for his pranks.

7. They have _____ the dinner bell.

8. If we had _____ the answer, we wouldn't have asked the question.

9. The student has _____ to do his best.

10. The gum has _____ under the desk.

PRACTICE 9: Writing Your Own Write a sentence of your own for each of the following past-participle verb forms.

1. has known _____

2. had told _____

3. have chosen _____

4. have stolen _____

5. has broken _____

USING *-ING* VERBS CORRECTLY

Verbs ending in *-ing* describe action that is going on or that was going on for a while. To be a complete verb, an *-ing* verb is always used with a helping verb. Two common errors occur with *-ing* verbs:

1. Using *be* or *been* instead of the correct helping verb

2. Using no helping verb at all

Learn the correct forms, and proofread carefully to catch these errors.

Incorrect	Correct
The boys **be going** home.	The boys **are going** home.
	The boys **were going** home.
The boys **been going** home.	The boys **have been going** home.
	The boys **had been going** home.
We **eating** a snack.	We **are eating** a snack.
	We **have been eating** a snack.
	We **were eating** a snack.
	We **had been eating** a snack.

Reviewing *-ing* Verb Errors

What two kinds of errors occur with -ing verbs?

_____

_____

How can you prevent these errors?

_____

_____

PRACTICE 10: Identifying and Correcting

A. Put an X next to the sentence if the underlined helping verb or *-ing* form is incorrect.

1. _____ They <u>had been going</u> to college.

2. _____ We <u>running</u> in a race.

3. _____ The roof <u>been raised</u>.

4. _____ The sun <u>was rising</u> over the horizon.

5. _____ The lawn <u>dying</u> in this hot sun.

6. _____ Spiders <u>running</u> up my arm!

7. _____ The motorist <u>is going</u> the wrong way.

8. _____ We <u>be listening</u> very carefully.

9. _____ The clothes <u>be sitting</u> in the dryer.

10. _____ The printer <u>printing</u> out your document now.

B. Correct the verb errors in Practice 10A by rewriting each incorrect sentence.

PRACTICE 11: Completing Fill in each blank in the following sentences with a helping verb and *-ing* form that make sense.

1. The crowd _____ _____ for more.

2. I _____ when you called.

3. The wolves _____ at the moon.

4. Many people _____ to the movie.

5. She _____ for a walk to relax.

6. The moths _____ too close to the flame.

7. The photographer _____ still-life photos.

8. That night, we _____ to a professional performer.

9. Your help _____ me out of a lot of trouble.

10. A few weeks ago, I _____ with a friend.

PRACTICE 12: Writing Your Own Write a sentence of your own for each of the following verbs.

1. is leaving _____

2. were cooking _____

3. had been writing _____

4. are feeling _____

5. have been promising _____

PROBLEMS WITH *BE*

The verb *be* can cause problems in both the present tense and the past tense. The following chart demonstrates these problems. Learn how to use these forms correctly, and then always proofread your written work carefully to avoid these errors.

The Verb *be*

Present Tense

Singular		Plural	
INCORRECT	CORRECT	INCORRECT	CORRECT
NOT *I be/ain't*	*I **am/am not***	**NOT** *we be/ain't*	*we **are/are not***
NOT *you be/ain't*	*you **are/are not***	**NOT** *you be/ain't*	*you **are/are not***
NOT *he, she, it be/ain't*	*he, she, it **is/is not***	**NOT** *they be/ain't*	*they **are/are not***

Past Tense

Singular		Plural	
INCORRECT	CORRECT	INCORRECT	CORRECT
NOT *I were*	*I **was***	**NOT** *we was*	*we **were***
NOT *you was*	*you **were***	**NOT** *you was*	*you **were***
NOT *he, she, it were*	*he, she, it **was***	**NOT** *they was*	*they **were***

Reviewing Problems with *be*

What are two common errors made with be?

_____

_____

How can you prevent these errors?

_____

_____

PRACTICE 13: Identifying and Correcting

A. Put an X next to the sentence if the underlined form of *be* is incorrect.

1. _____ These balloons <u>be</u> the ones for the party.

2. _____ I <u>ain't</u> going to travel by bus.

3. _____ They <u>was</u> outside in the rain.

4. _____ I <u>am</u> switching phone services.

5. _____ I <u>were</u> the one who broke the stereo.

6. _____ You <u>were</u> the only one who showed up.

7. _____ You <u>was</u> so much fun at the party.

8. _____ The pens and pencils <u>are</u> in the supply cabinet.

9. _____ Those clothes <u>was</u> for charity.

10. _____ He <u>were</u> asleep when you called.

B. Correct the verb errors in Practice 13A by rewriting each incorrect sentence.

PRACTICE 14: Completing Fill in each blank in the following sentences with the correct form of *be* in the tense indicated.

1. I _____ a runner in school. (past)

2. You _____ the most generous person I know. (present)

3. Yesterday, the sheep _____ on that hill. (past)

4. At this moment, I _____ very happy. (present)

5. It _____ dark outside, so you had better stay home. (present)

6. He _____ my brother. (present)

7. The humidity and the flies _____ torturous in Africa. (present)

8. You _____ my favorite aunt. (present)

9. The dog in that picture _____ named Old Man Ruff. (past)

10. It _____ never polite to point at people. (present)

PRACTICE 15: Writing Your Own Write a sentence of your own for each of the following forms of *be*.

1. am _____

2. were _____

3. is _____

4. are _____

5. was _____

PROBLEMS WITH *DO*

Another verb that causes sentence problems in the present and past tenses is *do*. The following chart shows these problems. Learn the correct forms, and proofread to avoid errors.

The Verb *do*

Present Tense

Singular		Plural	
INCORRECT	CORRECT	INCORRECT	CORRECT
NOT *I does*	*I* **do**	**NOT** *we does*	*we* **do**
NOT *you does*	*you* **do**	**NOT** *you does*	*you* **do**
NOT *he, she, it do*	*he, she, it* **does**	**NOT** *they does*	*they* **do**

Past Tense

Singular		Plural	
INCORRECT	CORRECT	INCORRECT	CORRECT
NOT *I done*	*I did*	**NOT** *we done*	*we did*
NOT *you done*	*you did*	**NOT** *you done*	*you did*
NOT *he, she, it done*	*he, she, it did*	**NOT** *they done*	*they did*

Reviewing Problems with *do*

What are two common errors made with do?

_____

_____

How can you prevent these errors?

_____

_____

PRACTICE 16: Identifying and Correcting

A. Put an X next to the sentence if the underlined form of *do* is incorrect.

1. _____ He <u>do</u> his laundry at three in the morning.

2. _____ I <u>done</u> a quick patch on the tire.

3. _____ My uncle and aunt <u>do</u> the cooking all the time.

4. _____ Some people <u>does</u> their hair funny.

5. _____ The young worker <u>does</u> the dishes.

6. _____ We <u>done</u> everything we could think of.

7. _____ The camera <u>done</u> the work.

8. _____ He <u>do</u> his work on time.

9. _____ He <u>does</u> a hilarious comedy act.

10. _____ You <u>did</u> all the chores.

B. Correct the verb errors in Practice 16A by rewriting each incorrect sentence.

PRACTICE 17: Completing Fill in each blank in the following sentences with the correct forms of *do* in the tense indicated.

1. I _____ the jig last night. (past)

2. She _____ her papers quickly. (present)

3. They _____ the job easily. (past)

4. They _____ the weather at 6:00 and 10:00. (present)

5. Last quarter, we _____ basic training together. (past)

6. You _____ math every night to keep up. (present)

7. She _____ wash her hair every day. (present)

8. The man _____ the books for my uncle's business. (present)

9. Tomas _____ the training for Carlos. (past)

10. I _____ the lettering on the poster. (past)

PRACTICE 18: Writing Your Own Write a sentence of your own for each of the following forms of *do*.

1. do _____

2. did _____

3. does _____

4. does _____

5. did _____

PROBLEMS WITH *HAVE*

Along with *be* and *do*, the verb *have* causes sentence problems in the present and past tenses. The following chart demonstrates these problems. Learn the correct forms, and proofread to avoid errors with *have*.

The Verb *have*

Present Tense

Singular		Plural	
INCORRECT	CORRECT	INCORRECT	CORRECT
NOT *I has*	*I* **have**	**NOT** *we has*	*we* **have**
NOT *you has*	*you* **have**	**NOT** *you has*	*you* **have**
NOT *he, she, it have*	*he, she, it* **has**	**NOT** *they has*	*they* **have**

Past Tense

Singular		Plural	
INCORRECT	CORRECT	INCORRECT	CORRECT
NOT *I has*	*I **had***	**NOT** *we has*	*we **had***
NOT *you have*	*you **had***	**NOT** *you has*	*you **had***
NOT *he, she, it have*	*he, she, it **had***	**NOT** *they has*	*they **had***

> ### Reviewing Problems with *have*
>
> *What are two common errors made with* have?
>
> _____
>
> _____
>
> *How can you prevent these errors?*
>
> _____
>
> _____

PRACTICE 19: Identifying and Correcting

A. Put an X next to the sentence if the underlined form of *have* is incorrect.

   1. _____ We <u>had</u> a wonderful time last night.

   2. _____ Samantha <u>has</u> some good news for you.

   3. _____ I <u>has</u> the worst sinus headache.

   4. _____ The nurses <u>has</u> time off.

   5. _____ Yesterday, Aziz <u>has</u> on the most expensive suit.

   6. _____ I <u>have</u> everything I need for the trip.

   7. _____ Brian <u>has</u> the story wrong.

   8. _____ The scarf <u>have</u> a small flaw.

   9. _____ The trees in the front yard <u>has</u> no leaves.

   10. _____ It <u>have</u> many inches of snow on top.

B. Correct the verb errors in Practice 19A by rewriting each incorrect sentence.

PRACTICE 20: Completing Fill in each blank in the following sentences with the correct form of *have* in the tense indicated.

1. The boys and girls _____ an early bedtime. (present)

2. I _____ a strange dream last night. (past)

3. We _____ fun at the beach. (past)

4. This _____ the directions for the party. (present)

5. We _____ an obligation to the court. (present)

6. Islands _____ many weather changes throughout the day. (present)

7. She _____ the answer all along. (past)

8. Cleo, my cat, _____ a small white star on her head. (past)

9. You _____ the bride's ring just a few minutes ago. (past)

10. Now you _____ the broken one. (present)

PRACTICE 21: Writing Your Own Write a sentence of your own for each of the following forms of have.

1. have _____

2. has _____

3. had _____

4. had _____

5. have _____

CHAPTER REVIEW

Did you know you lose points for every incorrect answer (as well as when you take hints) in the Grammar Apply?

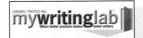

Reviewing Verb Tense

To review this material before you complete the Review Practices, watch the **Verb Tense** video at **MyWritingLab.com** one more time. This time, keep the video open as you complete the rest of the practices in this chapter. For best results, do the **MyWritingLab** exercises online as well as the Chapter Review practices in the book.

REVIEW PRACTICE 1: Identifying Underline the incorrect verb forms in each of the following sentences.

1. The children laughs at the clown's funny faces.

2. Veronica and Mike done the dance moves perfectly.

3. Maisy has forget her pager again.

4. Yesterday, you ask me the funniest thing.

5. We been the best of friends.

6. Oh no! You has a bug in your hair.

7. The monkeys plucks fleas off of each other.

8. I were filthy from the dust storm.

9. We eating everything in sight.

10. He have the worst cold ever.

 **Practicing Verb Tense**

Now complete the **Recall** activity for **Verb Tense** at **MyWritingLab.com**. Remember to read the answers carefully. If you're having a difficult time with a question, open up the video in the lower right-hand corner for some help.

REVIEW PRACTICE 2: Correcting Correct the errors in Review Practice 1 by rewriting each incorrect sentence.

 **Practicing Verb Tense**

Next, complete the **Apply** activity for **Verb Tense** at **MyWritingLab.com**. If you're stuck, you can click on the hint button.

REVIEW PRACTICE 3: Writing Your Own Write a paragraph describing your best friend. Be careful to use all verbs in the correct tense. Check in particular for errors with *be, do,* and *have.*

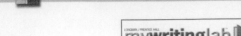

Practicing Verb Tense

For more practice, complete the **Write** activity for **Verb Tense** at **MyWritingLab.com.** Pay close attention to which verbs have tense errors.

EDITING THE STUDENT WRITING

Return to the student paragraph at the beginning of this chapter, and do the following activities.

Individual Activity Review your underlining. Did you find the 23 verbs? Next, place an X above the nine verb errors.

Collaborative Activity Team up with a partner, and use what you have learned in this chapter to correct these errors. Rewrite the paragraph with your corrections.

EDITING YOUR OWN WRITING

Exchange paragraphs from Review Practice 3 with another student, and do the following:

1. Underline any incorrect tenses.

2. Circle any incorrect verb forms.

Then return the paper to its writer, and use the information in this chapter to correct any verb errors in your own paragraph. Record your errors on the Error Log in Appendix 1.

Subject–Verb Agreement

The following paragraph, written by a student, contains examples of correct and incorrect Subject–verb agreement. Read the paragraph, and underline each of the subjects and verbs. Cross out the 21 prepositional phrases first.

It is very strange, but I loves the smell of oil, gas, and exhaust from cars. Most says these things smell like burning fumes, but for me they smell of warm, carefree days spent with my dad. Dad has a passion for fixing up old cars, and I am his assistant. Dad and I spends our summer days in the shed in the back of the house. Either he are underneath the car or in the car's engine. Hovering nearby is his willing assistant, me, with wrenches, oil, rags—anything Dad need. In the summer by mid-day, the shed gets so hot that I can actually see the fumes from the oil, gas, and exhaust in the air. I breathe deeply: There are the smell of my father and me. My gang of friends do not understand why I spend my summer in a hot shed with my dad. But I knows this: Here is my fondest memories.

Almost every day, we come across situations that require us to reach an agreement with someone. For example, you and a friend might have to agree on which movie to see, or you and your manager might have to agree on how many hours you'll work in the coming week. Whatever the issue, agreement is essential in most aspects of life—including writing. In this chapter, you will learn how to resolve conflicts in your sentences by making sure your subjects and verbs agree.

SUBJECT–VERB AGREEMENT

Subject–verb agreement simply means that singular subjects must be paired with singular verbs and plural subjects with plural verbs. Look at this example:

Singular: **She lives** in California.

The subject *she* is singular because it refers to only one person. The verb *lives* is singular and matches the singular subject. Here is the same sentence in plural form:

Plural: **They live** in California.

The subject *they* is plural, referring to more than one person, and the verb *live* is also plural.

Reviewing Subject–Verb Agreement

What is the difference between singular and plural?

_____

_____

What kind of verb goes with a singular subject?

_____

_____

What kind of verb goes with a plural subject?

_____

_____

Understanding Subject–Verb Agreement

To expand your understanding of this subject, go to **MyWritingLab.com**, and watch the video on **Subject–Verb Agreement.** Then, return to this chapter, which will go into more detail about this topic and give you opportunities to practice it. Finally, you will apply your understanding of subject–verb agreement to your own writing.

PRACTICE 1: Identifying and Correcting

A. Put an X next to the sentence if its subject and verb do not agree. Underline the subject and verb.

1. _____ We envies athletic ability.

2. _____ Disgruntled employees are difficult to control.

3. _____ Ian believes in his girlfriend.

4. _____ The paintings sells for a lot of money.

5. _____ Adriana try to study hard.

6. _____ The friends fights over stupid things.

7. _____ The new TV shows has great potential.

8. _____ Most kids loves rock music.

9. _____ Stella drives very fast.

10. _____ The play are about to begin.

B. Correct the subject–verb agreement errors in Practice 1A by rewriting each incorrect sentence.

PRACTICE 2: Completing Fill in each blank with a present-tense verb that agrees with its subject. Avoid *is, are, was,* and *were.*

1. The nudity in the movie _____ inappropriate.

2. They _____ the trip will be exciting.

3. The computer automatically _____ the latest version of your document every few minutes.

4. After the holidays, Cassandra _____ for two weeks.

5. Cheerleaders _____ for the school's team to win.

6. Looking out my office window, I _____ at a brick wall.

7. Jack _____ he got the lead for the play.

8. Race car drivers _____ at very high speeds.

9. Eating carrots _____ people's eyesight.

10. Fire fighters _____ several fires in a week.

PRACTICE 3: Writing Your Own Write a sentence of your own using each of the following words as subjects.

1. a backpack _____

2. Mike _____

3. the cars _____

4. his dogs _____

5. the computer _____

WORDS SEPARATING SUBJECTS AND VERBS

With sentences as simple and direct as *She lives in California*, checking that the subject and verb agree is easy. But problems can arise when words come between the subject and the verb. Often the words between the subject and verb are prepositional phrases. If you follow the advice given in Chapter 3 you will be able to find the subject and verb: *Cross out all the prepositional phrases in a sentence. The subject and verb will be among the words that are left.* Here are some examples:

                                  s   v

Prepositional Phrases: The **donation** ~~for the charity center~~ **is** ~~in my car~~.

When you cross out the prepositional phrases, you can tell that the singular subject, *donation*, and the singular verb, *is*, agree.

                                    s   v

Prepositional Phrases: The **stars** ~~in the sky~~ **twinkle** ~~at night~~.

When you cross out the prepositional phrases, you can tell that the plural subject, *stars*, and the plural verb, *twinkle*, agree.

Reviewing Words Separating Subjects and Verbs

What words often come between subjects and verbs?

_____

What is an easy way to identify the subject and verb in a sentence?

_____

PRACTICE 4: Identifying and Correcting

A. Place an X next to the sentence if its subject and verb do not agree. Cross out the prepositional phrases first. Then underline the subjects and verbs.

1. _____ The teacher in the audience seem familiar with the speaker.

2. _____ Roman architecture still influences architecture today.

3. _____ Penn and Teller is famous magicians.

4. _____ The reports on my desk belong to the finance department.

5. _____ Ranch dressing on a salad taste the best.

6. _____ The workers in the yard wants overtime work.

7. _____ Horror films and suspense dramas at the theatre gives me nightmares.

8. _____ The keys on the sofa fits the back door.

9. _____ The motorists on that highway drive too fast.

10. _____ One of her many talents are dancing.

B. Correct the subjects and verbs that do not agree in Practice 4A by rewriting each incorrect sentence.

PRACTICE 5: Completing Fill in each blank in the following sentences with a verb that agrees with its subject and makes sense. Cross out the prepositional phrases first.

1. Many travelers on this trip _____ trains to planes.

2. Our award-winning roses on the back patio _____ throughout the summer.

3. The decorative dragons on this silk _____ good fortune.

4. The beef and the noodles on the stove _____ seasoning.

5. The clothes in the dryer _____ folding.

6. A pool above the ground _____ value to a house.

7. The Alamo Dome in Texas _____ many sporting events and concerts.

8. The four of us _____ watching scary movies.

9. Tom Hanks _____ many types of characters.

10. The woman with the poodle and funny glasses always _____ me laugh.

PRACTICE 6: Writing Your Own Write a sentence of your own for each of the following prepositional phrases.

1. behind the couch _____

2. around that mountain _____

3. with the red hair _____

4. in our company _____

5. on our team _____

MORE THAN ONE SUBJECT

Sometimes a subject consists of more than one person, place, thing, or idea. These subjects are called **compound** (as discussed in Chapter 3). Follow these three rules when matching a verb to a compound subject:

1. When compound subjects are joined by *and*, use a plural verb.

   Plural: **Maria** and **Tom were** my best friends.

   The singular words *Maria* and *Tom* together make a plural subject. Therefore, the plural verb *were* is needed.

2. When the subject appears to have more than one part but the parts refer to a single unit, use a singular verb.

   Singular: **Vinegar and oil** is great on a salad.

   Vinegar is one item and *oil* is one item, but one is not eaten without the other, so they form a single unit. Because they are a single unit, they require a singular verb—*is*.

3. When compound subjects are joined by *or* or *nor*, make the verb agree with the subject closest to it.

   Singular: Neither **bananas** nor **chicken was** available at the store.

   The part of the compound subject closest to the verb is *chicken*, which is singular. Therefore, the verb must be singular—*was*.

   Plural: Neither **chicken** nor **bananas were** available at the store.

   This time, the part of the compound subject closest to the verb is *bananas*, which is plural. Therefore, the verb must be plural—*were*.

Reviewing Subject–Verb Agreement with More than One Subject

Do you use a singular or plural verb with compound subjects joined by and?

_____

Why should you use a singular verb with a subject like macaroni and cheese?

_____

If one part of a compound subject joined by or *or* nor *is singular and the other is plural, how do you decide whether to use a singular or plural verb?*

_____

PRACTICE 7: Identifying and Correcting

A. Put an X next to the sentence if its subjects and verb do not agree. Cross out the prepositional phrases first. Then underline the subject and verb.

1. _____ Neither the fish nor the ham were cooked well.

2. _____ "Ball and chain" are an expression referring to one's spouse.

3. _____ Paper and an ink cartridge for the printer need to be ordered.

4. _____ Sam and Jim from my school draws very well.

5. _____ Louisiana and Georgia are humid states.

6. _____ Either the flies or the heat in the summer annoy me.

7. _____ Sour cream and onion on chips are my favorite dip.

8. _____ Either the movers or I are responsible for packing the glasses.

9. _____ Ham and cheese with mayonnaise makes a great sandwich.

10. _____ Pens and pencils belongs in the third drawer.

B. Correct the subjects and verbs that do not agree in Practice 7A by rewriting each incorrect sentence.

PRACTICE 8: Completing Fill in each blank in the following sentences with a verb that agrees with its subject and makes sense. Avoid *is, are, was,* and *were* when possible. Cross out the prepositional phrases first.

1. The balloons and streamers for the party _____ in the back-seat of the car.

2. Neither the picture nor the wall hangings _____ good on the wall.

3. Colds and flus _____ usually caught in the winter.

4. Peanut butter and jelly _____ good for lunch.

5. Dinner and a movie with someone you like _____ a good date.

6. Sun and water _____ plants grow.

7. The managers and the staff in this office _____ a break.

8. Either this lotion or this oil _____ me to break out.

9. Neither the girls nor the boys from the third grade well.

10. The CDs and the DVDs _____ in the entertainment center.

PRACTICE 9: Writing Your Own Write a sentence of your own using the following words as subjects.

1. beer and peanuts _____

2. neither my father nor mother _____

3. the actors and their bodyguards _____

4. either the sweater or the pants _____

5. the rabbits and chickens _____

VERBS BEFORE SUBJECTS

When the subject follows its verb, the subject may be hard to find, which makes the process of agreeing subjects and verbs difficult. Subjects come after verbs in two particular situations—when the sentence begins with *Here* or *There* and when a question begins with *Who, What, Where, When, Why,* or *How.* Here are some examples:

Verb Before Subject: Here **are** the **contestants** ~~for the game~~.

Verb Before Subject: There **is paper** ~~in the filing cabinet~~.

In sentences that begin with *Here* or *There*, the verb always comes before the subject. Don't forget to cross out prepositional phrases to help you identify the subject. One of the words that's left will be the subject, and then you can check that the verb agrees with it.

Verb Before Subject: Where **are** the **keys** ~~to this lock~~?

Verb Before Subject: When **are you** graduating ~~from college~~?

In questions that begin with *Who, What, When, Where, Why,* and *How,* the verb comes before the subject, as in the first example, or is split by the sub-ject, as in the last example.

Reviewing Verbs Before Subjects

Where will you find the verb in sentences that begin with Here *or* There?

_____

Where will you find the verb in questions that begin with Who, What, Where, When, Why, *and* How?

_____

PRACTICE 10: Identifying and Correcting

A. Put an X next to the sentence if the subject and verb do not agree. Cross out the prepositional phrases first. Then underline the subject and verb.

1. _____ There are several reasons for this strategy.

2. _____ Who is the nurses for this procedure?

3. _____ What is you doing with all those leftovers?

4. _____ Here sit the dogs for the parade.

5. ____ There jumps the frogs from the pond.

6. _____ Whom are you taking to the baseball game?

7. _____ Why is you wearing those clothes?

8. _____ Here is the new TV.

9. _____ How are your back today?

10. _____ Here is the cleaning people for your house.

B. Correct the subjects and verbs that do not agree in Practice 10A by rewriting each incorrect sentence.

PRACTICE 11: Completing Fill in each blank in the following sentences with a verb that agrees with its subject and makes sense. Avoid *is*, *are*, *was*, and *were* when possible. Cross out the prepositional phrases first.

1. Here _____ our horses after the ride.

2. There _____ the nervous father-to-be.

3. Who _____ that girl with the red blouse?

4. What _____ Ling thinking?

5. There _____ the coals from last night's fire.

6. How _____ the beginning of the poem?

7. Where _____ Jane and Jill last week?

8. Here _____ the water from the creek.

9. Here _____ the performers for tonight's show.

10. Where _____ those old shoes?

PRACTICE 12: Writing Your Own Write a sentence of your own beginning with each of the following words.

1. here _____

2. there _____

3. who _____

4. what _____

5. how _____

COLLECTIVE NOUNS

Collective nouns name a group of people or things. Examples include such nouns as *army*, *audience*, *band*, *class*, *committee*, *crew*, *crowd*, *family*, *flock*, *gang*, *jury*, *majority*, *minority*, *orchestra*, *senate*, *team*, and *troop*. Collective nouns can be singular or plural. They are singular when they refer to a group as a single unit. They are plural when they refer to the individual actions or feelings of the group members.

s   v

Singular: The **orchestra plays** every Friday.

Orchestra refers to the entire unit or group. Therefore, it requires the singular verb *plays*.

s   v

Plural: The **orchestra play** different instruments.

Here *orchestra* refers to the individual members, who each play an instrument, so the plural verb *play* is used.

Reviewing Collective Nouns

When is a collective noun singular?

_____

_____

When is a collective noun plural?

_____

_____

PRACTICE 13: Identifying and Correcting

A. Put an X next to the sentence if the subject and verb do not agree. Cross out the prepositional phrases first. Then underline the subjects and verbs.

1. _____ My gang of friends is going to Magic Mountain.

2. _____ The committee for finance decide money issues.

3. _____ A crew of sailors whistles every time she walks by.

4. _____ The majority of the voters plans a vote on Monday.

5. _____ The jury are passing the verdict on the accused.

6. _____ The flock of birds is flying in formation.

7. _____ The band play "Wipe Out" at every game.

8. _____ My family visits one another for every holiday.

9. _____ A troupe of entertainers performs in our town once a year.

10. _____ My brother's class of graduating students like the new caps and gowns.

B. Correct the subjects and verbs that do not agree in Practice 13A by rewriting each incorrect sentence.

PRACTICE 14: Completing Fill in each blank in the following sentences with a verb that agrees with its subject and makes sense. Avoid *is*, *are*, *was*, and *were* when possible. Cross out the prepositional phrases first.

1. The team of football players _____ silently going through individual preparations for the game.

2. The majority _____ the voice of the minority.

3. The committee _____ taken a break from the long meeting.

4. Our class always _____ the most money for charity.

5. The orchestra in the pit _____ playing badly.

6. The family _____ going on vacation this summer.

7. The army _____ across the land.

8. Only a minority of the citizens _____ cheated by the new tax.

9. The crowd of onlookers _____ shocked by the scene.

10. The class with the most rowdy students pleased _____ with the teacher.

PRACTICE 15: Writing Your Own Write a sentence of your own using each of the following collective nouns as subjects.

1. crowd _____

2. army _____

3. family _____

4. senate _____

5. audience _____

INDEFINITE PRONOUNS

Indefinite pronouns do not refer to anyone or anything specific. Some indefinite pronouns are always singular, and some are always plural. A few can be either singular or plural, depending on the other words in the sentence. When an indefinite pronoun is the subject of a sentence, the verb must agree with the pronoun. Here is a list of indefinite pronouns.

Indefinite Pronouns

ALWAYS SINGULAR		ALWAYS PLURAL	EITHER SINGULAR OR PLURAL
another	neither	both	all
anybody	nobody	few	any
anyone	none	many	more
anything	no one	others	most
each	nothing	several	some
either	one		
everybody	other		
everyone	somebody		
everything	someone		
little	something		
much	whoever		

>   s   v
Singular: **Something changes** at home every day.

>   s   v
Everybody hates this hot weather.

>   s   v
Plural: **Several are making** the long hike.

>   s   v
Many stay longer than necessary.

The pronouns that can be either singular or plural are singular when they refer to singular words and plural when they refer to plural words.

          s   v
Singular: **Some** of Sarah's water **was** gone.

Some is singular because it refers to *water*, which is singular. The singular verb *was* agrees with the singular subject *some*.

          s   v
Plural: **Some** of Sarah's friends **were** at her graduation.

Some is plural because it refers to *friends*, which is plural. The plural verb *were* agrees with the plural subject *some*.

Reviewing Indefinite Pronouns

What is an indefinite pronoun?

_____

_____

When are all, any, more, most, *and* some *singular or plural?*

_____

_____

PRACTICE 16: Identifying and Correcting

A. Put an X next to the sentence if its subject and verb do not agree. Cross out the prepositional phrases first. Then underline the subject and verb.

1. _____ Several of the diners eats only vegetarian meals.

2. _____ Many of the people trip on the first step.

3. _____ Nothing in this refrigerator taste good to me today.

4. _____ More of the wild animals is moving into the city.

5. _____ Both of the students in the class tries very hard.

6. _____ Everybody pretends to like her.

7. _____ All of the money are for your business trip.

8. _____ Most of the crime scene have been destroyed.

9. _____ No one paces the floor as much as you do.

10. _____ Few of the invited guests plans to arrive late.

B. Correct the subjects and verbs that do not agree in Practice 16A by rewriting each incorrect sentence.

PRACTICE 17: Completing Fill in each blank in the following sentences with a verb that agrees with its subject and makes sense. Cross out the prepositional phrases first.

1. A few of the cats _____ their shots.

2. Some of the water _____ on the carpet.

3. Someone _____ eating my lunch.

4. Both of the boys _____ late for their appointments.

5. Nothing _____ more important than your health.

6. Somebody in this room _____ keeping a secret.

7. Several of the videos _____ destroyed in the heat.

8. Most of the mud _____ on me.

9. All of the barking dogs _____ to the neighbor.

10. Each person _____ a different superstition.

PRACTICE 18: Writing Your Own Write a sentence of your own using the following indefinite pronouns as subjects, and combine them with one of the following verbs: *is, are, was, were.*

1. each _____

2. others _____

3. several _____

4. most _____

5. some _____

CHAPTER REVIEW

Reviewing Subject–Verb Agreement

To review this material before you complete the Review Practices, watch the **Subject–Verb Agreement** video at **MyWritingLab.com** one more time. This time, keep the video open as you complete the rest of the practices in this chapter. For best results, do the **MyWritingLab** exercises online as well as the Chapter Review practices in the book.

In the **Subject–Verb Agreement** video, pay special attention to compound, indefinite, and collective nouns, which many students find confusing.

REVIEW PRACTICE 1: Identifying Underline the incorrect verbs in each of the following sentences. Cross out the prepositional phrases first.

1. We speaks in clear, forceful voices.

2. The rabbits and the chickens in the back shed shares the same feed.

3. A few of the memos for today's meeting was misplaced.

4. The committee of new employees ask a lot of questions.

5. Somebody take the erasers from this classroom every day.

6. Either the stereo or the TV in the living room require a new plug.

7. There is many books on the shelf.

8. Christy water the flowers in the planters.

9. What is you watching on the TV?

10. The team of synchronized swimmers compete in the finals every year.

Practicing Subject–Verb Agreement

Now complete the **Recall** activity for **Subject–Verb Agreement** at **MyWritingLab.com.** Remember to read the answers carefully because many of them look similar.

REVIEW PRACTICE 2: Correcting Correct the errors in Review Practice 1 by rewriting each incorrect sentence.

Practicing Subject–Verb Agreement

Next, complete the **Apply** activity for **Subject–Verb Agreement** at **MyWritingLab.com.** Pay close attention to the directions and only click on what you're asked to.

REVIEW PRACTICE 3: Writing Your Own Write a paragraph about an experience you have had participating on a team or observing a team. This could be in athletics, at work, in a club, at home, or at church.

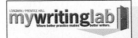

Practicing Subject–Verb Agreement

For more practice, complete the **Write** activity for **Subject–Verb Agreement** at **MyWritingLab.com.** Pay close attention to which subjects and verbs do not agree.

EDITING THE STUDENT WRITING

Return to the student paragraph at the beginning of this chapter, and do the following activities.

Individual Activity   Review your underlining. Did you find all the subjects and verbs? Now, underline the nine agreement errors in the paragraph twice.

Collaborative Activity   Team up with a partner, and use what you have learned in this chapter to correct these errors. Rewrite the paragraph with your corrections.

EDITING YOUR OWN WRITING

Exchange paragraphs from Review Practice 3 with another student, and do the following:

1. Underline the subject once in each sentence.

2. Underline the verbs twice.

3. Put an X by any verbs that do not agree with their subjects.

Then return the paper to its writer, and use the information in this chapter to correct any subject–verb agreement errors in your own paragraph. Record your errors on the Error Log in Appendix 1.

CHAPTER 9

More on Verbs

The following paragraph, written by a student, contains examples of active and passive verbs. Read the paragraph, and underline each of the 26 verbs.

I hate doing household chores, but I especially hated emptying the dishwasher. Since I'm short, emptying the dishwasher has two basic stages: the places I can reach and the places I can't reach. The silverware is emptied by me first because I can reach the drawer where it belongs. Then all the plastic containers are unloaded, which I coordinate by color. I put these away in the bottom cupboard, which, of course, I will be able to reach. Last and most hated comes the dinnerware and glasses. I take the plates and bowls out of the dishwasher and stacked them on the kitchen counter. The glasses are done in the same manner. Then I make a little room on the counter and will climb up. This is the only way I can reach the cupboards above the kitchen counter. Since the glasses are on the top shelf, I have to stand up, which usually made me dizzy. One of these days, I'm going to look down only to find the ground rushing up to meet me. Maybe then my roommate will not ask me to empty the dishwasher anymore.

Verbs communicate the action and time of each sentence. So it is important that you use verb tense consistently. Also, you should strive to write in the active, not the passive, voice. This chapter provides help with both of these sentence skills.

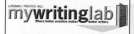
Understanding More on Verbs

Student Comment:
"This video on **Verb Tense and Active Voice** helped me understand verbs better because they were fresh in my mind when I went back and wrote my papers. No more verb errors for me!"

To learn more about verbs, go to **MyWritingLab.com,** and view the video on **Consistent Verb Tense and Active Voice.** Then, return to this chapter, which will go into more detail on verbs and give you opportunities to practice them. Finally, you will apply your understanding of verbs to your own writing.

CONSISTENT VERB TENSE

Verb tense refers to the time an action takes place—in the present, the past, or the future. The verb tenses in a sentence should be consistent. That is, if you start out using one tense, you should not switch tenses unless absolutely necessary. Switching tenses can be confusing. Here are some examples:

NOT	*Present* When the doorbell **rings** all evening and the ghosts *Present* *Past* and goblins **come** out for candy, then it **was** Halloween.
CORRECT	*Present* When the doorbell **rings** all evening and the ghosts *Present* *Present* and goblins **come** out for candy, then it **is** Halloween.

NOT	*Past* *Present* They **rushed** to the hospital when they **hear** that you were having the baby.
CORRECT	*Past* *Past* They **rushed** to the hospital when they **heard** that you were having the baby.

NOT	*Future* *Present* We **will send** you a postcard, and we **buy** you some souvenirs from the Virgin Islands.
CORRECT	*Future* *Future* We **will send** you a postcard, and we **will buy** you some souvenirs from the Virgin Islands.

Reviewing Consistent Verb Tenses

Why should verb tenses be consistent?

_____

What problem do inconsistent verb tenses create?

_____

PRACTICE 1: Identifying and Correcting

A. Put an I next to the sentence if the tenses of the underlined verbs are inconsistent.

1. _____ You <u>need</u> to water the lawn so that the grass <u>did</u> not <u>die</u>.

2. _____ The baby <u>cried</u> all last night, and I <u>paced</u> the floor.

3. _____ The cows <u>escaped</u> from the pasture and <u>will roam</u> into town.

4. _____ *Scooby Doo* <u>is</u> my favorite cartoon, and I <u>watched</u> it every day.

5. _____ This dress <u>looks</u> lovely while you <u>were wearing</u> it.

6. _____ Timmy <u>poured</u> milk on the carpet and <u>cleaned</u> it up with paper towels.

7. _____ You <u>are</u> the neatest person, and you never <u>leave</u> a mess.

8. _____ The cups and saucers <u>were broken</u> during the move, but the glasses <u>are</u> not.

9. _____ Food <u>cooks</u> quickly in the microwave, but it <u>tastes</u> better from the oven.

10. _____ Barbie's laugh <u>is</u> very irritating, and she <u>laughed</u> all the time.

B. Correct the inconsistent verbs in Practice 1A by rewriting each incorrect sentence.

PRACTICE 2: Completing Fill in each blank in the following sentences with a consistent verb that makes sense.

1. I _____ over the toys in the living room and _____ my ankle.

2. The students _____ to the convention in Spain, where they _____ their presentations.

3. When Jackson _____, he _____ me his new address.

4. The papers _____ behind the desk, but I _____ them anyway.

5. Some people _____ sports, and others just _____ them.

6. I _____ over the fence and _____ into the house.

7. Most people _____ because they _____ happy.

8. Vitamin B _____ you energy and _____ your body heal faster.

9. Exercise _____ stress while it _____ the body.

10. The leaves _____ from the trees in autumn and _____ back in the spring.

PRACTICE 3: Writing Your Own Write a sentence of your own for each of the following sets of verbs, making sure your tenses are consistent.

1. love, hate _____

2. wash, clean _____

3. plant, grow _____

4. run, jump _____

5. smell, taste _____

USING THE ACTIVE VOICE

In the **active voice,** the subject performs the action. In the **passive voice,** the subject receives the action. Compare the following two examples:

Passive Voice: The clothes **were washed** yesterday **by Valerie.**

Active Voice: **Valerie washed** the clothes yesterday.

The active voice adds energy to your writing. Here is another example. Notice the difference between active and passive.

Passive Voice: The picture **was painted** for this office **by my brother.**

Active Voice: **My brother painted** the picture for this office.

Reviewing Active and Passive Voice

What is the difference between the active and passive voice?

_____

_____

Why is the active voice usually better than the passive?

_____

_____

PRACTICE 4: Identifying and Correcting

A. Put a P next to each sentence that is in the passive voice.

1. _____ Jarrett played with Issa today.

2. _____ The flowers were delivered to the wedding by the florist.

3. _____ A ticket was given to the driver by a police officer.

4. _____ The clothes were dried by the sun.

5. _____ We mailed invitations to our family and friends.

6. _____ The bleach was spilled on my shirt by Jean.

7. _____ A message was received in secret.

8. _____ Ants invaded my kitchen.

9. _____ The man was attacked by the dog.

10. _____ The new baby was placed in its mother's arms by the doctor.

B. Rewrite each passive-voice sentence in Practice 4A in the active voice.

PRACTICE 5: Completing Fill in each blank in the following sentences with an active-voice verb that makes sense.

1. The news _____ current events around the nation.

2. I _____ calamine lotion on my mosquito bites.

3. The TV in my bedroom _____ a fuse when I turned it on.

4. Dexter _____ the presents in the car.

5. My favorite soda _____ Coca-Cola.

6. Clive _____ his appointment with time to spare.

7. The scientists _____ a new gene.

8. The winds _____ over 100 mph.

9. The computer _____ to me, "You've got mail."

10. Fifi _____ chasing the ducks in the park.

PRACTICE 6: Writing Your Own Write a sentence of your own putting each of the following subjects and verbs in the passive voice.

1. my mom gives _____

2. he feels _____

3. the twins bought _____

4. the team threw _____

5. prisoners made _____

CHAPTER REVIEW

Reviewing More on Verbs

To review this material before you complete the Review Practices, watch the **Consistent Verb Tense and Active Voice** video at **MyWritingLab.com** one more time. This time, keep the video open as you complete the rest of the practices in this chapter. For best results, do the **MyWritingLab** exercises online as well as the Chapter Review practices in the book.

Remember that clicking "Hint" will give you helpful information about an exercise.

REVIEW PRACTICE 1: Identifying Underline any inconsistent or passive verbs in each of the following sentences.

1. When the phone rings, I refused to answer it.

2. The boat was tugged to shore by the fisherman.

3. This new recipe was created by my uncle.

4. They parked in the lot and walk a mile to the park's entrance.

5. The students were taken on an off-campus field trip.

6. Tim and Bill will fish this summer, and then they camped.

7. Since I love chocolate, I ate it all the time.

8. The kitten was cleaned by its mother.

9. The solar panels heat up when the sun came out.

10. The corrections were made by Mrs. Smith.

Practicing More on Verbs

Now complete the **Recall** activity for **Consistent Verb Tense and Active Voice** at **MyWritingLab.com.** If you're having a difficult time with a question, open up the video in the lower right-hand corner for some help.

REVIEW PRACTICE 2: Correcting Correct the verb errors in Review Practice 1 by rewriting each incorrect sentence.

Practicing More on Verbs

Next, complete the **Apply** activity for **Consistent Verb Tense and Active Voice** at **MyWritingLab.com.** If you're stuck, you can click on the hint button.

REVIEW PRACTICE 3: Writing Your Own Write a paragraph about your favorite college course. What do you like most about it? Why is it your favorite? Stay in the present tense, and use the active voice.

Practicing More on Verbs

For more practice, complete the **Write** activity for **Consistent Verb Tense and Active Voice** at **MyWritingLab.com.** Pay close attention to the use of active voice and verb tense consistency.

EDITING THE STUDENT WRITING

Return to the student paragraph at the beginning of this chapter, and do the following activities.

Individual Activity Review your underlining in the paragraph. Did you find the 26 verbs? Now, underline the eight inconsistent and passive-voice verbs twice.

Collaborative Activity Team up with a partner, and use what you have learned in this chapter to correct these errors. Rewrite the paragraph with your corrections.

EDITING YOUR OWN WRITING

Exchange paragraphs from Review Practice 3 with another student, and do the following:

1. Circle all verbs that are not consistent in tense.

2. Underline any verbs in the passive voice.

Then return the paper to its writer, and use the information in this chapter to correct any verb consistency or voice errors in your own paragraph. Record your errors on the Error Log in Appendix 1.

UNIT QUIZZES

Here are some exercises that test your understanding of all the material in this unit: Regular and Irregular Verbs, Verb Tense, Subject–Verb Agreement, and More on Verbs.

Unit Quiz 1 Identifying

Underline the verb errors in each of the following sentences.

1. The boys done a great job with the backyard.

2. My brother cutted his leg.

3. George and Martha is two characters from an Edward Albee play.

4. When the full moon rises over the mountains, the wolves howled.

5. I flirted with the girl next to me and make her smile.

6. The football players has run around the field 10 times.

7. Jared has ate all the macaroon cookies again.

8. We eatted dinner before the movie.

9. Here is several good reasons for this meeting.

10. The shortest boy on the track team run the fastest.

11. She will fly into Boston on the third and gave her speech on the fourth.

12. The criminals fledded from the scene of the crime.

13. The choir have sung that song many times.

14. Jonathon bended the pipe with his car.

15. What is you doing in the garage every night?

16. Last night, all of the food will be eaten by the guests.

17. The dogs been barking at the tree all night.

18. The children hidded from their babysitter.

19. Jenny eats whatever she wants but didn't gain weight.

20. There are no reason for this chaos.

Unit Quiz 2 Correcting

Correct the verb errors in Unit Quiz 1 by rewriting each incorrect sentence.

Unit Quiz 3 Identifying

Underline the verb errors in the following paragraph.

My mother has the most whimsical sense of style. She loves frogs. In the living room are a frog lamp, a frog hanging from the bathroom towel rack, and a huge concrete frog will sit in the entryway, which everybody stumble over. And if you looks closely, you can find little figurines all over the house. Geese of various sizes is scattered around the entertainment center. A pack of hunting dogs was placed on the kitchen counter by my mom. Little rabbits, turtles, and cats snuggles in the warm earth in the household plants. But the most whimsical and cherished decoration of all are the hand-carved totem pole that stands in the living room. This has come through the generations, even though nobody know who made it. Fanciful woodland animals appear all around it. Merry little sprites and elves dances through the woods as a maiden rests in her bower. I have spent hours tracing the designs with my fingers, fantasizing about the story behind the maiden's smile. Some day this will belong to me, and I passed it down to my children. I hope it sparks their imagination as much as it has mine.

Unit Quiz 4 Correcting

Correct the verb errors in Unit Quiz 3 by rewriting the paragraph.

UNIT WRITING ASSIGNMENTS

1. Have you ever had a misunderstanding with a friend or relative that wasn't your fault? How did the misunderstanding come about? Was anyone to blame, or was the situation simply a misunderstanding? Who was involved? What did you do? How did this event make you feel?

2. Have you ever performed an act of kindness with no thought to yourself? What did you do, and why did you do it? What kind of sacrifice, if any, did you make? How did your actions make you feel?

3. We often see things differently when we are children, like our impressions of our parents. As we grow older, we begin to see things from a more mature perspective. Is there a situation, such as getting punished, or a person that you now understand differently from how you did in your childhood? What did you think as a child, and what do you think now? What has made your perceptions change? Do you have a better understanding of the situation or person?

Pronouns

Pronouns generally go almost unnoticed in writing and speaking, even though these words can do anything nouns can do. In fact, much like your inborn sense of balance, pronouns work in sentences to make your writing precise and coherent. Without pronouns, writers and speakers would find themselves repeating nouns over and over, producing sentences that are unnatural and boring. For example, notice how awkward the following paragraph would be without pronouns:

Robert wrote a rough draft of Robert's essay last night. Then Robert asked Robert's girlfriend to read over Robert's essay with Robert. After Robert's girlfriend helped Robert find errors, Robert made corrections. Then Robert set aside the essay for a day before Robert took the essay out and began revising again.

When we let pronouns take over and do their jobs, we produce a much more fluent paragraph:

Robert wrote a rough draft of his essay last night. Then he asked his girlfriend to read over his essay with him. After she helped Robert find errors, he made corrections. Then he set aside the essay for a day before he took it out and began revising again.

Problems with pronouns occur when the words pronouns refer to aren't clear or when pronouns and their antecedents—the words they refer to—are too far apart. In this unit, we will deal with the following aspects of pronouns:

Chapter 10: Pronoun Problems
Chapter 11: Pronoun Reference and Point of View
Chapter 12: Pronoun Agreement

Pronoun Problems

The following student paragraph contains examples of correct and incorrect pronoun usage. Read the paragraph, and underline the 40 pronouns.

My's first date almost turned me against dating forever. It was a blind date to an amusement park set up by my best friend, Claire, who was going with her boyfriend, Roger. They and us made small talk during the two-hour drive. Once there, Norman was a perfect gentleman, buying Claire and I souvenirs, holding the door open for she and me, and always saying thank you. But all of that there changed once we decided to ride the Boomerang. Norman bought a huge lemonade right before we got on the ride. I told him that I didn't think it was a good idea to take the drink on the ride since we were going to be slung up and down from one end of the ride to the other. "Don't worry," he said, "it has a lid." Sure enough, as we accelerated forward and upward, the lid popped off, and lemonade went everywhere. By the time the ride stopped, I was covered in the sweet, sticky stuff. Needless to say, I was angry with him. He didn't even apologize, just asked me what my problem was and told me that he was a better sport than me. Unfortunately, this here wasn't the worst part of the date. As we were leaving the park, I got attacked by a bee and was stung on my neck. I had to ride home covered in lemonade with a throbbing bee sting on my neck and Norman, the person responsible for my torment, at my side. There was no small talk this time.

Pronouns are words that take the place of nouns. They help us avoid repeating nouns. In this chapter, we'll discuss five types of pronoun problems: (1) using the wrong pronoun as a subject, (2) using the wrong pronoun as an object, (3) using an apostrophe with a possessive pronoun, (4) misusing pronouns in comparisons, and (5) misusing demonstrative pronouns.

Student Comment: "With **MyWritingLab**, I can try as many times as possible and not feel stupid."

Understanding Pronouns

To help you understand this topic, go to **MyWritingLab.com,** and watch the video on **Pronoun Case.** Then, return to this chapter, which will go into more detail about pronouns and give you opportunities to practice them. Finally, you will apply your understanding of pronoun case to your own writing.

PRONOUNS AS SUBJECTS

Single pronouns as subjects usually don't cause problems.

Subject Pronoun: **I** gave to charity.
Subject Pronoun: **They** flew to Dallas.

You wouldn't say "*Me* gave to charity" or "*Them* flew to Dallas." But an error often occurs when a sentence has a compound subject and one or more of the subjects is a pronoun.

NOT   The boys and **us** played ball.
Correct: The boys and **we** played ball.

NOT   **Him** and **me** rode together.
Correct: **He** and **I** rode together.

To test whether you have used the correct form of the pronoun in a compound subject, try each subject alone:

Subject Pronoun? **The boys and us** played ball.

Test: **The boys** played ball. **YES**

Test: **Us** played ball. **NO**

Test: **We** played ball. **YES**

Correction: **The boys and we** played ball.

Here is a list of subject pronouns.

Subject Pronouns

SINGULAR	PLURAL
I	*we*
you	*you*
he, she, it	*they*

Reviewing Pronouns as Subjects

Name two subject pronouns.

_____

How can you test whether you are using the correct pronoun as the subject of a sentence?

_____

PRACTICE 1: Identifying and Correcting

A. Put an X next to the sentence if the underlined pronoun is incorrect.

1. _____ Last night, <u>him</u> and I helped with the dishes.

2. _____ The dogs and <u>us</u> ran wild across the playground.

3. _____ He and <u>me</u> are going to the Madonna concert.

4. _____ We and <u>you</u> can fit in that phone booth.

5. _____ In the spring, you and <u>I</u> are going fly-fishing.

6. _____ Last year, Jim, Tanya, and <u>we</u> car-pooled together.

7. _____ You and <u>me</u> should be lab partners.

8. _____ <u>They</u> and the receptionist have all gone to lunch.

9. _____ My mother and <u>her</u> have known each other forever.

10. _____ <u>Him</u> and I felt that you were very kind.

B. Correct the pronoun errors in Practice 1A by rewriting each incorrect sentence.

PRACTICE 2: Completing Fill in each blank in the following sentences with a subject pronoun that makes sense.

1. Jamie and _____ decided to go to the same college and room together.

2. During the storm, Nicole, Brad, and _____ took shelter in the basement.

3. You and _____ need to come to an agreement.

4. After dinner, the students and _____ are going to the library to study.

5. She and _____ are getting married this June.

6. _____ and some of the parents have set up a reading area for the children.

7. The scientists and _____ are trying to discover a new planet in the solar system.

8. A famous graphic artist and _____ did the cover for this book.

9. The lifeguard and _____ both jumped in to save the swimmer.

10. Joseph, who is a great gardener, and _____, who is a wonderful decorator, designed my Asian garden.

PRACTICE 3: Writing Your Own Write a sentence of your own for each of the following compound subjects.

1. you and I _____

2. we and they _____

3. Sara and she _____

4. you and he _____

5. she and we _____

PRONOUNS AS OBJECTS

One of the most frequent pronoun errors is using a subject pronoun when the sentence calls for an object pronoun. The sentence may require an object after a verb, showing that someone or something receives the action of the verb. Or it may be an object of a preposition that is required (see page 17 for a list of prepositions).

NOT	She gave Alisha and **I** some candy.
Correct:	She gave Alisha and **me** some candy.

NOT	This is just between you and **I**.
Correct:	This is just between you and **me**.

Like the subject pronoun error, the object pronoun error usually occurs with compound objects. Also like the subject pronoun error, you can test whether you are using the correct pronoun by using each object separately.

Object Pronouns?	She gave Alisha and **I** some candy.
Test:	She gave **Alisha** some candy. **YES**
Test:	She gave **I** some candy. **NO**
Test:	She gave **me** some candy. **YES**
Correction:	She gave **Alisha and me** some candy.

Here is a list of object pronouns:

Object Pronouns

SINGULAR	PLURAL
me	*us*
you	*you*
him, her, it	*them*

Reviewing Pronouns as Objects

In what two places are pronouns used as objects?

_____

How can you test whether you have used the correct pronoun as the object in a sentence?

_____

PRACTICE 4: Identifying and Correcting

A. Put an X next to the sentence if the underlined pronoun is incorrect.

1. _____ Kendra invited John and <u>I</u> to the movies.

2. _____ The cutest boys in the class danced with her and <u>I</u>.

3. _____ The baby ducks are waddling behind <u>they</u> and us.

4. _____ Jim and George are bouncing the ball to Sandy and <u>her</u>.

5. _____ The argument is between <u>she</u> and him.

6. _____ I found my little sister with <u>him</u> and her.

7. _____ The chaperones are walking in front of Elkie and <u>he</u>.

8. _____ Margot can go down the water slide after John and <u>he</u>.

9. _____ The competition is between <u>them</u> and us.

10. _____ The doctor gave Valerie and <u>we</u> some candy after the shot.

B. Correct the pronoun errors in Practice 4A by rewriting each incorrect sentence.

PRACTICE 5: Completing Fill in each blank in the following sentences with an object pronoun that makes sense.

1. Jeremy took off running after Judy and _____

2. Between you and _____, we can do anything.

3. The actor read his lines to them and _____.

4. We watched the children and _____.

5. Thanks to _____ and her, we have raised enough money for the trip.

6. Your mom is seated in the middle of _____ and the Turners.

7. The karate instructor made _____ and you perform in front of the class.

8. I was in awe of Cassandra and _____.

9. Charles gave the food not to Jimmy but to _____.

10. The high winds almost blew us and _____ over.

PRACTICE 6: Writing Your Own Write a sentence of your own for each of the following compound object pronouns.

1. you and me _____

2. him and her _____

3. us and them _____

4. Ben and him _____

5. Shawna and her _____

POSSESSIVE PRONOUNS

Possessive pronouns show ownership (***my** boat*, ***his** bed*, ***our** horse*). (See page 9 for a list of pronouns.) An apostrophe is used with nouns to show ownership (***Jack's** cat*, *the **worker's** tools*, *the **committee's** vote*). But an apostrophe is never used with possessive pronouns.

Possessive Pronouns

SINGULAR	PLURAL
my, mine	*our, ours*
your, yours	*you, yours*
his, her, hers	*their, theirs*

NOT	That truck is **their's.**
Correct:	That truck is **theirs.**
NOT	The apple on the counter is **your's.**
Correct:	The apple on the counter is **yours.**
NOT	The cat licked **its'** paws.
Correct:	The cat licked **its** paws.

Reviewing Possessive Pronouns

When do you use an apostrophe with a noun?

_____

Do possessive pronouns take apostrophes?

_____

PRACTICE 7: Identifying and Correcting

A. Put an X next to the sentence if the underlined pronoun is incorrect.

1. _____ <u>His</u> cell phone rang in class.

2. _____ <u>Her's</u> clothes are muddy.

3. _____ These assignments are <u>your's</u>.

4. _____ Those water balloons are <u>their's</u>.

5. _____ <u>Their</u> gifts were the most expensive.

6. _____ The dirty clothes on the floor are <u>our's</u>.

7. _____ <u>His</u> charm will not get him out of this situation.

8. _____ The horse swished <u>it's</u> tail in agitation.

9. _____ That plane behind the barn is <u>theirs</u>.

10. _____ <u>My's</u> hair is falling out.

B. Correct the pronoun errors in Practice 7A by rewriting each incorrect sentence.

PRACTICE 8: Completing Fill in each blank in the following sentences with a possessive pronoun that makes sense.

1. This brand-new truck is _____.

2. Those punk rock clothes are definitely _____.

3. The artwork is _____.

4. _____ ghost is haunting this house.

5. _____ dog barks at everybody.

6. According to _____ notes, we should have turned left.

7. People have the right to _____ own beliefs.

8. Those are _____ goals and ambitions for the future.

9. My father rolled _____ eyes at my suggestions.

10. You spent _____ money!

PRACTICE 9: Writing Your Own Write a sentence of your own for each of the following possessive pronouns.

1. my _____

2. theirs _____

3. hers _____

4. yours _____

5. its _____

PRONOUNS IN COMPARISONS

Sometimes pronoun problems occur in comparisons with *than* or *as*. An object pronoun may be mistakenly used instead of a subject pronoun. To find out if you are using the right pronoun, you should finish the sentence as shown here.

NOT She can crochet better than **me.**

Correct: She can crochet better than **I** [can crochet].

NOT Beatrice is as good a runner as **him.**

Correct: Beatrice is as good a runner as **he** [is].

Hint: Sometimes an object pronoun is required in a *than* or *as* comparison. But errors rarely occur in this case because the subject pronoun sounds so unnatural.

NOT Elaine likes him more than she likes **I.**

Correct: Elaine likes him more than she likes **me.**

Reviewing Pronouns in Comparisons

What causes pronoun problems in comparisons?

_____

_____

How can you test whether to use a subject pronoun or an object pronoun in a than or as comparison?

_____

_____

PRACTICE 10: Identifying and Correcting

A. Put an X next to the sentence if the underlined pronoun is incorrect.

1. _____ He can read out loud better than <u>me</u>.

2. _____ Gabriel has more skill than <u>them</u>.

3. _____ Cynthia is as good a race-car driver as <u>he</u> is.

4. _____ Reyna can hold her breath longer than <u>him</u>.

5. _____ Veronica can jump higher than <u>I</u>.

6. _____ Carla is more popular than <u>her</u>.

7. _____ Manuel isn't as creative as <u>she</u>.

8. _____ He is as cold as <u>her</u>.

9. _____ We are just as friendly as <u>they</u>.

10. _____ Cordelia confides in you more than she confides in <u>I</u>.

B. Correct the pronoun errors in Practice 10A by rewriting each incorrect sentence.

PRACTICE 11: Completing Fill in each blank in the following sentences with pronouns that are correct.

1. He quits his job even more often than _____.

2. Every day, I like you more than I like _____.

3. I do believe that I am more tired than _____.

4. They are trying to recover the ball just as hard as _____.

5. Vinny and Clark are more suave than _____.

6. They push their children harder than _____ do.

7. Glenda isn't as selfish as _____.

8. Isabella likes Nolan more than she likes _____.

9. We have a better defense than _____.

10. I bet that I can play chess better than _____ can.

PRACTICE 12: Writing Your Own Write a sentence of your own using each of the following pronouns in comparisons.

1. I _____

2. they _____

3. she _____

4. he _____

5. we _____

DEMONSTRATIVE PRONOUNS

There are four demonstrative pronouns: *this, that, these,* and *those*. **Demonstrative pronouns** point to specific people or objects. Use *this* and *these* to refer to items that are near and *that* and *those* to refer to items farther away. Look at the following examples.

Demonstrative (near):	**This** is my new computer.
Demonstrative (near):	**These** are library books.
Demonstrative (farther):	**That** is the bank.
Demonstrative (farther):	**Those** are the frames for the pictures.

Sometimes demonstrative pronouns are not used correctly.

	Incorrect	Correct
NOT	this here, that there	this, that
NOT	these here, these ones	these
NOT	them, those there, those ones	those
NOT	**Them** are the memos she typed.	
Correct:	**Those** are the memos she typed.	

NOT	I'll give you **these here**.
Correct:	I'll give you **these**.
NOT	**Those ones** were in the garage.
Correct:	**Those** were in the garage.
NOT	**Those there** are the cards.
Correct:	**Those** are the cards.

When demonstrative pronouns are used with nouns, they become adjectives.

Pronoun:	**That** is your dog.
Adjective:	**This dog** is his.
Pronoun:	**Those** are memories you will always cherish.
Adjective:	You will always cherish **those memories.**

The problems that occur with demonstrative pronouns can also occur when these pronouns act as adjectives.

NOT	Please hand me **that there** pen.
Correct:	Please hand me **that** pen.

Reviewing Demonstrative Pronouns

Name the four demonstrative pronouns.

_____ _____

_____ _____

Give two examples of errors with demonstrative pronouns.

_____

_____

PRACTICE 13: Identifying and Correcting

A. Put an X next to the sentence if the underlined demonstrative pronoun is incorrect.

1. _____ <u>Those</u> were reserved for VIPs.

2. _____ <u>This here</u> is the best meal I've ever made.

3. _____ <u>Them</u> are the color swatches from the decorator.

4. _____ <u>These</u> are the keys you thought you'd lost.

5. _____ Will you put <u>these here</u> in the mail?

6. _____ <u>Those</u> were the best days of my life.

7. _____ <u>That</u> will never do.

8. _____ Before you go, <u>these here</u> need to be fixed.

9. _____ <u>Those ones</u> are for you, and <u>these ones</u> are for me.

10. _____ <u>Those there</u> on the sofa belong to my dad.

B. Correct the pronoun errors in Practice 13A by rewriting each incorrect sentence.

PRACTICE 14: Completing Fill in each blank in the following sentences with a demonstrative pronoun that is correct.

1. _____ is the old bell from the tower.

2. _____ was the worst experience I have ever had.

3. What is? _____

4. _____ of you standing at the back of the line should be patient.

5. Please take _____ to the dry cleaner.

6. Where did you find? _____

7. _____ should make the long hike more bearable.

8. Nolan stored _____ in the basement.

9. _____ are the exercises we have to have finished by Monday.

10. _____ was the longest day I've ever lived through!

PRACTICE 15: Writing Your Own Write a sentence of your own for each of the following demonstrative pronouns. Make sure you use them as pronouns and not as adjectives.

1. this _____

2. that _____

3. these _____

4. those _____

CHAPTER REVIEW

You can save your work in the Apply exercise and come back to it later.

Reviewing Pronouns

To review this material before you complete the Review Practices, watch the **Pronoun Case** video at **MyWritingLab.com** one more time. This time, keep the video open as you complete the rest of the practices in this chapter. For best results, do the **MyWritingLab** exercises online as well as the Chapter Review practices in the book.

REVIEW PRACTICE 1: Identifying Underline the pronoun errors in each of the following sentences.

1. This here is a mystery.

2. You told she and I different stories.

3. These funky glasses are his'.

4. Noemi isn't as good with punctuation as him.

5. The whale blew air out it's blowhole.

6. Them are definitely mine.

7. We have to keep the surprise between you and I.

8. Julianna can talk faster than her.

9. The students and us took a rest from the examinations.

10. Jessica, Andy, and me decided to eat out tonight.

Practicing Pronouns

Now complete the **Recall** activity for **Pronoun Case** at **MyWritingLab.com.** Remember to read the answers carefully because many of them look similar.

REVIEW PRACTICE 2: Correcting Correct the pronoun errors in Review Practice 1 by rewriting each incorrect sentence.

Practicing Pronouns

Next, complete the **Apply** activity for **Pronoun Case** at **MyWritingLab.com.** Remember that spelling counts.

REVIEW PRACTICE 3: Writing Your Own Write your own paragraph about the town you grew up in. What is one vivid memory you have of this place?

Practicing Pronouns

For more practice, complete the **Write** activity for **Pronoun Case** at **MyWritingLab.com.** Pay close attention to the case of all the pronouns.

EDITING THE STUDENT WRITING

Return to the student paragraph at the beginning of this chapter, and do the following activities.

Individual Activity Review your underlining in the student paragraph. Did you find the 40 pronouns? Place an X above the seven pronoun errors in the paragraph.

Collaborative Acitivty Team up with a partner, and use what you have learned in this chapter to correct these errors. Rewrite the paragraph with your corrections.

EDITING YOUR OWN WRITING

Exchange paragraphs from Review Practice 3 with another student, and do the following:

1. Circle all pronouns.

2. Put an X through any that are not in the correct form. Check that all the subject and object pronouns are used correctly. Also check that possessive pronouns, pronouns used in comparisons, and demonstrative pronouns are used correctly.

Then return the paper to its writer, and use the information in this chapter to correct the pronoun errors in your own paragraph. Record your errors on the Error Log in Appendix 1.

Pronoun Reference and Point of View

The following student paragraph contains examples of correct and incorrect pronoun usage. Read the paragraph, and underline each of the 19 pronouns.

They say that women are gatherers and men are hunters. You never truly understood this statement until I watched a man for a good hour at the mall. I knew he was married, or at least attached, by the mounds of shopping bags—but no female—surrounding him. The obviously overwhelmed man was slumped on a bench with only his upper torso visible due to all the shopping clutter. Eventually, the man's significant other relieved him of the packages, dropped off their 10-year-old son, and proceeded to search the mall for an outfit to match the shoes that she bought on sale. The bewildered yet relieved man took his son's hand, looked around, stood up, sat down, checked his watch, and yawned. Then he heard a sports announcer yell, "Touchdown!" It was on. The man and his son tracked the sound to a 64-inch big-screen TV just inside a department store entrance. Slowly he circled his prey, sniffing out the accessories. Then, decisively, he moved in for the kill. "Charge it!" he said.

Anytime you use a pronoun, it must clearly refer to a specific word. The word it refers to is called its **antecedent.** Two kinds of problems occur with pronoun references: The antecedent may be unclear, or the antecedent may be missing altogether. You should also be careful to stick to the same point of view in your writing. If, for example, you start out talking about "I," you should not shift to "you" in the middle of the sentence.

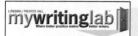 **Understanding Pronoun Reference and Point of View**

To find out more about these pronoun features, go to **MyWritingLab.com,** and view the video on **Pronoun Reference and Point of View.** Then, return to this chapter, which will go into more detail about these topics and give you opportunities to practice them. Finally, you will apply your understanding of pronoun reference and point of view to your own writing.

PRONOUN REFERENCE

Sometimes a sentence is confusing because the reader can't tell what a pronoun refers to. The confusion may occur because the pronoun's antecedent is unclear or is completely missing.

Unclear Antecedents

In the following examples, the word each pronoun refers to is unclear.

Unclear: A box and a key lay on the beach. As Miguel reached for **it,** the surf came in. (Was Miguel reaching for the box or the key? Only Miguel knows for sure.)

Clear: A box and a key lay on the beach. As Miguel reached for **the box,** the surf came in.

Clear: A box and a key lay on the beach. As Miguel reached for **the key,** the surf came in.

Unclear: Sandra told Denise that **she** shouldn't wear that color. (Does *she* refer to Sandra or Denise? Only the writer knows.)

Clear: Sandra told Denise that **Sandra** shouldn't wear that color.

Clear: Speaking with Denise, **Sandra** told **her** not to wear that color.

How can you be sure that every pronoun you use has a clear antecedent? First, you can proofread carefully. Probably an even better test, though, is to ask a friend to read what you have written and tell you if your meaning is clear or not.

Missing Antecedents

Every pronoun should have a clear antecedent—the word it refers to. But what happens when there is no antecedent at all? The writer's message is not communicated. Two words in particular should alert you to the possibility of missing antecedents: *it* and *they*.

The following sentences have missing antecedents:

Missing Antecedent:	In a survey, it shows that most people are happy with the president. (What does *it* refer to? It has no antecedent.)
Clear:	**A recent survey** shows that most people are happy with the president.
Missing Antecedent:	**They** say that the wise know when to speak and when not to. (Who is *they*?)
Clear:	**An old saying** states that the wise know when to speak and when not to.

Reviewing Pronoun Reference

What is an antecedent?

_____

_____

How can you be sure every pronoun you use has a clear antecedent?

_____

_____

What two words warn you that an antecedent may be missing?

_____   _____

PRACTICE 1: Identifying and Correcting

A. Put an X next to each sentence with a missing or unclear antecedent.

　　1. _____ They always tell me to look both ways before crossing the street.

　　2. _____ Talking to Tomás, Jim asked if he was interested in a job.

　　3. _____ It says that we can expect a booming economy.

4. _____ My grandparents always tell me that "pretty is as pretty does."

5. _____ Jon and Carlos decided to buy the same costume for the masquerade party, but he looks dumb in it.

6. _____ Even though Cindy and Lena like each other, she picks fights all the time.

7. _____ According to the news, we can expect more rain.

8. _____ Jeff told Marc that he would be leaving his job soon.

9. _____ In last year's poll, they revealed the cause of the crises.

10. _____ When I spoke to Randy and Gage, they told me where everyone was meeting.

B. Correct the pronoun errors in Practice 1A by rewriting each incorrect sentence.

PRACTICE 2: Completing Fill in each blank in the following sentences with either a pronoun or a noun to make the sentence clear.

1. César, James, and Juan have gone to pick out a new car for _____.

2. I tried to grab the coffeepot and cups, but _____ fell to the ground first.

3. When she spoke to Esther, _____ said that you couldn't go.

4. After you saw Harim and David, what did _____ have to say?

5. I looked for my lost shoe and sweater and found the _____ under my bed.

6. When Jack and Frank argue, _____ always wins.

7. When the proud parents and _____ saw the new baby, they expressed their joy.

8. The roses and the jasmine both require direct sunlight, but the _____ need more water.

9. Whenever I look at Misty and Kelly, _____ always smiles.

10. I went to the market for bread and eggs, but I forgot _____ when I got to the checkout line.

PRACTICE 3: Writing Your Own Write a sentence of your own using pronouns that refer to the following antecedents.

1. Mary and Jane _____

2. The cash and the grocery list _____

3. Heath, Eddie, and Emilio _____

4. the news _____

5. an old saying _____

SHIFTING POINT OF VIEW

Point of view refers to whether a statement is made in the first, second, or third person. Each person—or point of view—requires different pronouns. The following chart lists the pronouns for each point of view.

Point of View

First Person:	*I, we*
Second Person:	*you, you*
Third Person:	*he, she, it, they*

If you begin writing from one point of view, you should stay in that point of view. Do not shift to another point of view. For example, if you start out writing "I," you should continue with "I" and not shift to "you." Shifting point of view is a very common error in college writing.

Shift: If **a person** doesn't save money, **you** will have nothing left for retirement.

Correct: If **a person** doesn't save money, **he or she** will have nothing left for retirement.

Shift: I moved to Los Angeles because **you** can meet movie stars there.

Correct: I moved to Los Angeles because **I** can meet movie stars there.

Reviewing Point of View

What is point of view?

_____

_____

> *What does it mean to shift point of view?*
>
> _____
>
> _____

PRACTICE 4: Identifying and Correcting

A. Put an X next to the sentence if the underlined pronouns shift point of view.

1. _____ I am nice to all strangers because <u>you</u> never know whom you might meet.

2. _____ People can't be too careful with <u>our</u> money.

3. _____ A body needs lots of water to keep <u>you</u> healthy.

4. _____ The workers decided to cross the picket line because <u>they</u> wanted to end the strike.

5. _____ People are not an island unto themselves, even if <u>you</u> think you are.

6. _____ I like going to rock concerts because <u>they</u> find <u>it</u> both exciting and relaxing.

7. _____ A person can get a great deal right now at the car dealership if <u>he</u> or <u>she</u> has good credit.

8. _____ John ate so many cookies that <u>he</u> got sick.

9. _____ One shouldn't listen at closed doors; <u>you</u> will never hear anything nice.

10. _____ A person should ask for help when <u>you</u> are in trouble.

B. Correct the pronoun errors in Practice 4A by rewriting each incorrect sentence.

PRACTICE 5: Completing Fill in each blank in the following sentences with pronouns that stay in the same point of view.

1. I should listen to these different types of music since _____ never know what _____ will like.

2. They have had a wonderful time, and _____ plan on returning soon.

3. I buy my groceries in bulk because _____ know that _____ am getting a bargain.

4. Since you are the one in love with her, _____ should call her.

5. We have always loved this spot for picnics, and _____ intend to meet here at least once a year.

6. You can find the best sales at discount centers if _____ know how to look.

7. Marion ran for two miles before _____ ran out of energy.

8. They can't leave this issue alone; _____ are determined to re-solve it tonight.

9. I enjoy walking in the park because _____ feel that nature relieves stress.

10. I won't admit to seeing the alien since _____ believe no one will listen.

PRACTICE 6: Writing Your Own Write a sentence of your own for each of the following pronouns. Be sure the pronouns have clear antecedents, and do not shift point of view.

1. you _____

2. they _____

3. it _____

4. I _____

5. we _____

CHAPTER REVIEW

Remember you can watch the video while answering questions if you need to review any of the material in this chapter.

Reviewing Pronoun Reference and Point of View

To review this material before you complete the Review Practices, watch the **Pronoun Reference and Point of View** video at **MyWritingLab.com** one more time. This time, keep the video open as you complete the rest of the practices in this chapter. For best results, do the **MyWritingLab** exercises online as well as the Chapter Review practices in the book.

REVIEW PRACTICE 1: Identifying Label each of the following sentences U if the antecedent is unclear, M if the antecedent is missing, or S if the sentence shifts point of view.

1. _____ Both Tina and Abigail asked Jim out on a date, but he only said yes to her.

2. _____ It says that there is a big dance tonight.

3. _____ In a current medical study, it shows that more women are suffering heart attacks than ever before.

4. _____ I love to read in the bathtub because it relaxes you.

5. _____ Everyone is so busy that they didn't send Christmas cards this year.

6. _____ I put the cell phone and the credit card right here, but now I can't find it.

7. _____ In this poll, it says that more people are for the new law than against it.

8. _____ Jesse told Kevin that he was going to cook dinner that night.

9. _____ I am going to wear my fake Rolex watch and carry my fake Gucci purse because everyone will think you're rich.

10. _____ They say love is worth the pain.

Practicing Pronoun Reference and Point of View

Now complete the **Recall** activity for **Pronoun Reference and Point of View** at **MyWritingLab.com.** Remember to read the answers carefully because many of them look similar.

REVIEW PRACTICE 2: Correcting Correct the pronoun errors in Review Practice 1 by rewriting each sentence.

Practicing Pronoun Reference and Point of View

Next, complete the **Apply** activity for **Pronoun Reference and Point of View** at **MyWritingLab.com.** Pay close attention to the directions, and click only on what you're asked to.

REVIEW PRACTICE 3: Writing Your Own Using a variety of pronouns, write a paragraph about something you have learned from your friends this week.

Practicing Pronoun Reference and Point of View

For more practice, complete the **Write** activity for **Pronoun Reference and Point of View** at **MyWritingLab.com.** Pay close attention to whether or not your pronouns have a clear reference.

EDITING THE STUDENT WRITING

Return to the student paragraph at the beginning of this chapter, and do the following activities.

Individual Activity   Review your underlining in the student paragraph. Did you find the 19 pronouns? Put an X above the five pronoun errors in the paragraph.

Collaborative Activity   Team up with a partner, and use what you have learned in this chapter to correct these errors. Rewrite the paragraph with your corrections.

EDITING YOUR OWN WRITING

Exchange paragraphs from Review Practice 3 with another student, and do the following:

1. Underline all pronouns.

2. Draw arrows to the words they modify.

3. Put an X through any pronouns that do not refer to a clear antecedent or that shift point of view.

Then return the paper to its writer, and use the information in this chapter to correct any pronoun-reference and point-of-view errors in your own paragraph. Record your errors on the Error Log in Appendix 1.

Pronoun Agreement

The following student paragraph contains correct and incorrect pronoun usage. Read the paragraph, then underline the pronouns once and their antecedents twice. There are 32 pronouns.

I know how to write. I know how to structure my thoughts in an organized, cohesive manner, and I can convey those thoughts in written form. However, I cannot write on command. To say to me "OK, you have X amount of time to answer this midterm prompt" causes instant paralysis of the brain. I brainstorm. I pray. I want to throw up. But my brain doesn't open. According to the teacher, anybody can pass a timed writing exam if he is prepared. But that is not the case when I face a written exam. I can study for a week straight, draft outlines, and remember important facts. But all of these efforts magically disappear when I receive the test. I look around and notice everyone with their heads bent, frantically writing away. I hear somebody tapping his pencil on the desk and wonder if they are as nervous as I am. Then the fear of judgment settles in. Each teacher, in her infinite wisdom, doesn't seem to realize that she's passing judgment on *me*, not just my writing, for my writing is a reflection of myself.

As you learned in Chapter 3, subjects and verbs must agree for clear communication. If the subject is singular, the verb must be singular; if the subject is plural, the verb must be plural. The same holds true for pronouns and the words they refer to—their *antecedents*. They must agree in number—both singular or both plural.

Usually, pronoun agreement is not a problem, as these sentences show:

Singular: **Mr. Parker** dropped **his** pager.

Plural: **Marianne** and **Marvin** gave **their** opinions.

Understanding Pronoun Agreement

For more information about this topic, go **to MyWritingLab.com,** and view the video on **Pronoun Antecedent Agreement.** Then, return to this chapter, which will go into more detail about pronoun agreement and give you opportunities to practice it. Finally, you will apply your understanding of pronoun agreement to your own writing.

INDEFINITE PRONOUNS

Pronoun agreement may become a problem with indefinite pronouns. Indefinite pronouns that are always singular give writers the most trouble.

NOT   **One** of the contestants did **their** dance routine.

(How many students did the dance routine? Only *one*, so use a singular pronoun.)

Correct: **One** of the contestants did **her** dance routine.

Correct: **One** of the contestants did **his** dance routine.

NOT   **Somebody** left the lights on in **their** car.

(How many people left their lights on? *One person*, so use a singular pronoun.)

Correct: **Somebody** left the lights on in **her** car.

Correct: **Somebody** left the lights on in **his** car.

Correct: **Somebody** left the lights on in **his or her** car.

(if you don't know whose car it is)

Here is a list of indefinite pronouns that are always singular.

Singular Indefinite Pronouns

another	*everybody*	*neither*	*one*
anybody	*everyone*	*nobody*	*other*
anyone	*everything*	*none*	*somebody*
anything	*little*	*no one*	*someone*
each	*much*	*nothing*	*something*
either			

Hint: A few indefinite pronouns can be either singular or plural, depending on their meaning in the sentence. These pronouns are *any*, *all*, *more*, *most*, and *some*.

Singular: **Most** of the senior class had **its** orientation today.

Plural: **Most** of the seniors had **their** orientation today.

In the first sentence, *class* is considered a single body, so the singular pronoun *its* is used. In the second sentence, the *seniors* are individuals, so the plural pronoun *their* is used.

Reviewing Indefinite Pronouns

Why should a pronoun agree with the word it refers to?

_____

Name five indefinite pronouns that are always singular.

_____

PRACTICE 1: Identifying and Correcting

A. Put an X next to the sentence if the underlined pronoun does not agree with its antecedent.

1. _____ Paula and Rebecca got help revising <u>their</u> papers.

2. _____ Any one of the sculptors will have <u>his or her</u> cell phone on.

3. _____ Another of the officers turned <u>their</u> siren on.

4. _____ Everyone had <u>their</u> immunization shots.

5. _____ All of the man's hair has lost <u>their</u> color.

6. _____ At least one of the actresses will have <u>her</u> agent with her.

7. _____ Someone is remembering <u>their</u> childhood.

8. _____ Nobody knows where <u>their</u> tickets are.

9. _____ Each of the boys practiced <u>his</u> lessons.

10. _____ Anybody traveling with <u>their</u> children should board the plane first.

B. Correct the pronoun errors in Practice 1A by rewriting each incorrect sentence.

PRACTICE 2: Completing Fill in each blank in the following sentences with a pronoun that agrees with its antecedent and makes sense.

1. Somebody is playing _____ stereo too loud.

2. Another of the beauty queens needs _____ dress fixed.

3. All of the cars had _____ engines overhauled.

4. Everyone should listen to _____ elders.

5. Each of my dogs had _____ hair groomed today.

6. Some of the singers lost _____ voices.

7. Something has _____ claws in me!

8. Any of the pantsuits, with _____ matching scarves, will look good on you.

9. Most of the roads have had _____ potholes fixed.

10. Everybody has _____ warmest clothes on.

PRACTICE 3: Writing Your Own Write a sentence of your own for each of the following sets of pronouns.

1. anybody, his or her _____

2. most, their _____

3. something, its _____

4. each, its _____

5. all, their _____

AVOIDING SEXISM

In the first section of this chapter, you learned that you should use singular pronouns to refer to singular indefinite pronouns. For example, the indefinite pronoun *someone* requires a singular pronoun, *his* or *her*, not the plural *their*. But what if you don't know whether the person referred to is male or female? Then you have a choice: (1) You can say "he or she" or "his or her"; (2) you can make the sentence plural; or (3) you can rewrite the sentence to avoid the problem altogether. What you should not do is ignore half the population by referring to all humans as males.

NOT	If **anyone** has questions, **they** should ask us.
NOT	If **anyone** has questions, **he** should ask us.

Correct: If **anyone** has questions, **he or she** should ask us.

Correct: If **people** have questions, **they** should ask us.

NOT   **Everyone** forgot to bring **their** spending money.

NOT   **Everyone** forgot to bring **his** spending money.

Correct: **Everyone** forgot to bring **his or her** spending money.

Correct: **All the travelers** forgot to bring **their** spending money.

Sexism in writing can also occur in ways other than with indefinite pronouns. We often assume that doctors, lawyers, and bank presidents are men and that nurses, teachers, and secretaries are women. But that is not accurate.

NOT   Each **policeman** is assigned **his** own locker.

        (Why automatically assume that every member of the police force is male?)

Correct: Each **police officer** is assigned **his or her** own locker.

NOT   The **chairman** should run all department meetings.

        (Because both men and women can head departments, boards, and committees, a more appropriate term is *chairperson* or *chair*.)

Correct: The **chair** should run all department meetings.

NOT   A good **receptionist** keeps **her** area clear of clutter.

        (Why leave the men who are receptionists out of the sentence?)

Correct: A good **receptionist** keeps **his or her** area clear of clutter.

Correct: Good **receptionists** keep **their** areas clear of clutter.

Reviewing Sexism in Writing

What is sexism in writing?

_____

_____

What are two ways to get around the problem of using male pronouns to refer to both women and men?

_____   _____

Give two other examples of sexism in writing.

_____

_____

PRACTICE 4: Identifying and Correcting

A. Put an X next to the sentence if it has sexist references.

1. _____ A nurse left her name tag on the counter.

2. _____ Each of my co-workers was rewarded for submitting his or her ideas.

3. _____ A firefighter learns how to fight his way through smoke and flames.

4. _____ Ask a teacher if she knows the answer.

5. _____ A whistle tells the construction worker when it is time to eat his or her lunch.

6. _____ Each of the students passed his midterm exam.

7. _____ Somebody forgot to turn off her computer in the computer lab.

8. _____ Every mail carrier must deliver all the mail in his bag every day.

9. _____ A good manager always listens to his employees.

10. _____ The doctors gave their patients good advice.

B. Correct the pronoun errors in Practice 4A by rewriting each incorrect sentence.

PRACTICE 5: Completing Fill in each blank in the following sentences with a pronoun that is correct.

1. I heard that one of the gardeners broke _____ truck.

2. An opera singer can stretch _____ vocal cords to many octaves.

3. No customer in our restaurant will have _____ MasterCard refused.

4. Each child should bring a permission slip signed by _____ parents.

5. All of the dentists have _____ teeth checked once a year.

6. Ask one of the chefs if you can taste _____ dish.

7. Scuba divers should check _____ air tanks periodically.

8. If a mechanic wants to make more money, _____ should stay open for business on the weekends.

9. Someone trimmed _____ hair in the bathroom and left a mess.

10. A race-car driver's main priority is _____ tires.

PRACTICE 6: Writing Your Own Write a sentence of your own for each of the following antecedents. Include at least one pronoun in each sentence.

1. politician _____

2. flight attendant _____

3. dancer _____

4. secret agent _____

5. trucker _____

CHAPTER REVIEW

Reviewing Pronoun Agreement

To review this material before you complete the Review Practices, watch the **Pronoun Antecedent Agreement** video at **MyWritingLab.com** one more time. This time, keep the video open as you complete the rest of the practices in this chapter. For best results, do the **MyWritingLab** exercises online as well as the Chapter Review practices in the book.

Be sure to read the instructions for the Apply exercise carefully. You will be asked to click only on the pronoun, <u>not</u> the antecedent. You will also often have to change the verb of the sentence as well.

REVIEW PRACTICE 1: Identifying Underline the pronoun or sexist errors in each of the following sentences.

1. Everyone who wants his parking validated should see the receptionist.

2. If a surfer isn't careful, she could get hit by her surfboard.

3. Anyone can look like they're rich, even if they aren't.

4. Most of the birds have built its nests.

5. A good writer keeps her notebook close by.

6. It is a law that a motorcyclist must wear his helmet.

7. A policeman gave warnings to the speeding motorists.

8. Somebody left their laundry at the laundromat.

9. Each of the cherries had their pit removed.

10. Waitresses work hard for their tips.

Practicing Pronoun Agreement

Now complete the **Recall** activity for **Pronoun Antecedent Agreement** at **MyWritingLab.com.** If you're having a difficult time with a question, open up the video in the lower right-hand corner for some help.

REVIEW PRACTICE 2: Correcting Correct the pronoun errors, including sexist references, in Review Practice 2 by rewriting each incorrect sentence.

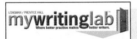

Practicing Pronoun Agreement

Next, complete the **Apply** activity for **Pronoun Antecedent Agreement** at **MyWritingLab.com.** If you're stuck, you can click on the hint button.

REVIEW PRACTICE 3: Writing Your Own Write a paragraph explaining what you think the qualities of a good teacher are.

Practicing Pronoun Agreement

For more practice, complete the **Write** activity for **Pronoun Antecedent Agreement** at **MyWritingLab.com.** Make sure to pay close attention to whether or not your pronouns and antecedents agree.

EDITING THE STUDENT WRITING

Return to the student paragraph at the beginning of this chapter, and do the following activities.

Individual Activity   Review your underlining in the student paragraph. Did you find the 32 pronouns and their antecedents? Next, put an X above the six pronoun errors in the paragraph.

Collaborative Activity   Team up with a partner, and use what you have learned in this chapter to correct these errors. Rewrite the paragraph with your corrections.

EDITING YOUR OWN WRITING

Exchange paragraphs from Review Practice 3 with a classmate, and do the following:

1. Underline any pronouns.

2. Circle any pronouns that do not agree with the words they refer to.

Then return the paper to its writer, and use the information in this chapter to correct any pronoun agreement errors in your own paragraph. Record your errors on the Error Log in Appendix 1.

UNIT QUIZZES

Here are some exercises that test your understanding of all the material in this unit: Pronoun Problems, Pronoun Reference and Point of View, and Pronoun Agreement.

Unit Quiz 1 Identifying

Underline the pronoun errors in each of the following sentences.

1. You are just as big hearted as him.

2. I will make my's own destiny.

3. I casually surveyed the room over the rim of my dark glasses, but you couldn't see anyone.

4. Alyssa and Martha both ran as fast as they could, but she won the race.

5. A sitter should spend some time simply playing with her charges.

6. Jeremy and her are designing my furniture.

7. Anybody can become familiar with his own writing process.

8. Them in the back seat are going to storage.

9. Somebody has their hands in my cookie jar!

10. They say a bird in the hand is worth two in the bush.

11. One of the accountants left his calculator behind.

12. Diane loses her patience more with Jim than with I.

13. In last year's books, it shows a marked rise in profits.

14. You cannot eat those there; they will spoil your appetite.

15. During the outdoor symphony, him and her proposed to one another at the same time.

16. When Julia heard Cindy and he yell, she went racing toward them.

17. These lemon cakes are her's.

18. Each of the toys came with their own batteries.

19. People shouldn't fear the sun altogether since you do get several essential vitamins from its light.

20. These here were left outside and are ruined.

Unit Quiz 2 Correcting

Correct the pronoun errors in Unit Quiz 1 by rewriting each sentence.

Unit Quiz 3 Identifying

Underline the pronoun errors in the following paragraph.

They say that the apple doesn't fall far from the tree, and I guess that's true. My mom is a chocolate lover. Brittany and Jennifer, my twin sisters, and me are chocolate lovers too. Perhaps the word "love" isn't the right choice because this here is not just a craving, but an obsession. We will eat any kind: dark, light, white, Swiss, German, with nuts, without nuts, and so on. I remember when Brittany and Jennifer were just five years old. Mom had given them and I these huge chocolate bunnies for Easter. Being the older sister, I was entitled to a percentage of that chocolate. So I bullied the twins into giving I the ears. I fell asleep that night dreaming of all that warm, smooth, sweet stuff until I was rudely awakened by the sound of fire engines and my screaming family. Our living room was on fire. The firemen said that the fire was started in the fireplace. Somebody had tried to burn their chocolate bunny. The bubbling chocolate spilled onto the carpet and caught fire. Imagine mine surprise to learn the bunny was mine. In this case, revenge wasn't so sweet. Mom and Dad denied us our chocolate for one month. From that moment on, I respected my sisters' rights to have and to hold her own chocolate. I have to admit that the twins' passion for chocolate is greater than me because she opened up her own chocolate shop, *Sweet Chocolate,* which Mom now manages. The other twin is now the chief executive officer of a top-name chocolate factory, and she loves her job. But I too am doing my part in this legacy: I am a wife and a mother who is passing on her's chocolate genetics—in moderation, of course—to her children.

Unit Quiz 4 Correcting

Correct the pronoun errors in Unit Quiz 3 by rewriting the paragraph.

UNIT WRITING ASSIGNMENTS

1. Your best friend has asked you to design the cover of his first rap CD, *Incognito.* What would your design be? Why this design? What colors would you use and why? How effective do you think your cover will be in marketing your friend's CD?

2. If you had to pick one word to describe your room, what would it be? Give examples of things in your room to help explain why you chose this word.

3. Most people feel there is a right way and a wrong way to do a particular chore, such as washing the car or mowing the lawn. Is there a particular chore that you insist be done a certain way? What is the chore? Explain the right way to go about doing it and the reason your way is the best.

Modifiers

Words that modify—usually called adjectives and adverbs—add details to sentences, describing, limiting, or identifying so that sentences become more vivid and interesting. They work like accessories in our everyday lives. Without jewelry, scarves, ties, and cuff links, we are still dressed. But accessories give a little extra flair to our wardrobe. Without modifiers, our writing would be bland, boring, and lifeless. However, to use adjectives and adverbs correctly, you need to learn about their different forms and functions.

In the chapters in this unit, you will learn about adjectives, adverbs, and various problems with the placement of these words in sentences:

Adjectives

The following paragraph, written by a student, contains examples of correct and incorrect adjective usage. Read the paragraph, and underline the 14 adjectives. Look specifically for comparative and superlative adjectives.

One thing that I have always wanted to invent is an automatic vacuum for the house. It would be like the ones used in swimming pools, only more better. Since my parents started making me vacuum our house five years ago, it has been my least favorite chore. I hate dragging the heavy vacuum up and down the stairs, and the cord is never long enough. If I could invent an automatic vacuum, it would have a more thinner body, so it could go easily down the halls. It would also have a more longer cord and more powerful suction. A person could just turn it on and let it go. Of course, it would suck up anything in its path, so a person would have to be careful about what was left on the ground. Overall, though, I think it would make vacuuming the most easiest task.

Adjectives are modifiers. They help us communicate more clearly (I have a *brown* jacket; I want a *black* one) and vividly (the concert was *loud* and *wild*). Without adjectives, our language would be drab and boring.

Understanding Adjectives

To understand more about this part of speech, go to **MyWritingLab.com**, and watch the video on **Adjectives.** Then, return to this chapter, which will go into more detail about adjectives and give you opportunities to practice using them. Finally, you will apply your understanding of these modifiers to your own writing.

USING ADJECTIVES

Adjectives are words that modify—or describe—nouns or pronouns. Adjectives often tell how something or someone looks: *dark, light, tall, short, large, small.* Most adjectives come before the words they modify, but with linking verbs (such as *is, are, look, become,* and *feel*), adjectives follow the words they modify.

Adjectives Before a Noun: We walked down the **narrow, winding** path.

Adjectives After a Linking Verb: The path was **narrow** and **winding.**

Reviewing Adjectives

What are adjectives?

_____

Where can you find adjectives in a sentence?

_____

PRACTICE 1: Identifying and Correcting

A. Put an X next to the sentence if the underlined word is not an adjective.

    1. _____ <u>This</u> is a boring day.

    2. _____ The computer was <u>old</u>.

    3. _____ You <u>wrote</u> a good essay.

    4. _____ My brother is <u>strong</u> and <u>brave</u>.

5. _____ Our last vacation was in <u>May</u>.

6. _____ Could you hand <u>me</u> the yellow pencil?

7. _____ The new <u>telephone</u> rang loudly.

8. _____ <u>Jimmy</u> was nervous and worried.

9. _____ My English professor <u>would</u> not accept my late assignment.

10. _____ *The Rover* is a funny <u>play</u>.

B. Correct the errors in Practice 1A by listing the correct adjectives.

PRACTICE 2: Completing Fill in each blank in the following paragraph with an adjective that makes sense.

Yesterday, I drove to the department store to buy a pair of (1) _____ shoes. I needed them to match my (2) _____ dress, which I bought for the (3) _____ party. The shoes looked (4) _____ and (5) _____ . When I got to the store, the parking lot was (6) _____ , and I had a (7) _____ time finding a place to park. Then I reached for my purse, and I was (8) _____ when I realized that I had left it in my apartment. I had to drive all the way back home to retrieve my (9) _____ purse because that's where all of my money was. When I finally got back to the store, it took me (10) _____ minutes to find another parking spot. At that point, I was determined to find that pair of shoes!

PRACTICE 3: Writing Your Own Write a sentence of your own for each of the following adjectives.

1. pretty _____

2. scared _____

3. friendly _____

4. hopeful _____

5. blue _____

COMPARING WITH ADJECTIVES

Most adjectives have three forms: a **basic** form, a **comparative** form (used to compare two items or indicate a greater degree), and a **superlative** form (used to compare three or more items or indicate the greatest degree).

For positive comparisons, adjectives form the comparative and superlative in two different ways.

1. For one-syllable adjectives and some two-syllable adjectives, use *-er* to compare two items and *-est* to compare three or more items.

Basic	Comparative (used to compare two items)	Superlative (used to compare three or more items)
large	larger	largest
cool	cooler	coolest
rain	rainier	rainiest
happy	happier	happiest

2. For some two-syllable adjectives and all longer adjectives, use *more* to compare two items and *most* to compare three or more items.

Basic	Comparative (used to compare two items)	Superlative (used to compare three or more items)
loyal	more loyal	most loyal
hopeful	more hopeful	most hopeful
beautiful	more beautiful	most beautiful
trustworthy	more trustworthy	most trustworthy

For negative comparisons, use *less* to compare two items and *least* to compare three or more items.

Basic	Comparative (used to compare two items)	Superlative (used to compare three or more items)
wild	less wild	least wild
silly	less silly	least silly
enormous	less enormous	least enormous

Hint: Some adjectives are not usually compared. For example, one person cannot be "more dead" than another. Here are some more examples.

broken	*final*	*square*
empty	*impossible*	*supreme*
equal	*singular*	*unanimous*

Reviewing Adjective Forms

When do you use the comparative form of an adjective?

_____

When do you use the superlative form of an adjective?

_____

How do one-syllable and some two-syllable adjectives form the comparative and superlative in positive comparisons?

_____

How do some two-syllable adjectives and all longer adjectives form the comparative and superlative in positive comparisons?

_____

How do you form negative comparisons?

_____

PRACTICE 4: Identifying and Correcting

A. Underline the adjectives in each of the following sentences. Do not count possessive pronouns as adjectives.

1. This month was hotter than last month.

2. Our hotel was more expensive than yours.

3. I have less valuable jewelry than my sister.

4. This was the most stressful day of the week.

5. Bong Yul gave the longest presentation of anyone in the class.

6. My dad was less worried about my grades than about my job at the department store.

7. Chris's car is more economical than mine.

8. The longest line is the one for tickets.

9. I know that you are richer than I am.

10. Tabitha was the least likely person to cut class.

B. Change the positive comparisons in Practice 4A to negative and the negative comparisons to positive.

PRACTICE 5: Completing Fill in each blank in the following paragraph with the correct comparative or superlative form of the adjective in parentheses.

I was cleaning out the refrigerator when I realized that there were three packs of sandwich meat. I threw out the (1) _____ (old) one and put the other two on a shelf where I would remember to use them. The orange juice that I made a week ago tasted (2) _____ (bitter) than I thought it should, so I threw that away also. But those were not the (3) _____ (gross) things in there. I found a piece of fruit that was (4) _____ (black) than chocolate, and I think it used to be a peach. I also found a bag of grapes that looked (5) _____ (wrinkled) than raisins, a jar of jelly with furry white spots on top, and some leftover Chinese food that smelled (6) _____ (rotten) than an old gym sock. When I opened the freezer, I found that the ice cream was (7) _____ (frozen) than the meat, which had turned a yucky gray color. There was freezer burn on everything but the frozen burritos, which were the (8) _____ (appetizing) things in there. I couldn't believe it had been two months or (9) _____ (long) since we had cleaned the refrigerator and freezer! When my roommate got home, she shook her head and thanked me for doing the (10) _____ (disgusting) job in the house.

PRACTICE 6: Writing Your Own Write a sentence of your own for each of the following comparative and superlative forms.

1. most frustrated _____

2. less hassled _____

3. more flexible _____

4. least friendly _____

5. most pleasant _____

COMMON ADJECTIVE ERRORS

Two types of problems occur with adjectives used in comparisons.

1. Instead of using one method for forming the comparative or superlative, both are used. That is, both -er and *more* or *less* are used to compare two items or both -est and most or *least* are used to compare three or more items.

   NOT   The new glue was **more weaker** than the old glue.

   Correct: The new glue was **weaker** than the old glue.

   NOT   Derrick was the **most smartest** employee of the company.

   Correct: Derrick was the **smartest** employee of the company.

2. The second type of error occurs when the comparative or superlative is used with the wrong number of items. The comparative form should be used for two items and the superlative for three or more items.

   NOT   Post-it Notes were the **newest** of the two products.

   Correct: Post-it Notes were the **newer** of the two products.

   NOT   Superglue was the **stickier** of the many 3M products.

   Correct: Superglue was the **stickiest** of the many 3M products.

Reviewing Common Adjective Errors

Can you ever use -er + more or -est + most?

_____

When do you use the comparative form of an adjective?

_____

When do you use the superlative form of an adjective?

_____

PRACTICE 7: Identifying and Correcting

A. Underline the incorrect adjective forms in each of the following sentences.

1. *Lord of the Rings: The Return of the King* was the most longest movie I have ever seen.

2. My brother is the shortest of the two of us.

3. This class is the most boring of my five classes.

4. Seth is watching his most favoritest cartoon.

5. Yours is the prettiest house on the block.

6. Vanity is the ugliest sin.

7. The fruit at the farmer's market was less fresh than at the roadside stand.

8. Ray is the most friendliest of all of my friends.

9. My voice is the louder among all of my family members.

10. Janette likes the most confusing mystery novels.

B. Correct the five adjective errors in Practice 7A by rewriting each incorrect sentence.

PRACTICE 8: Completing Fill in each blank in the following paragraph with the correct adjective form.

Science is the (1) _____ (more difficult/most difficult) subject for me to understand. No matter how hard I study, I never get (2) _____ (higher/more higher) grades than C's on my science exams. My sister Kimber and I usually have the same GPA, but I have always considered myself to be a little (3) _____ (smarter/more smarter) than she is. Most subjects just seem (4) _____ (easier/more easier) for me. However, when it comes to the sciences, she is definitely the (5) _____ (more talented/most talented) one. She takes good notes, so studying is usually a lot (6) _____ (least stressful/less stressful) for her. I personally hate studying, but maybe that's because my notes are (7) _____ (more unorganized/most unorganized) than Kimber's. I think that science itself is the (8) _____ (scariest/most scariest) thing I've ever had to learn. If someone could find a way to make science classes (9) _____ (more enjoyable/most enjoyable), I think I would learn to be (10) _____ (more relaxed/most relaxed) about them.

PRACTICE 9: Writing Your Own Write a sentence of your own for each of the following adjectives.

1. kindest _____

2. more helpful _____

3. most gorgeous _____

4. smaller _____

5. more pleasant _____

USING *GOOD* AND *BAD* CORRECTLY

The adjectives *good* and *bad* are irregular. They do not form the comparative and superlative like most other adjectives. Here are the correct forms for these two irregular adjectives:

Basic	Comparative (used to compare two items)	Superlative (used to compare three or more items)
good	better	best
bad	worse	worst

Problems occur with *good* and *bad* when writers don't know how to form their comparative and superlative forms.

NOT	more better, more worse, worser, most best, most worst, bestest, worstest
Correct:	better, worse, best, worst

These errors appear in sentences in the following ways:

NOT	These overexposed pictures are the **bestest** mistake that we ever made.
Correct:	These overexposed pictures are the **best** mistake that we ever made.

NOT	The drought got **more worse** with each dry day.
Correct:	The drought got **worse** with each dry day.

Reviewing *Good* and *Bad*

What are the three forms of good?

_____   _____

_____

What are the three forms of bad?

_____   _____

_____

PRACTICE 10: Identifying and Correcting

A. In the following sentences, underline the forms of *good* and *bad* used correctly, and circle the forms of *good* and *bad* used incorrectly.

1. This was the worst day of my life.

2. That's the bestest decision I have heard so far.

3. I liked the movie, but I thought the ending could have been better.

4. After she stood out in the rain, Charity's cold got worse.

5. Carmenita likes take-and-bake pizza better than delivery.

6. I don't know anything more worse than your news.

7. I ate at the best Mediterranean restaurant in town.

8. Lee was surfing the Internet to find the most best deal on a Chevy Blazer.

9. My cats always behave more good than my dogs.

10. Of all my friends, Jameson has the worse handwriting.

B. Correct the five adjective errors in Practice 10A by rewriting each incorrect sentence.

PRACTICE 11: Completing Fill in each blank in the following paragraph with the correct form of *good* and *bad*.

Last Tuesday, I was having a really (1) _____ day. I was late to work, which made my boss think that I was the

(2) _____ employee he has. While I was on my lunch break, my car broke down, and the mechanic said I had a (3) _____ transmission. To make matters (4) _____, he said it would cost $500 to replace it. I had to borrow my (5) _____ friend's bicycle to get home, and then I got a ticket for not wearing a helmet. I honestly thought that day was never going to get (6) _____. When I finally got home, I checked my mail and found some (7) _____ news. There was a card from my grandma with a $20 bill inside, thanking me for being the (8) _____ granddaughter she has. (I happen to be the *only* granddaughter she has, but that's another story.) Grandma wished me a (9) _____ day and reminded me to call her. At that point, I realized that I am very lucky to have someone who wants to talk to me, even when I have nothing (10) _____ to talk about.

PRACTICE 12: Writing Your Own Write a sentence of your own using the following forms of *good* and *bad*.

1. good _____

2. better _____

3. worse _____

4. bad _____

5. best _____

CHAPTER REVIEW

Reviewing Adjectives

To review this material before you complete the Review Practices, watch the **Adjectives** video at **MyWritingLab.com** one more time. This time, keep the video open as you complete the rest of the practices in this chapter. For best results, do the **MyWritingLab** exercises online as well as the Chapter Review Practices in the book.

To accompany the exercises on this topic, make a chart on a sheet of paper, labeling the three forms of an adjective: basic, comparative, and superlative. In this way, not only do you find out the answers to the questions, but you are also compiling a list of word forms as you go along.

REVIEW PRACTICE 1: Identifying Underline the incorrect adjectives in each of the following sentences.

1. The bestest job I ever had was at Mike's Pizza.

2. Tiffany was more lazier than Sally was today.

3. The most biggest flag flies over the gas station.

4. Of the two boys, John was the tallest.

5. When Cheyenne got engaged, she couldn't have been more happier.

6. Yesterday I felt lousy, but today I feel worser.

7. We have small mice in our attic that are the most cutest things I've ever seen.

8. There are 12 pine trees on our street, and the taller one is in our front yard.

9. Your first essay was good, but this is even more good.

10. The bananas on the counter are more riper today.

 **Practicing Adjectives**

Now complete the **Recall** activity for **Adjectives** at **MyWritingLab.com.** Remember to read the answers carefully because many of them look similar.

REVIEW PRACTICE 2: Correcting Correct the incorrect adjectives in Review Practice 2 by rewriting the sentences.

 **Practicing Adjectives**

Next, complete the **Apply** activity for **Adjectives** at **MyWritingLab.com.** Remember that spelling and spacing count.

REVIEW PRACTICE 3: Writing Your Own Write a paragraph describing one of the most memorable people you have ever met. What did the person look like? How did he or she talk? What did he or she wear? Where did you meet this person? Why is this person so memorable?

 **Practicing Adjectives**

For more practice, complete the **Write** activity for **Adjectives** at **MyWritingLab.com.** Pay close attention to which adjectives are used incorrectly.

EDITING THE STUDENT WRITING

Return to the student paragraph at the beginning of this chapter, and do the following activities.

Individual Activity Review your underlining. Did you find the 14 adjectives? Next, put an X above the four adjectives in the paragraph that are not in the correct form.

Collaborative Activity Team up with a partner, and use what you have learned in this chapter to correct these errors.

EDITING YOUR OWN WRITING

Exchange paragraphs from Review Practice 3 with a classmate, and do the following:

1. Underline all the adjectives.

2. Circle those that are not in the correct form.

Then return the paper to its writer, and use the information in this chapter to correct any adjective errors in your own paragraph. Record your errors on the Error Log in Appendix 1.

14

Adverbs

The following student paragraph contains correct and incorrect adverb usage. Read the paragraph, and underline the 18 adverbs.

I will never forget the day I received my driver's license. I thought I was *real* important, and I honestly thought I could conquer the world. Though I didn't have no driving experience, I convinced my parents to let me take their new convertible for a joy ride. They were reluctant at first, but they most generously agreed to my foolish request. I immediately drove to my best friend's house, and we eventually found three other guys. We then drove proud to the pizza place where students often gather. After visiting with some friends for about an hour, we decided to leave and see a movie. However, as I was backing *slow* out of my parking spot, I bumped into a post. I couldn't believe it! I hadn't never seen that post before, and I know I looked behind me when I put the car in reverse. Well, there was only minor damage to the bumper, but I knew my parents would be awful upset. With that in mind, we decided to see the movie and deal with my parents later.

Like adjectives, adverbs help us communicate more clearly (she walked *quickly*) and more vividly (he sat *comfortably*). They make sentences more interesting.

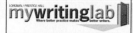
Understanding Adverbs

To learn more about these modifiers, go to **MyWritingLab.com,** and watch the video on **Adverbs.** Then, return to this chapter, which will go into more detail about adverbs and give you opportunities to practice using them. Finally, you will apply your understanding of this part of speech to your own writing.

USING ADVERBS

Adverbs modify verbs, adjectives, and other adverbs. They answer the questions *how? when? where? how often?* and *to what extent?* Look at the following examples.

How:	The air bag inflated **instantly** during the accident.
When:	My car **always** breaks down when I have an important date.
Where:	Don't park your car **there.**
How often:	Maggie drives to Los Angeles **weekly.**
To what extent:	Traffic is **extremely** heavy on the weekends.

Some words are always adverbs, including *here, there, not, never, now, again, almost, often,* and *well.*

Other adverbs are formed by adding *-ly* to an adjective:

Adjective	Adverb
light	lightly
loud	loudly
busy	busily

Hint: Not all words that end in *-ly* are adverbs. Some, such as *friendly, early, lonely, chilly,* and *lively,* are adjectives.

Reviewing Adverbs

What are adverbs?

_____

What five questions do adverbs answer?

_____   _____

_____   _____

_____

List four words that are always adverbs.

_____   _____

_____   _____

How do many adverbs end?

_____

PRACTICE 1: Identifying and Correcting

A. Put an X next to the sentence if the underlined word is not an adverb.

1. _____ I spoke quietly to my <u>best</u> friend in class.

2. _____ My girlfriend sent me <u>lovely</u> flowers on my birthday.

3. _____ <u>Rock</u> the baby gently.

4. _____ Will you be able to help me <u>now</u>?

5. _____ Grace is very <u>happy</u> about her new job.

6. _____ The CD is permanently <u>stuck</u> in the computer.

7. _____ My books got quite <u>wet</u> in the rain.

8. _____ Jason learned to type <u>quickly</u>.

9. _____ I will not make that mistake <u>again</u>.

10. _____ Luis receives a <u>salary</u> bonus annually.

B. Correct the errors in Practice 1A by listing the actual adverbs, including those that were identified correctly.

PRACTICE 2: Completing Fill in each blank in the following paragraph with an adverb.

One day, I (1) _____ volunteered to take my two friends home from school. The rain was falling (2) _____ on the ground, so we ran (3) _____ to my car. It was parked on the far side of the parking lot, and I could (4) _____ remember where it was. I (5) _____ pulled out my keys, and we (6) _____ jumped inside. After we had driven around the corner, my friend (7) _____ remembered that she had (8) _____ forgotten to pick up her financial aid check. She said she (9) _____ needed the money, and she (10) _____ begged me to go back to campus. I finally gave in, and we turned the car around.

PRACTICE 3: Writing Your Own Write a sentence of your own for each of the following adverbs.

1. wildly _____

2. honestly _____

3. almost _____

4. kindly _____

5. never _____

COMPARING WITH ADVERBS

Like adjectives, most adverbs have three forms: a **basic** form, a **comparative** form (used to compare two items), and a **superlative** form (used to compare three or more items).

For positive comparisons, adverbs form the comparative and superlative forms in two different ways:

1. One-syllable adverbs use *-er* and *-est* to form the comparative and superlative.

Basic	Comparative (used to compare two items)	Superlative (used to compare three or more items)
soon	sooner	soonest
fast	faster	fastest

2. Adverbs of two or more syllables use *more* to compare two items and *most* to compare three or more items.

Basic	Comparative (used to compare two items)	Superlative (used to compare three or more items)
quickly	more quickly	most quickly
gently	more gently	most gently
easily	more easily	most easily

For negative comparisons, adverbs, like adjectives, use *less* to compare two items and *least* to compare three or more items.

Basic	Comparative (used to compare two items)	Superlative (used to compare three or more items)
quickly	less quickly	least quickly
gently	less gently	least gently
easily	less easily	least easily

Hint: Like adjectives, certain adverbs are not usually compared. Something cannot last "*more* eternally" or work "*more* invisibly." The following adverbs cannot logically be compared.

endlessly	*eternally*	*infinitely*
equally	*impossibly*	*invisibly*

Reviewing Adverb Forms

When do you use the comparative form of an adverb?

_____

When do you use the superlative form of an adverb?

_____

How do one-syllable adverbs form the comparative and superlative in positive comparisons?

_____

How do adverbs of two or more syllables form the comparative and superlative in positive comparisons?

_____

How do adverbs form negative comparisons?

_____

PRACTICE 4: Identifying and Correcting

A. Underline the adverbs in each of the following sentences.

1. The river is flowing less swiftly than usual.

2. I use the library more frequently than my roommate.

3. I like to go shopping there.

4. I was absent less often than my friend.

5. I am taking that class again.

6. We were both upset about the service, but Cammy spoke more angrily to the server.

7. They are most likely to be at the dance.

8. Rachel walked less gracefully after her knee surgery.

9. The other actors were brave, but I said my lines more timidly.

10. Of all the children in day care, my son was screaming the loudest.

B. Change the positive comparisons in Practice 4A to negative ones and the negative comparisons to positive ones.

PRACTICE 5: Completing Fill in each blank in the following paragraph with the correct comparative or superlative form of the adverb in parentheses.

I was 15 pounds overweight last summer because I had been eating (1) _____ (foolishly) than usual. I was also exercising (2) _____ (regularly) because I had taken on a second job. My friend introduced me to a new diet that was the (3) _____ (sensibly) organized one I had ever heard of. According to this diet, breakfast and lunch would be (4) _____ (strictly) planned than dinner. I could eat a piece of fruit or a bagel, but I couldn't snack between meals. I didn't really like the food options I had, but I was (5) _____ (seriously) worried that a piece of fruit wouldn't be enough to satisfy my appetite. Snacking between meals was my biggest problem, and I was visiting the snack machine at work (6) _____ (often) than the water fountain. In fact, that scenario had to be completely reversed. I had to drink lots and lots of water, which meant that I made visits to the bathroom (7) _____ (frequently) than I ever had before. My co-workers cracked jokes about my trips to the bathroom, but the one who was (8) _____ (genuinely) supportive was Bill. Apparently, Bill wanted to start a diet too, and he was (9) _____ (honestly) interested in the success of my weight loss than in the side effects of drinking so much water. When I eventually lost the 15 pounds, Bill hugged and congratulated me, but even (10) _____ (importantly), he said that I looked great.

PRACTICE 6: Writing Your Own Write a sentence of your own for each of the following adverb forms.

1. the superlative form of *sweetly* _____

2. the positive basic form of *wisely* _____

3. the comparative form of *patiently* _____

4. the negative superlative form of *harshly* _____

5. the comparative form of *boldly* _____

ADJECTIVE OR ADVERB?

One of the most common modifier errors with modifiers is using an adjective when an adverb is called for. Keep in mind that adjectives modify nouns and pronouns, whereas adverbs modify verbs, adjectives, and other adverbs. Adverbs *do not* modify nouns or pronouns. Here are some examples.

NOT She fastened the seat belt **tight.** [adjective]
Correct: She fastened the seat belt **tightly.** [adverb]

NOT We were **real** frightened after the accident. [adjective]
Correct: We were **really** frightened after the accident. [adverb]

> ### Reviewing the Difference Between Adjectives and Adverbs
>
> *How do you know whether to use an adjective or an adverb in a sentence?*
>
> _____
>
> _____

Give an example of an adverb in a sentence.

_____

_____

Give an example of an adjective in a sentence.

_____

_____

PRACTICE 7: Identifying and Correcting

A. Underline the incorrect adverb forms in the following sentences.

1. You tied your shoelaces too loose, and your shoes are falling off your feet.

2. I set up my computer real quickly, and I think I missed something.

3. She peeked quietly into the room where the baby was sleeping.

4. We sat sleepily in our chairs.

5. When we left the party, we told Joe that we had a really good time.

6. Run quick to the phone to call the police!

7. If you want the best deal, you have to shop wise.

8. Tina wants to go very bad, but she doesn't have enough money.

9. He signed his name sloppily on the paper.

10. If you had built the cabinet proper, it wouldn't be falling apart.

B. Correct the five adverb errors in Practice 7A by rewriting each incorrect sentence.

PRACTICE 8: Completing Fill in each blank in the following paragraph with the correct form of the modifier in parentheses.

I (1) _____ (recent/recently) discovered that I am not very good at interior decorating. I had been watching a special on the Home Improvement channel, and I saw this (2) _____ (real/really) neat way to paint a wall. It's called woodgraining, and it looked very easy when the experts did it on TV. They painted the wall a dark brown and then went over it (3) _____ (slow/slowly) with a special brush, which gave the wall a woodgrain effect. The brush has ridges in it that catch the paint and drag it (4) _____ (careful/carefully) into lines. I just knew my dining room would look great with this technique, so I drove (5) _____ (quick/quickly) to the hardware store and bought the necessary supplies. As I began the project, I (6) _____ (sudden/suddenly) realized that it was going to take longer than I had (7) _____ (original/originally) expected. I had no idea how to control the brush, and I (8) _____ (soon/soonly) became frustrated. I practiced and practiced, and it looked better (9) _____ (eventual/eventually), but it was not (10) _____ (near/nearly) as beautiful as the wall the experts painted. Next time, I'm hiring a professional.

PRACTICE 9: Writing Your Own Write a sentence of your own using each of the following adverbs correctly.

1. really _____

2. faithfully _____

3. poorly _____

4. happily _____

5. amazingly _____

DOUBLE NEGATIVES

Another problem that involves adverbs is the **double negative**—the use of two negative words in one clause. Examples of negative words include *no, not, never, none, nothing, neither, nowhere, nobody, barely,* and *hardly.* A double negative creates the opposite meaning of what is intended.

> **NOT**   I **never** had **no** seat belts in my car.

The actual meaning of these double negatives is "I did have seat belts in my car."

> **Correct:**   I **never** had seat belts in my car.
> **NOT**   My brother does**n't** wear seat belts **nowhere.**

The actual meaning of these double negatives is "My brother wears seat belts somewhere."

> **Correct:**   My brother does**n't** wear seat belts **anywhere.**

Double negatives often occur with contractions.

NOT   There are**n't hardly** any cars in the parking lot.

The actual meaning of these double negatives is "There are quite a few cars in the parking lot."

Correct: There are **hardly** any cars in the parking lot.

Using two negatives is confusing and grammatically wrong. Be on the lookout for negative words, and use only one per clause.

Reviewing Double Negatives

What is a double negative?

_____

List five negative words.

_____

Why should you avoid double negatives?

_____

PRACTICE 10: Identifying and Correcting

A. Underline the incorrect negatives in the following sentences.

   1. Nobody never attended the meetings.

   2. There isn't nowhere I'd rather be than here with you.

   3. My best friend isn't barely one month younger than I am.

   4. I didn't have no choice.

   5. Lara is nice, but she isn't no saint.

   6. Ramell can't get out of bed no more.

   7. Nobody left me no food in the house.

   8. The phone rang for ten minutes, but there wasn't no answer.

   9. I didn't want a date for the Christmas party, and I didn't go with nobody.

   10. That fish isn't hardly cooked.

B. Correct the negative errors in Practice 10A by rewriting the incorrect sentences.

PRACTICE 11: Completing Fill in each blank in the following paragraph with the correct negative adverb in parentheses.

Caring for a puppy is (1) _____ (hardly/not hardly) as easy as it looks. Puppies require lots of attention, and many dog owners complain that they (2) _____ (don't ever/don't never) have enough time to spend with their pets. It is especially important to remember that puppies need lots of training, and if they (3) _____ (aren't never/aren't ever) given the training when they're young, they (4) _____ (won't ever/won't never) be well behaved when they get older. Also, puppies have a great deal of energy. There (5) _____ (isn't anything/isn't nothing) they won't chew on or tear up if they get a chance. It doesn't seem to matter (6) _____ (none/any) whether the puppy is male or female, because all puppies share those personality traits. Nonetheless, I can't think of (7) _____ (anyone/no one) who couldn't benefit from a puppy's unconditional love. I don't have (8) _____ (no/any) doubt that this is the reason people keep adopting puppies into their homes. People wouldn't (9) _____ (ever/never) take on the trouble of raising a dog if it wasn't so darn cute. And there isn't (10) _____ (anything/nothing) that compares to the feeling a person gets after being licked in the face by such a faithful friend.

PRACTICE 12: Writing Your Own Write a sentence of your own using the following negative words correctly.

1. never _____

2. nobody _____

3. nowhere _____

4. barely _____

5. none _____

USING *GOOD/WELL* AND *BAD/BADLY* CORRECTLY

The pairs *good/well* and *bad/badly* are so frequently misused that they deserve special attention.

Good is an adjective; *well* is an adverb or an adjective.

Use *good* with a noun (n) or after a linking verb (lv).

                                                      n

Adjective: Wearing your seat belt is a **good** idea.

                        lv

Adjective: He looks **good.**

Use *well* for someone's health or after an action verb (av).

                        lv

Adjective: She is **well** again. [health]

                        av

Adverb: The car drives **well** since we changed the oil.

Bad is an adjective; *badly* is an adverb.
Use *bad* with a noun (n) or after a linking verb (lv). Always use *bad* after *feel* if you are talking about emotions.

                                    n

Adjective: He uses **bad** language.

                        lv

Adjective: I feel **bad** that I got a ticket.

Use *badly* with an adjective (adj) or after an action verb (av).

                                          adj

Adverb: The car was **badly** damaged.

                        av

Adverb: He drives **badly.**

Reviewing *Good/Well* and *Bad/Badly*

When should you use the adjective good?

_____

When should you use the adjective well? *The adverb* well?

_____

When should you use the adjective bad?

_____

When should you use the adverb badly?

_____

PRACTICE 13: Identifying and Correcting

A. Underline the incorrect forms of *good*, *well*, *bad*, and *badly* in the following sentences.

1. If you do your job good, you'll probably get a raise.

2. Anika felt well about her decision.

3. The police are often portrayed bad in movies.

4. She spoke bad about her parents.

5. Gabrielle was in the hospital for pneumonia, but now she is good again.

6. Diane's pregnancy is going bad, and she has been very sick.

7. We feel badly that you can't come to our housewarming party.

8. Do you know that girl very good?

9. I know you like Tyrone, but I think his attitude is badly.

10. Jackie is learning what sports she can play good.

B. Correct the adjective and adverb errors in Practice 13A by rewriting each incorrect sentence.

PRACTICE 14: Completing Fill in each blank in the following paragraph with the correct word in parentheses.

　　James wanted so (1) _____ (bad/badly) to make the baseball team that he practiced long and hard all summer. When school started in the fall, he went to a really (2) _____ (good/well) baseball camp, and he spent eight weeks training with the best coaches in town. He became very (3) _____ (good/well) at pitching, and he could hit home runs (4) _____ (good/well) too. Practice finally began for baseball. James came early to every practice and tried his best, but he was so nervous that sometimes he handled the ball (5) _____ (bad/badly). He couldn't throw the ball as (6) _____ (good/well) and was having trouble pitching fastballs. He didn't look (7) _____ (good/well) swinging the bat either. It was as if something had invaded his body just to make him look (8) _____ (bad/badly) in front of everyone. He felt so

(9) _____ (bad/badly) about his performance at practice that he made even more errors. Finally, his coach took him aside and told him to relax. He spent the weekend calming down and concentrating, and the following week he was a (10) _____ (good/well) baseball player again.

PRACTICE 15: Writing Your Own Write a sentence of your own using the following words correctly.

1. good _____

2. badly _____

3. well _____

4. bad _____

5. good _____

CHAPTER REVIEW

Reviewing Adverbs

For this topic, be sure to look at the grammar of the sentence to determine if it is correct rather than just listen to the way the sentence sounds.

To review this material before you complete the Review Practices, watch the **Adverbs** video at **MyWritingLab.com** one more time. This time, keep the video open as you complete the rest of the practices in this chapter. For best results, do the **MyWritingLab** exercises online as well as the Chapter Review practices in the book.

REVIEW PRACTICE 1: Identifying Underline the incorrect adverb forms in the following sentences.

1. Hold on tight to this rope!

2. I thought you did really good in the play.

3. Becky made a real bad mistake.

4. The groom stood proud at the altar, watching his bride.

5. My father doesn't show me no respect.

6. This soup tastes badly.

7. Listen quiet to the CD because I'm trying to study.

8. The Rodriguez family never go nowhere without their dog.

9. I didn't do nothing to hurt you.

10. You drive so bad that other drivers are afraid of you.

 **Practicing Adverbs**

Now complete the **Recall** activity for **Adverbs** at **MyWritingLab.com.** If you're having a difficult time with a question, open up the video in the lower right-hand corner for some help.

REVIEW PRACTICE 2: Correcting Correct the adverb errors in Review Practice 1 by rewriting the sentences.

 **Practicing Adverbs**

Next, complete the **Apply** activity for **Adverbs** at **MyWritingLab.com.** Pay close attention to the directions, and only click on what you're asked to.

REVIEW PRACTICE 3: Writing Your Own Write a paragraph explaining a favorite pastime of yours. What does the activity involve? Why do you like it? What does it do for you?

 **Practicing Adverbs**

For more practice, complete the **Write** activity for **Adverbs** at **MyWritingLab.com.** Make sure to pay close attention to which adverbs are used incorrectly.

EDITING THE STUDENT WRITING

Return to the student paragraph at the beginning of this chapter, and do the following activities.

Individual Activity   Review your underlining. Did you find the 18 adverbs? Next, put an X above the four adverb errors in the paragraph. Underline the two double negatives twice.

Collaborative Activity   Team up with a partner, and use what you have learned in this chapter to correct these errors. Rewrite the paragraph with your corrections.

EDITING YOUR OWN WRITING

Exchange paragraphs from Review Practice 3 with a classmate, and do the following:

1. Underline all the adverbs.

2. Circle those that are not in the correct form.

3. Put an X above any double negatives.

Then return the paper to its writer, and use the information in this chapter to correct any adverb errors in your own paragraph. Record your errors on the Error Log in Appendix 1.

Modifier Errors

The following paragraph, written by a student, contains examples of correct and incorrect modifier usage. Read the paragraph, and underline as many modifiers as you can. Don't forget modifiers of more than one word.

My favorite invention is the toaster oven. The toaster is in the kitchen with a glass door. To make toast and bagels, every morning it is used. Being the oldest of four children, it is usually very difficult to prepare a quick breakfast for everyone. But the toaster is very helpful and easy to use. To determine the appropriate cook time, the dial must be set on the chosen temperature. Opening the glass door, the rack inside is where the toast or bagel is placed. Then the door is shut, and the lever on the front is pressed down. After cooking for the specified time, a bell will ring to signal that the food is ready to eat. I will be moving into the dorms next quarter, and my mom promised to buy a new toaster oven for me yesterday. I just know that having a toaster oven in my dorm room will earn me a reputation as a great cook.

As you know, a modifier describes another word or group of words. Sometimes, however, a modifier is too far from the words it refers to (*misplaced modifier*), or the word it refers to is missing altogether (*dangling modifier*). As a result, the sentence is confusing.

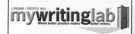
Understanding Modifier Errors

To expand your understanding of modifier errors, go to **MyWritingLab.com,** and view the video on **Misplaced or Dangling Modifiers.** Then, return to this chapter, which will go into more detail about these errors and give you opportunities to practice correcting them. Finally, you will apply your understanding of modifier errors to your own writing.

MISPLACED MODIFIERS

A modifier should be placed as close as possible to the word or words it modifies, but this does not always happen. A **misplaced modifier** is too far from the word or words it refers to, making the meaning of the sentence unclear. Look at these examples.

NOT The gardener prunes the tree that grows in the backyard **in May.**
    (Does the tree in the backyard grow only in May? Probably not. But the gardener prunes it only in May. So the modifier *in May* needs to be moved closer to the word it actually modifies.)

Correct: **In May,** the gardener prunes the tree that grows in the backyard.

NOT I need to upgrade the computer in that office **that doesn't have a mouse.**
    (It is the computer, not the office, that doesn't have a mouse. So the modifier *that doesn't have a mouse* needs to be moved closer to the word it modifies.)

Correct: I need to upgrade the computer **that doesn't have a mouse** in that office.

Certain modifiers that limit meaning are often misplaced, causing problems. Look at how meaning changes by moving the limiting word *only* in the following sentences:

Only Rachel plans to meet Sally for lunch at The Pepper.
(No one but Rachel will meet Sally.)

Rachel **only** plans to meet Sally for lunch at The Pepper.
(Rachel plans to meet her but might not show up.)

Rachel plans **only** to meet Sally for lunch at The Pepper.
(Rachel plans to meet Sally for lunch and do nothing else.)

Rachel plans to meet **only** Sally for lunch at The Pepper.
(Rachel plans to meet no one but Sally.)

Rachel plans to meet Sally **only** for lunch at The Pepper.
(Rachel does not plan to meet for any other reason.)

Rachel plans to meet Sally for lunch **only** at The Pepper.
(Rachel plans to have lunch there but no other meals.)

Rachel plans to meet Sally for lunch at The Pepper **only.**
(Rachel does not plan to meet at any other place.)

Here is a list of common limiting words.

almost	*hardly*	*merely*	*only*
even	*just*	*nearly*	*scarcely*

Reviewing Misplaced Modifiers

What is a misplaced modifier?

_____

How can you correct a misplaced modifier?

_____

PRACTICE 1: Identifying and Correcting

A. Underline the misplaced modifiers in each of the following sentences.

1. Anne lost a filling while shopping from a molar.

2. I told them that we would have lunch today in the park last weekend.

3. As a young child, my parents tried not to spoil me.

4. Paul sold his bike to me after he got a new one as a present for $150.

5. Eunice used shampoo on her hair from the beauty salon.

6. The best movie ever made was *Jaws* in 3D.

7. Thomas told Renee that to pass the exam she would be wise.

8. I need to check out the book about Edgar Allen Poe with the blue spine.

9. The basketball team held a car wash from our college.

10. My diary is in the closet under my collection of quarters.

B. Correct the modifier errors in Practice 1A by rewriting each incorrect sentence.

PRACTICE 2: Completing Fill in each blank in the following paragraph with a modifier. Include at least two phrases.

When Stephanie was born, her parents owned a (1) _____ car that had many miles on it. They took many vacations in the car, even going (2) _____ one year. It was a dependable car, but it was very small and (3) _____. Needless to say, when Stephanie came along, her parents realized their need for (4) _____ transportation. They (5) _____ started shopping around for (6) _____ roomy vehicles that would fit her baby car seat and still have room for (7) _____. A salesman talked them into buying a minivan, which they had initially thought was (8) _____. Eventually, they came to (9) _____ the car and found it was perfect for them. Sixteen years later, when Stephanie got her driver's license, the (10) _____ became her car, and her parents bought a new Toyota.

PRACTICE 3: Writing Your Own Write a sentence of your own for each of the following modifiers.

1. after the rain _____

2. since we arrived _____

3. while making dinner _____

4. before she saw him _____

5. though we couldn't hear it _____

DANGLING MODIFIERS

Modifiers are "dangling" when they have nothing to refer to in a sentence. **Dangling modifiers** (starting with an *-ing* word or with *to*) often appear at the beginning of a sentence. Here is an example.

NOT   **Surfing the Internet,** my computer mouse is very helpful.

A modifier usually modifies the words closest to it. So the phrase *Surfing the Internet* modifies *my computer mouse*. But my mouse doesn't surf the Internet. In fact, there is no logical word in the sentence that the phrase modifies. It is left dangling. You can correct a dangling modifier in one of two ways—by inserting the missing word referred to or by rewriting the sentence.

Correct:	**Surfing the Internet, I** find my computer mouse very helpful.
Correct:	**When I am surfing the Internet,** my computer mouse is very helpful.

NOT	**To play the lottery,** a ticket must be bought.
Correct:	**To play the lottery, you** must buy a ticket.
Correct:	You must buy a ticket if you want **to play the lottery.**

NOT	The bag for charity was full **after going through our old clothes.**
Correct:	**After going through our old clothes, we** had a full bag for charity.
Correct:	**After we went through our old clothes,** we had a full bag for charity.
Correct:	The bag for charity was full **after we went through our old clothes.**

Reviewing Dangling Modifiers

What is a dangling modifier?

_____

_____

How do you correct a dangling modifier?

_____

_____

PRACTICE 4: Identifying and Correcting

A. Underline the dangling modifiers in each of the following sentences.

1. Thinking the team would never win the tournament, the calendar marked the big day.

2. To remain in this fraternity, dues must be paid.

3. While drawing in the coloring book, the crayons broke.

4. Before jumping in the pool, the diving board was very slippery.

5. To visit South America, a passport must be obtained.

6. Flying first class in the commercial jet, the seat would not recline.

7. To upgrade the computer, more memory was installed.

8. To change the oil in my car, the filter must be replaced.

9. After waiting in line for an hour, the post office worker closed her window.

10. To feed the children dinner, macaroni and cheese was prepared.

B. Correct the modifier errors in Practice 4A by rewriting each incorrect sentence.

PRACTICE 5: Completing Fill in each blank in the following paragraph with a modifier. Include at least two phrases.

(1) _____, everything at Macy's goes on sale. The salespeople run around frantically, preparing (2) _____ clothes and other items. Hundreds of (3) _____ people show up at the doors, often arriving before the store opens. Within a few hours, shoppers are (4) _____, and all of the beautifully arranged items become (5) _____. I personally witnessed one of these big sales when (6) _____. It was (7) _____ to see the number of people fighting over everything in sight. I wondered if they really needed the items or were just (8) _____. After I made my few purchases, I left (9) _____. I was glad to be out of the confusion and back (10) _____.

PRACTICE 6: Writing Your Own Write a sentence of your own for each of the following phrases.

1. clear and sunny _____

2. taking my coat _____

3. to communicate with my parents _____

4. getting a haircut _____

5. to visit Paris _____

CHAPTER REVIEW

To complete these exercises, you might want to take notes, particularly writing down the words that limit meaning so you can look at them while you complete the exercises.

Reviewing Modifier Errors

To review this material before you complete the Review Practices, watch the **Misplaced or Dangling Modifiers** video at **MyWritingLab.com** one more time. This time, keep the video open as you complete the rest of the practices in this chapter. For best results, do the **MyWritingLab** exercises online as well as the Chapter Review practices in the book.

REVIEW PRACTICE 1: Identifying Underline any misplaced or dangling modifiers in the following sentences.

1. Joanne told Sam that she would take him to dinner tonight last Wednesday.

2. Checking the time, the clock said it was exactly 1:00 p.m.

3. Fishing in the lake, the boat sprang a leak.

4. To iron your shirts, spray starch is needed.

5. My souvenirs are on the table from Texas.

6. We made the floral arrangements from my garden with lots of daffodils.

7. To turn off the television, the remote must be used.

8. Scanning pictures from our vacation, my printer broke.

9. Moving the furniture for the carpet cleaners, the sofa landed on my toe.

10. Peter just bought a classic Mustang from a used-car dealer with white racing stripes.

Practicing Modifier Errors

Now complete the **Recall** activity for **Misplaced or Dangling Modifiers** at **MyWritingLab.com.** Remember to read the answers carefully because many of them look similar.

REVIEW PRACTICE 2: Correcting Correct the misplaced or dangling modifiers in Review Practice 1 by rewriting the sentences.

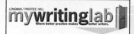

Practicing Modifier Errors

Next, complete the **Apply** activity for **Misplaced or Dangling Modifiers** at **MyWritingLab.com.** If you're stuck, you can go to the lower right-hand corner and open up the video again, or you can click on the hint button.

REVIEW PRACTICE 3: Writing Your Own Write your own paragraph about the career you hope to have after college and your plans to begin working in this field.

Practicing Modifier Errors

For more practice, complete the **Write** activity for **Misplaced or Dangling Modifiers** at **MyWritingLab.com.** Make sure to pay close attention to any modifier errors.

EDITING THE STUDENT WRITING

Return to the student paragraph at the beginning of this chapter, and do the following activities.

Individual Activity Review your underlining in the paragraph. Review the answers as a class to make sure you found all the modifiers. Now, put brackets around the seven modifier errors (four dangling modifiers and three misplaced modifiers).

Collaborative Activity Team up with a partner, and use what you have learned in this chapter to correct these errors. Rewrite the paragraph with your corrections.

EDITING YOUR OWN WRITING

Exchange paragraphs from Review Practice 3 with a classmate, and do the following:

1. Underline any misplaced modifiers.

2. Put brackets around any dangling modifiers.

Then return the paper to its writer, and use the information in this chapter to correct any modifier problems in your own paragraph. Record your errors on the Error Log in Appendix 1.

UNIT QUIZZES

Here are some exercises that test your understanding of all the material in this unit: Adjectives, Adverbs, and Modifier Errors.

Unit Quiz 1 Identifying

In each of the following sentences, underline the adverbs and adjectives used incorrectly. Put brackets around any misplaced or dangling modifiers.

1. That was the bestest meal I have ever eaten.

2. You did good on this report, so I think you'll get a pay raise.

3. To bake a cake, a greased pan is needed.

4. Fred started shopping here because the sales clerks are more friendlier than in any other store.

5. Devon couldn't never understand geometry, no matter how much he studied it.

6. Jogging to the dock, the boat left without us.

7. I tried real hard, but I just couldn't move that rock by myself.

8. Melanie went to the mall with Sheena,wearing her new jacket.

9. Of all the students in the class, Jade is the more intelligent.

10. I left the wallet on the cafeteria tablethat I got from my sister.

11. Sit quiet, so you don't disturb anyone.

12. You couldn't sing more worse than Toni.

13. Looking under the bed, my shoes were right in front of me.

14. I couldn't barely hear what you were whispering.

15. Between Konrad and Luke, Konrad is the tallest.

16. She did bad on the test, so she wants to do an assignment for extra credit.

17. Having lost his job, Mike didn't have nowhere to go.

18. I heard the song that we requested at the concertin the car.

19. There are 14 houses on this block, and mine is by far the bigger.

20. I think it would be more better if you sat with your family and I with mine.

Unit Quiz 2 Correcting

Correct the adjective, adverb, and modifier errors in Unit Quiz 1 by rewriting each incorrect sentence.

Unit Quiz 3 Identifying

In the following paragraph, underline the adverbs and adjectives used incorrectly. Put brackets around any misplaced or dangling modifiers.

During my first year of college, I wrote for the campus newspaper [about our sports teams]. I was assigned to cover the men's basketball games, the women's swim meets, and all of the tennis matches. Needless to say, I was kept quite busy going to real exciting sports events. Of the three sports, I thought the swim meets were more fun. Cheri and Julia were the two swim coaches, and they were so cooperative. The only problem I had was keeping up with the deadlines. [To get an article published in a weekly paper], a draft had to be submitted by Tuesday evening. Wednesday the editors reviewed it for corrections or changes, and Thursday it was laid out for press. This tight schedule didn't leave no room for procrastination; however, it made me a better writer. Because the deadlines were so strict, I had no choice but to sit down with my pen and paper. Something even more better was that I learned how to take good notes.[Listening for important details], my notes were very organized. I also learned how to manipulate the tone of my articles, making them sound positive even when the teams weren't doing so good. Writing for the paper was the most toughest experience I've had, but it was also the most rewarding.

Unit Quiz 4 Correcting

Correct the adjective, adverb, and modifier errors in Unit Quiz 3 by rewriting the paragraph.

UNIT WRITING ASSIGNMENTS

1. What is your personal writing process? What do you do to prepare yourself for writing? What are your favorite prewriting techniques? What do you look for in revision? Describe your writing process from beginning to end, using as many details as possible.

2. We all have our idiosyncrasies, especially when it comes to doing everyday tasks. How do you go about doing an everyday task, such as washing laundry or driving to school? Write about the process you go through to perform this activity.

3. Describe the first major holiday that you can remember. Who was there? What happened? How did you feel? Write about the holiday using as many details as you can.

Punctuation

Can you imagine streets and highways without stoplights or traffic signs? Driving would become a life-or-death adventure as motorists made risky trips with no signals to guide or protect them. Good writers, like conscientious drivers, prefer to leave little to chance. They observe the rules of punctuation to ensure that their readers arrive at their intended meaning. Without punctuation, sentences would run together, ideas would be unclear, and words would be misread. Writers need to use markers—like periods, commas, and dashes—to help them communicate as efficiently and effectively as possible.

Look at the difference punctuation makes in the meaning of the following letter.

Dear John:

I want a man who knows what love is all about. You are generous, kind, thoughtful. People who are not like you admit to being useless and inferior. You have ruined me for other men. I yearn for you. I have no feelings whatsoever when we're apart. I can be forever happy—will you let me be yours?   Susan

Dear John,

I want a man who knows what love is. All about you are generous, kind, thoughtful people, who are not like you. Admit to being useless and inferior. You have ruined me. For other men, I yearn. For you, I have no feelings whatsoever. When we're apart, I can be forever happy. Will you let me be?   Yours, Susan

This unit will help you write the love letter you actually want to write—with the punctuation that gets your message across. It will also provide you with guidelines for using the following punctuation.

Chapter 16: End Punctuation
Chapter 17: Commas
Chapter 18: Apostrophes
Chapter 19: Quotation Marks
Chapter 20: Other Punctuation Marks

End Punctuation

The following student paragraph contains nine incorrect or missing pieces of end punctuation. Read the paragraph, and underline the errors you find.

Last summer, I belonged to a book club. It was full of nice people, and I became good friends with many of the ones my age? Unfortunately, the club was growing too rapidly, and soon there were too many new members. When that happened, the structure of the club fell apart? Instead of discussing books, the people would get together just to eat munchies and complain about things! Soon the leaders sent out a survey, asking the club members for comments and suggestions. I thought this would be my chance to explain how uncomfortable I was feeling! They asked things like "What kinds of things could we do to make it a better? club!" and I answered all of the survey questions honestly. What I didn't expect was that one of the club leaders took all of my answers personally, and she was suddenly very mad at me. I was confused by her response, and I asked myself, "What could I possibly have said wrong?" She told me that my answers were sarcastic and mean. I was shocked? "How!" I tried to ask her, but she kept avoiding me. When I finally met with her, she began to cry. "You hurt me?" she yelled, and I was still in shock. I apologized profusely and tried to understand, and eventually I think she forgave me. Still, I don't think I'll be going back to that book club again.

End punctuation signals the end of a sentence in three ways: The **period** ends a statement, the **question mark** signals a question, and the **exclamation point** marks an exclamation.

Understanding End Punctuation

To improve your understanding of these forms of punctuation, go to **MyWritingLab.com,** and view the video on **Final Punctuation.** Then, return to this chapter, which will go into more detail about these punctuation marks and give you opportunities to practice them. Finally, you will apply your understanding of end punctuation to your own writing.

PERIOD

1. A **period** is used with statements, mild commands, and indirect questions.

Statement:	Michelangelo painted the Sistine Chapel.
Command:	Paint the Sistine Chapel.
Indirect Question:	I wonder if he had any help painting the Sistine Chapel.

2. A period is also used with abbreviations and numbers.

Abbreviations:	Mrs. Baker lives at 7901 Broad St., next door to Dr. Janet Rodriguez.
Numbers:	$15.85 10.5 $659.95 .075

Reviewing Periods

What are the three main uses of a period?

_____

What are two other uses of a period?

_____

PRACTICE 1: Identifying and Correcting

A. Put an X next to each sentence that contains a period error.

1. _____ I am taking the day off

2. _____ I want to know what you are doing.

3. _____ I can sell the chair for $3000, or about two hours of work.

4. _____ I wonder if Mr Thompson can help me.

5. _____ Will you be at Seventh St and Pine Ave this afternoon?

6. _____ My checking account has a balance of $105,90.

7. _____ Dr. Edwards, please check my blood pressure.

8. _____ Dr Otto is my math instructor.

9. _____ We need to take the trash out tonight

10. _____ I work for the US ambassador to Ecuador.

B. Correct the punctuation errors in Practice 1A by rewriting each incorrect sentence.

PRACTICE 2: Completing Add periods to the following paragraph.

The woman, Mrs. Chambers, rushed into the emergency room She was 38 weeks pregnant and going into labor Mr Chambers had been sitting at home while his wife ran errands He had no idea what was going on until he received a call from St Vincent's Hospital, telling him that his wife had been admitted Dr Bustamonte delivered their baby within the hour, and Mr Chambers arrived just in time. Unfortunately, in his hurry to get to the hospital, Mr Chambers forgot the camcorder, the camera, and even a change of clothes for his wife But aside from those minor details, the family went home with a healthy little boy and a bill for $1,56988

PRACTICE 3: Writing Your Own Write a sentence of your own for each of the following directions.

1. a statement about Mr. Guerra _____

2. an indirect question about Jefferson St. _____

3. a statement about $934.59 _____

4. a command to do the laundry _____

5. an indirect question about the weather _____

QUESTION MARK

The **question mark** is used after a direct question.

Question Mark: What do you know about Michelangelo?

Question Mark: "What do you know about Michelangelo?" the
                    teacher asked.

Reviewing Question Marks

What is the main role of a question mark?

_____

Give an example of a question.

_____

PRACTICE 4: Identifying and Correcting

A. Put an X next to each sentence that contains a question mark error.

1. _____ Are you kidding.

2. _____ I wonder if Steve registered for this class?

3. _____ Janie asked, "What is taking so long?"

4. _____ This cannot happen today?

5. _____ What seems to be the problem?

6. _____ I can't remember if Kimo is allergic to dairy products?

7. _____ "Would you like something to drink?" the waitress asked?

8. _____ You are planning to be there, right?

9. _____ I can't believe you haven't cleaned this room?

10. _____ Brigitte asked the teacher what she meant?

B. Correct the punctuation errors in Practice 4A by rewriting each incorrect sentence.

PRACTICE 5: Completing Add question marks to the following paragraph.

Being a professional photographer is not a glamorous job. Sometimes I ask myself, "Why are you doing this" because it definitely isn't easy. On more than one occasion, I have had to work with uncooperative people, and I wonder silently, "Why are they here if they don't want to smile for me Didn't they make this appointment Didn't they call *me* for *my* services" Nonetheless, I keep taking their pictures. At least three times I've had to ask men, "Will you please take the toothpick out of your mouth" And they look at me as if they really think the toothpick makes them look sexy. Can you imagine how uncivilized that is However, when I wake up each morning,

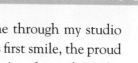
I really do look forward to seeing who will come through my studio door. I've had the opportunity to capture a baby's first smile, the proud sparkle in a new bride's eye, and a grandmother's soft touch as she read to her grandson. Now, what other job could give me that for my résumé

PRACTICE 6: Writing Your Own Write a question of your own for each of the following directions.

1. a question about gardening _____

2. a question Fawn asked about her car tires _____

3. a question about breakfast _____

4. a question Toni asked about computer paper _____

5. a question Matt asked about basketball _____

EXCLAMATION POINT

The **exclamation point** indicates strong feeling.

If it is used too often, it is not as effective as it could be. You shouldn't use more than one exclamation point at a time.

Exclamation Point:	Never!
Exclamation Point:	I can't believe it!
Exclamation Point:	That is insulting!
Exclamation Point:	"That is insulting!" he said.

Reviewing Exclamation Points

What is the main use of an exclamation point?

_____

Give an example of an exclamation.

_____

PRACTICE 7: Identifying and Correcting

A. Put an X next to each sentence that contains an exclamation point error.

1. _____ Did you tell me the truth!

2. _____ Don't you dare!

3. _____ Yeah, we won.

4. _____ "Thank God!" she said.

5. _____ What have you been doing in here!

6. _____ Can you tell me how to get to New Mexico!

7. _____ "It's going to explode," the man shouted!

8. _____ Chandra told the disc jockey, "My favorite artist is Whitney Houston!"

9. _____ Get off my bike!

10. _____ "That's it," Shannon screamed!

B. Correct the punctuation errors in Practice 7A by rewriting each incorrect sentence.

PRACTICE 8: Completing Add exclamation points to the following paragraph.

The last baseball game I saw was between the Texas Rangers and the Seattle Mariners during the summer of 2001. I am a big fan of the Rangers, even during their bad seasons. Posters saying "Go Rangers" hang proudly on my bedroom walls. Sometimes I even bring them to the games. During this particular game, the Rangers were up by one run at the bottom of the ninth inning. Seattle was at bat, and there were already two outs. Doug Davis was pitching for the Rangers, and Ichiro Suzuki was at bat. "Strike him out" I yelled from my seat, but the first pitch was a ball. "No way" I screamed. "That's a horrible call" Yet the next pitch was another ball. I couldn't believe it The bases were empty, and this was looking like a victory for Texas, but Davis was going to give it away. "Throw a strike" I shouted at the top of my lungs, and finally he did. "Two more, Davis" I begged. Whoosh The pitch flew by Suzuki at the speed of light, and the ump called out, "Strike" One more pitch went out—*whoosh* "Strike three" yelled the ump, and the stands erupted in applause. Victory for the Rangers! That was one of the happiest days of my life.

PRACTICE 9: Writing Your Own Write an exclamation of your own for each of the following directions.

1. an exclamation about cockroaches _____

2. an exclamation about childbirth _____

3. an exclamation by Brittany about a broken ankle _____

4. an exclamation by Steve about a touchdown _____

5. an exclamation about bad food _____

CHAPTER REVIEW

Reviewing End Punctuation

To help you decide on the correct end punctuation, you might want to read the sentences out loud.

To review this material before you complete the Review Practices, watch the **Final Punctuation** video at **MyWritingLab.com** one more time. This time, keep the video open as you complete the rest of the practices in this chapter. For best results, do the **MyWritingLab** exercises online as well as the Chapter Review practices in the book.

REVIEW PRACTICE 1: Identifying Underline the periods, question marks, and exclamation points that are used incorrectly in the following sentences.

1. Have you seen my little brother.

2. "Go?" Marcus yelled to Cho, who was preparing to bungee-jump at the fairgrounds.

3. "Will you come help me paint my house!" Vernon asked.

4. Get out of my way.

5. Can you open this jar of pickles for me.

6. I wonder if Tom knows his door is open?

7. "Yeah?" Isabel screamed when she learned she was pregnant.

8. My porch light is burned out?

9. "Could you repeat that!" she asked.

10. I can't remember where I left my wallet?

Practicing End Punctuation

Now complete the **Recall** activity for **Final Punctuation** at **MyWritingLab.com.** Remember to read the answers carefully because many of them look similar.

REVIEW PRACTICE 2: Correcting Correct the punctuation errors in Review Practice 1 by rewriting the incorrect sentences.

Practicing End Punctuation

Next, complete the **Apply** activity for **Final Punctuation** at **MyWritingLab.com.** If you're stuck, go to the lower right-hand corner and open up the video again, or you can click on the hint button.

REVIEW PRACTICE 3: Writing Your Own Write your own paragraph about the house you grew up in. Try to include each type of end punctuation—the period, the question mark, and the exclamation point.

Practicing End Punctuation

For more practice, complete the **Write** activity for **Final Punctuation** at **MyWritingLab.com.** Pay close attention to end punctuation in your paragraph.

EDITING THE STUDENT WRITING

Return to the student paragraph at the beginning of this chapter, and do the following activities.

Individual Activity   Review the end punctuation errors you found in the paragraph. Did you locate all nine errors in end punctuation?

Collaborative Activity   Team up with a partner, and compare the errors you both found. Then, working together, use what you have learned in this chapter about periods, question marks, and exclamation points to correct the errors you identified.

EDITING YOUR OWN WRITING

Exchange paragraphs from Review Practice 3 with a classmate, and do the following:

1. Circle any errors in end punctuation.

2. Suggest the correct punctuation above your circle.

Then return the paragraph to its writer, and use the information in this chapter to correct any end punctuation errors in your own paragraph. Record your errors on the Error Log in Appendix 1.

Commas

READING FOR COMMAS

The following paragraph, written by a student, is missing 15 commas. Read the paragraph, and add commas where you think they should be.

The students in my English class and the students in my theater class are very different. In theater the students just won't be quiet and settle down. This is probably because the theater students are talkative outgoing people. Usually the class gets out of hand which I don't like. When it gets really bad it sounds like there are 1000 people in one small classroom. Sometimes I just want to yell "Shut up!" The students in my English class however are very quiet and serious. They usually listen well pay close attention to the teacher and maintain order in the class. I think I probably learn more in this class but it can get boring at times. I'll just be glad when June 10 2011 comes because then I'll be a certified social worker and I'll be finished with my degree.

The **comma** is the most frequently used punctuation mark, but it is also the most often misused. Commas make reading sentences easier because they separate the parts of sentences. Following the rules in this chapter will help you write clear sentences that are easy to read.

Understanding Commas

To find out more about commas, go to **MyWritingLab.com,** and watch the video on **Commas.** Then, return to this chapter, which will go into more detail about this punctuation mark and give you opportunities to practice using it. Finally, you will apply your understanding of commas to your own writing.

COMMAS WITH ITEMS IN A SERIES

Use commas to separate items in a series.
This means you should put a comma between all items in a series.

Series: The class required that we read 2 novels, 20 short stories, and 12 poems.

Series: The students exchanged their essays, read them, and gave each other suggestions.

Series: Tonight I need to finish an essay, read a short story, and answer the questions on page 15.

Sometimes this rule applies to a series of adjectives in front of a noun, but sometimes it does not. Look at these two examples.

Adjectives with Commas: The **long, boring** lecture is finally over.

Adjectives without Commas: The **last red** encyclopedia is checked out of the library.

Both of these examples are correct. So how do you know whether or not to use commas? You can use one of two tests. One test is to insert the word "and" between the adjectives. If the sentence makes sense, use a comma. Another test is to switch the order of the adjectives. If the sentence still reads clearly, use a comma between the two words.

Test 1: The **long and boring** lecture is finally over. **OK, so use a comma**

Test 2: The **boring, long lecture** is finally over. **OK, so use a comma**

Test 1: The **last and red** encyclopedia is checked out of the library. **NO comma**

Test 2: The **red last** encyclopedia is checked out of the library. **NO comma**

Reviewing Commas with Items in a Series

Why use commas with items in a series?

_____

Where do these commas go?

_____

PRACTICE 1: Identifying and Correcting

A. Put an X next to the sentence if any commas in the underlined part of the sentence are missing or used incorrectly.

1. _____ If I win the lottery, I will <u>go to Paris, buy a new house, and pay off my student loans</u>.

2. _____ My best friend can play <u>tennis golf and, racquetball</u>.

3. _____ Charise's <u>fat brown</u> puppy is chewing on my sandals.

4. _____ <u>The piano, the desk, and the entertainment center</u> need to be dusted.

5. _____ I gave <u>my old jeans, my leather jacket and the television</u> to charity.

6. _____ When we went to the hockey game, we ate <u>ice cream popcorn and red licorice</u>.

7. _____ Every day, Debra <u>goes to work, goes to night school, and works out at the gym</u>.

8. _____ <u>*NCIS, ER, and NYPD Blue*</u> are all very interesting TV dramas.

9. _____ The <u>old red</u> barn needs to be painted.

10. _____ <u>The salmon the prime rib, and the crab legs</u> are this restaurant's signature dishes.

B. Correct the comma errors in Practice 1A by rewriting each incorrect sentence.

PRACTICE 2: Completing Add the missing commas to the following paragraph.

When the strangers arrived in the quiet town, they saw a private village a brick silo and a white house. Next to the house was a pigpen a chicken yard and a granary. Hard mud filled the pigpen, but there were no pigs. The doors of the house were dirty the rain gutters were hanging from the rooftops and two windows were broken. Beyond the barn was a small garden of geraniums roses and azaleas. The house appeared to be occupied by a young couple two small boys and a teenage girl. The scattered toys in the front yard gave the strangers this impression. It didn't look like anyone was home, but the strangers hoped the residents wouldn't be gone long. They just wanted a warm meal a soft bed and a pleasant conversation for one night.

PRACTICE 3: Writing Your Own Write a sentence of your own for each of the following series.

1. three kinds of animals _____

2. three places to spend money _____

3. three occupations _____

4. three things to do at the beach _____

5. three things to buy at the grocery store _____

COMMAS WITH INTRODUCTORY WORDS

Use a comma to set off an introductory word, phrase, or clause from the rest of its sentence.

If you are unsure whether to add a comma, try reading the sentence with your reader in mind. If you want your reader to pause after the introductory word or phrase, you should insert a comma.

Introductory Word:	**Yes,** I finished my essay.
Introductory Word:	**Actually,** the class was more interesting than I thought it would be.
Introductory Phrase:	**All in all,** this is a very competitive group.
Introductory Phrase:	**To save time,** I did my homework during my lunch break.
Introductory Clause:	**As the papers were being passed out,** everyone was nervous.
Introductory Clause:	**When the professor wrote on the chalkboard,** we began taking notes.

Reviewing Commas with Introductory Words

Why use commas with introductory words, phrases, and clauses?

_____

_____

How can you tell if a comma is needed?

_____

_____

PRACTICE 4: Identifying and Correcting

A. Put an X next to the sentence if any commas in the underlined part of the sentence are missing or used incorrectly.

1. _____ <u>To be totally honest,</u> I've never liked math classes.

2. _____ <u>Of course</u> I'd love to help you with that project.

3. _____ <u>Hoping, to see some changes</u> we all voted in the last student body election.

4. _____ <u>When they asked, for my opinion,</u> I spoke honestly.

5. _____ <u>Because Camille was with me,</u> I felt brave.

6. _____ <u>Not knowing, what we were up against,</u> we were a little nervous.

7. _____ <u>When she was tired</u> Sara drank lots of coffee.

8. _____ <u>Thank goodness,</u> the hardest part is over.

9. _____ <u>Fortunately Mike,</u> is on the panel too.

10. _____ <u>In hindsight</u> that was a bad decision.

B. Correct the comma errors in Practice 4A by rewriting each incorrect sentence.

PRACTICE 5: Completing Add the missing commas to the following paragraph.

Finally our squad is ready for the big cheerleading competition. Being one of the 10 men on the team I always feel lots of pressure and anxiety. The women count on us to lift, hold, and catch them without a flaw. Really it's not just dropping the girls that I worry about. Every minor mistake takes points away from our total score. When I was in high school cheerleading was just for girls. Now that I'm in college I have a whole different view. The cheerleading squad depends on big, strong men, and the best squads seem to have the most men. Unfortunately it is often difficult to recruit men to cheer. For some reason, many people don't think it's a "manly" thing to do. Personally I can't think of anything more manly than catching a petite cheerleader in a short skirt and swinging her up over my head. It always makes me think of Tarzan and Jane.

PRACTICE 6: Writing Your Own Write a sentence of your own for each of the following introductory words, phrases, or clauses.

1. Well _____

2. When I was in junior high _____

3. After the song started _____

4. Honestly _____

5. To be more specific _____

COMMAS WITH INDEPENDENT CLAUSES

Use a comma before *and, but, for, nor, or, so,* and *yet* when they join two independent clauses. (Remember that an independent clause must have both a subject and a verb.)

Independent Clauses:	The instructor put us in small groups**, and** she gave us a new assignment.
Independent Clauses:	The essay was difficult to read**, but** I learned some new vocabulary words.

Hint: Do not use a comma when a single subject has two verbs.

s v no comma v

The **instructor put** us in small groups and **gave** us a new assignment.

Adding a comma when none is needed is one of the most common errors in college writing assignments. Only if the second verb has its own subject should you add a comma.

s v comma s v

The **instructor put** us in small groups, and **she gave** us a new assignment.

Reviewing Commas with Independent Clauses

Name three coordinating conjunctions.

_____

When should you use a comma before a coordinating conjunction?

_____

Should you use a comma before a coordinating conjunction when a single subject has two verbs?

_____

PRACTICE 7: Identifying and Correcting

A. Put an X next to the sentence if any commas in the underlined part of the sentence are missing or used incorrectly.

1. _____ Mom went to the outlet <u>mall and</u> she bought a new jacket for me.

2. _____ My car ran out of <u>gas but</u> the gas gauge said I had a full tank.

3. _____ Greg organized a local baseball <u>league and</u> did lots of fund-raising.

4. _____ I can't stay <u>long for</u> I have a paper to write.

5. _____ My brother is out with his <u>girlfriend or</u> he's working late tonight.

6. _____ Junior is usually late to <u>class, but</u> he's always prepared.

7. _____ I've been <u>dieting yet</u> I haven't lost any weight.

8. _____ I'm going to order either the chicken <u>parmesan, or</u> the fettuccine Alfredo.

9. _____ James is taking a trip to <u>Missouri, and</u> he's visiting his grandparents.

10. _____ I have a doctor's appointment in 20 <u>minutes so</u> I have to leave right now.

B. Correct the comma errors in Practice 7A by rewriting each incorrect sentence.

PRACTICE 8: Completing Add the missing commas to the following paragraph.

The trainers at the Los Angeles Zoo watch the animals closely so they are usually prepared for anything. One of the elephants, Orion, was becoming extremely overweight and the trainers began to worry about him. Orion was very intelligent but he was also very lazy. The trainers started him on a cardiovascular exercise program and within a few months, Orion lost 600 pounds. Then the trainers worried that the exercise might be too much for Orion was 42 years old. They wondered if his heart would be able to take all of this activity, so they called in some veterinarians. The vets brought in an ultrasound machine but they could not detect Orion's heartbeat. They decided that his heart was too deep for the ultrasound to pick up or that his sternum was too thick for the ultrasound machine. Eventually, the vets found other instruments and they determined that Orion was a very healthy elephant. This was a very challenging experience yet it was also very helpful. The vets and trainers learned a great deal about the elephant's anatomy and that will help them deal with Orion in the future.

PRACTICE 9: Writing Your Own Write a sentence of your own using each of the following coordinating conjunctions with two independent clauses.

1. and _____

2. so _____

3. but _____

4. or _____

5. yet _____

COMMAS WITH INTERRUPTERS

Use a comma before and after a word or phrase that interrupts the flow of a sentence.

Most words that interrupt a sentence are not necessary for understanding the main point of a sentence. Setting them off makes it easier to recognize the main point.

Word: I didn't study for the exam, **however,** because I had to work late.

Word: The exchange student, **Frida,** is from Sweden.

Phrase: The city with the most hotels, **according to this travel journal,** is Las Vegas.

Phrase: This book, ***The Long Valley,*** is a collection of Steinbeck's short stories.

Phrase: James Whitaker, **the chair of the English Department,** is retiring.

A very common type of interrupter is a clause that begins with *who, whose, which, when,* or *where* and is not necessary for understanding the main point of the sentence:

Clause: The new instructor, **who came here from UC Berkeley,** is teaching the American literature class.

Because the information "who came here from UC Berkeley" is not necessary for understanding the main idea of the sentence, it is set off with commas.

Clause: The public library, **which is downtown,** provides several books on tape.

The main point here is that the public library provides books on tape. Since the other information isn't necessary to understanding the sentence, it can be set off with commas.

Hint: Do not use commas with *who, whose, which, when,* or *where* if the information is necessary for understanding the main point of the sentence.

My brother **who joined the Navy** came home for Christmas.

Because the information in the *who* clause is necessary to understand which brother came home for Christmas, you should not set it off with commas.

Hint: Do not use commas to set off clauses beginning with *that*.

The movie theater **that is on Elm Street** is showing *Jurassic Park III*.

Reviewing Commas with Interrupters

Why should you use commas to set off words and phrases in the middle of a sentence?

_____

_____

When should you use commas with who, whose, which, when, *or* where?

_____

_____

When should you not use commas before these words?

_____

_____

PRACTICE 10: Identifying and Correcting

A. Put an X next to the sentence if there are any comma errors in the underlined part of the sentence.

1. _____ I bought this <u>car however,</u> because of the extended warranty.

2. _____ Jimmy's favorite <u>character, Buzz Lightyear,</u> is from *Toy Story.*

3. _____ <u>Pink, a female musician</u> is in concert this weekend.

4. _____ The <u>vacuum cleaner which I hate,</u> is in the hall closet.

5. _____ My <u>aunt, who made this bread,</u> lives in New Mexico.

6. _____ The <u>remote control, that is on the coffee table,</u> works the TV,
   VCR, and DVD player.

7. _____ I need to go to the <u>office which is on the north side of the build-
   ing</u> to get the tickets.

8. _____ My next-door <u>neighbor, whose cat always torments mine,</u>
   works for the school district.

9. _____ Jack has been dating <u>Lisa the girl from Texas</u> for about five
   months.

10. _____ You are the <u>one, of course,</u> who will win this election.

B. Correct the comma errors in Practice 10A by rewriting each incorrect
sentence.

PRACTICE 11: Completing Add the missing commas to the following paragraph.

Doing laundry is my favorite household chore. I have to sort the
clothes of course before I throw them all into the washing machine,

but I am very picky about what items can be washed together. I put the colors the dark ones in one pile, and the whites go in another. But there are in-between colors like tans and beiges that I cannot put in either stack. Those colors get their own pile. The whites and only the whites are washed in hot water, and sometimes I will put in a little bleach. The colors are always washed in warm or cold usually cold because I don't want the colors to "bleed." I love my washing machine which was quite expensive because it can handle very large loads. Four people live in this house, so believe me their laundry stacks up quickly. Most of the other chores like washing dishes and dusting I will gladly give away, but save the laundry for me.

PRACTICE 12: Writing Your Own Write a sentence of your own using each of the following phrases or clauses as interrupters.

1. who was 16 years old _____

2. however _____

3. of course _____

4. which changes every year _____

5. whose bike is in my garage _____

COMMAS WITH DIRECT QUOTATIONS

Use commas to mark direct quotations.

A direct quotation records a person's exact words. Commas set off the exact words from the rest of the sentence, making it easier to understand who said what.

Direct Quotation:	The instructor said**,** **"The exam will be next Friday."**
Direct Quotation:	**"The exam will be next Friday,"** the instructor said.
Direct Quotation:	**"The exam,"** said the instructor**, "will be next Friday."**

Hint: If a quotation ends with a question mark or an exclamation point, do not use a comma. Only one punctuation mark is needed.

NOT	**"What was the question?,"** he asked.
Correct:	**"What was the question?"** he asked.

Reviewing Commas with Direct Quotations

Why should you use commas with a direct quotation?

_____

Should you use a comma if the quotation ends with a question mark or an exclamation point? Why or why not?

_____

PRACTICE 13: Identifying and Correcting

A. Put an X next to the sentence if there are any comma errors in the underlined part of the sentence.

   1. _____ Shawn <u>said, "I</u> think this is a good day for tennis."

   2. _____ "Take me <u>dancing"</u> said Helen Hunt's character in *As Good As It Gets*.

   3. _____ "I can't <u>believe" she said, "that</u> you are going to miss the big event."

   4. _____ "We got the <u>loan!" Simone</u> shouted in glee.

   5. _____ Julian <u>asked "Where</u> are we supposed to meet?"

   6. _____ "Do these pants make me look <u>fat?," she</u> asked.

   7. _____ "Go to <u>work," he said, "and</u> I'll take you to dinner when you get home."

   8. _____ "If you <u>insist," she said, "then</u> that's the way it will be."

   9. _____ Tara <u>snapped "Get</u> back in line!"

   10. _____ "Is this fish <u>fresh?" I</u> asked the waitress.

B. Correct the comma errors in Practice 13A by rewriting each incorrect sentence.

PRACTICE 14: Completing Add the missing commas to the following paragraph.

"I'm looking for some plants for my garden" Annabel told the man at the nursery. "What kinds of plants did you have in mind?" he asked her. "Well, something that can tolerate heat" she said "because my garden gets lots of sun." "If you want flowers" he said "roses are always nice, and these petunias would do well." Annabel thought about them and said "I need something that spreads out, too like a ground cover." "Oh" he said "I have just the thing for you! Try this verbena." "Will it spread out pretty far?" she asked. "Absolutely" he assured her "and it will be full of little flowers." "I'll take it" she said, pulling out her wallet.

PRACTICE 15: Writing Your Own Write a sentence of your own for each of the following quotations.

1. a direct quotation about the weather _____

2. a direct quotation about your job _____

3. a direct quotation about television _____

4. a direct quotation about dinner _____

5. a direct quotation about attending class regularly _____

OTHER USES OF COMMAS

Other commas clarify information in everyday writing.

Numbers: What is **2,667,999** divided by **10,300?**

Dates: Mike and Melissa were married on **August 1, 2000,** in Cincinnati.

Notice that there is a comma both before and after the year.

Addresses: Nicole moved from **Lamont, California,** to **8900 New Fork Lane, Aspen, CO 81612.**

Notice that there is no comma between the state and the zip code.

States: They moved from San Antonio, Texas, to Phoenix, Arizona.

Notice that there is a comma both before and after a state.

Letters: **Dear Alyson,**
Yours truly,

Reviewing Other Uses of Commas

Give one example of commas in each of the following situations:

Numbers _____

Dates _____

Addresses _____

Letters _____

Why are these commas important?

_____

PRACTICE 16: Identifying and Correcting

A. Put an X next to the sentence if there are any comma errors in the under-lined part of the sentence.

1. _____ My grandmother lives at <u>3,230 Eureka Street</u>.

2. _____ On <u>June 10, 2006</u> I will graduate from this university.

3. _____ The boys are camping in <u>Denver, Colorado</u>.

4. _____ This stadium holds <u>300,00 people</u>.

5. _____ We moved from <u>Jackson, Mississippi,</u> to Oakland, California.

6. _____ We were married on <u>December 3 2003</u>.

7. _____ I only paid <u>$1566</u> for my new bedroom furniture.

8. _____ There are approximately <u>450000</u> people living in this city.

9. _____ William built a house at <u>2244 Knoxbury Street, Miami, FL, 33012</u>.

10. _____ The winner of the contest will receive <u>$5000,00</u> in prize money.

B. Correct the comma errors in Practice 16A by rewriting each incorrect sentence.

PRACTICE 17: Completing Add the missing commas to the following paragraph.

My cousin joined the Marines on June 20 1996 and after boot camp, he was sent to Okinawa Japan. At this base, he worked in communications. Since he was such a quick learner, he advanced in rank very quickly. Soon he was responsible for more than 1500 other Marines. His paychecks were not very much—approximately $2000 each month—however, he was single and didn't have any big bills. After three years and many other tours, the Marines asked him if he was planning to stay in the service. He had a great reputation, and they wanted him to keep advancing in rank. My cousin thought about it for a long time, but he decided that he would be happier back in the civilian world. After his discharge, he bought a house in Topeka Kansas and fell in love with a wonderful girl. Several of my cousin's Marine friends were at their wedding on November 16 2001 to share in their happiness.

PRACTICE 18: Writing Your Own Write a sentence of your own for each of the following items.

1. your current address _____

2. the date you were born _____

3. the number of students at your school _____

4. the amount of money you would like to make in one year _____

5. the address of your campus library _____

CHAPTER REVIEW

Many of the questions in the Recall exercise are similar (other than the comma placement), so you need to read them carefully.

Reviewing Commas

To review this material before you complete the Review Practices, watch the **Commas** video at **MyWritingLab.com** one more time. This time, keep the video open as you complete the rest of the practices in this chapter. For best results, do the **MyWritingLab** exercises online as well as the Chapter Review practices in the book.

REVIEW PRACTICE 1: Identifying Underline the incorrect and missing commas in each of the following sentences.

1. When we went to the store we forgot to buy milk.

2. Cesar tried to move the refrigerator, but it was too heavy.

3. Fortunately this is the last chemistry class that I have to take.

4. "Really" she said, "I never meant to hurt your feelings."

5. I sat next to Carter, my best friend at the concert.

6. We started this class on September 7 2004.

7. Chaney brought chips salsa, and soft drinks to the party.

8. The empty deserted farmhouse caught fire yesterday.

9. We need to raise $100 500 in donations.

10. I found the special paper pen and ink that I need at a stationery store.

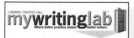

Practicing Commas

Now complete the **Recall** activity for **Commas** at **MyWritingLab.com**. If you're having a difficult time with a question, open up the video in the lower right-hand corner for some help.

REVIEW PRACTICE 2: Correcting Correct the comma errors in Review Practice 1 by rewriting each incorrect sentence.

Practicing Commas

Next, complete the **Apply** activity for **Commas** at **MyWritingLab.com**. Pay close attention to the directions and only click on when prompted.

REVIEW PRACTICE 3: Writing Your Own Write your own paragraph about one of your neighbors. What are some identifying qualities of this person? Do you like him or her?

Practicing Commas

For more practice, complete the **Write** activity for **Commas** at **MyWritingLab.com**. Pay close attention to which sentences might contain comma errors.

EDITING THE STUDENT WRITING

Return to the student paragraph at the beginning of this chapter, and do the following activities.

Individual Activity   Go over the commas you added to the paragraph. Make sure you found 15.

Collaborative Activity   Team up with a partner, and check to make sure you have identified the same missing commas in the paragraph. Then, working together, use what you have learned in this chapter to label each comma from the following list.

1. Commas with items in a series

2. Commas with introductory words

3. Commas with independent clauses

4. Commas with interrupters

5. Commas with direct quotations

6. Commas with numbers, dates, addresses, and letters

Finally, rewrite the paragraph with your corrections.

EDITING YOUR OWN WRITING

Exchange paragraphs from Review Practice 3 with a classmate, and do the following:

1. Circle any misplaced commas.

2. Add any missing commas.

3. Suggest corrections for the incorrect commas.

Then return the paper to its writer, and use the information in this chapter to correct any comma errors in your own paragraph. Record your errors on the Error Log in Appendix 1.

Apostrophes

The following student paragraph contains correct and incorrect apostrophe usage. Read the paragraph, and underline the 12 words with apostrophes.

I like to talk, especially when I have an audience. I'm usually the one coming up with conversation topic's, trying to make people laugh, and "breaking the ice." Sometimes in a classroom situation, though, its different. I dont mind answering question's that the instructor poses, but sometimes Im afraid that Ill say the wrong thing and make a fool of myself. The difference is that in social situations, I'm not being judged. Everyone's trying to be friend's and have fun. In a classroom, the instructor is waiting to see if I know what Im talking about. The instructor's always judging me, but that's the instructors job. Though I'm not always the one to dominate class discussion's, I do like to participate in them. I'd much rather we talk in groups than listen to lectures. I like to hear other students opinions, because sometimes they'll bring up very interesting points. Although talking in front of people can sometimes be intimidating, its a very good way to learn about yourself.

The **apostrophe** looks like a single quotation mark. Its two main purposes are to indicate where letters have been left out and to show ownership.

Understanding Apostrophes

To help you understand this form of punctuation, go to **MyWritingLab.com,** and view the video on **Apostrophes.** Then, return to this chapter, which will go into more detail about apostrophes and give you opportunities to practice using them. Finally, you will apply your understanding of this punctuation mark to your own writing.

MARKING CONTRACTIONS

Use an apostrophe to show that letters have been omitted to form a contraction.

A **contraction** is the shortening of one or more words. Our everyday speech is filled with contractions.

I will	=	I'll (*w* and *i* have been omitted)
do not	=	don't (*o* has been omitted)
let us	=	let's (*u* has been omitted)

Here is a list of commonly used contractions.

Some Common Contractions

I am	=	*I'm*	*you will*	=	*you'll*
I would	=	*I'd*	*he is*	=	*he's*
I will	=	*I'll*	*she will*	=	*she'll*
you have	=	*you've*	*it is*	=	*it's*
we have	=	*we've*	*do not*	=	*don't*
we will	=	*we'll*	*did not*	=	*didn't*
they are	=	*they're*	*have not*	=	*haven't*
they have	=	*they've*	*could not*	=	*couldn't*

Hint Two words frequently misused are *it's* and *its*.

    it's = contraction: it is (or it has)   **It's** too late to go to the movie.

    its = pronoun: belonging to it   **Its** eyes are really large.

To see if you are using the correct word, say the sentence with the words *it is.* If that is what you want to say, add an apostrophe to the word.

    ?   I wonder if **its** on the dresser.

    Test: I wonder if **it is** on the dresser.   **YES, add an apostrophe**

This sentence makes sense with *it is*, so you should write *it's*.

Correct: I wonder if **it's** on the dresser.

? The horse stomped **its** foot.

Test: The horse stomped **it is** foot.   **NO, so no apostrophe**

This sentence does not make sense with *it is*, so you should not use the apostrophe in *its*.

Correct: The horse stomped **its** foot.

Reviewing Contractions

What is the purpose of an apostrophe in a contraction?

_____

Write five contractions and tell which letters have been omitted.

_____   _____

_____   _____

_____   _____

_____   _____

_____   _____

What is the difference between it's and its?

_____

PRACTICE 1: Identifying and Correcting

A. Put an X next to the sentence if an apostrophe is missing or used incorrectly.

1. _____ Youve got to leave before my parents get home.

2. _____ My sister said that she's applying to UCLA.

3. _____ I think wel'l be able to make it.

4. _____ Amber did'nt have a ride to class.

5. _____ We're going to the mountains on Friday.

6. _____ Its a nice day today.

7. _____ He said they've been here before.

8. _____ Can you write the report while Im making the display?

9. _____ The cat knocked it's bowl over last night.

10. _____ Hows this plan going to work?

B. Correct the apostrophe errors in Practice 1A by rewriting each incorrect sentence.

PRACTICE 2: Completing Add apostrophes to the contractions in the following paragraph.

Gordon Foster couldnt drive fast enough to pick up his wife, Betsy, from the airport. Shed been at a conference in Tennessee for five days, and he couldnt wait to see her again. Shes one of the nutritionists for the city's hospital, and theyre always being sent to meetings and lectures out of state. When shes gone, Gordon cant stand it. Theyve only got two children, and the kids are now in high school, so its not that hes stuck changing diapers or preparing bottles. He just doesnt like being without Betsy. Sometimes shell shake her head and laugh at how dependent Gordon is. But its pretty obvious that she enjoys being missed so much.

PRACTICE 3: Writing Your Own Write a sentence of your own for each of the following contractions.

1. he's _____

2. they'll _____

3. couldn't _____

4. doesn't _____

5. we'd _____

SHOWING POSSESSION

Use an apostrophe to show **possession.**

1. For a singular word, use 's to indicate possession or ownership. You can always replace a possessive with *of* plus the noun or pronoun.

the team**'s** leader   =   the leader **of the team**
                                  (the team possesses the leader)

Edward**'s** car   =   the car **of Edward**
                                  (Edward possesses the car)

the teacher's rules = the rules **of the teacher**
(the teacher possesses the rules)

tomorrow's weather = the weather **of tomorrow**
(tomorrow "owns" or "possesses" the
weather)

2. For plural nouns ending in -s, use only an apostrophe.

the students' books = the books **of the students**

the sisters' bedroom = the bedroom **of the sisters**

the writers' convention = the convention **of the writers**

the tourists' hotel = the hotel **of the tourists**

3. For plural nouns that do not end in -s, add 's.

the men's bathroom = the bathroom **of the men**

the children's toys = the toys **of the children**

the women's tea party = the tea party **of the women**

Reviewing Possessives

How do you mark possession or ownership for a singular word?

_____

*How do you mark possession or ownership for a plural word that
ends in -s?*

_____

*How do you mark possession or ownership for a plural word that
doesn't end in -s?*

_____

PRACTICE 4: Identifying and Correcting

A. Put an X next to the sentence if an apostrophe is missing or used
incorrectly.

1. _____ Jennifer's dad is on his way to Boston.

2. _____ Dustin wrecked his moms car last night.

3. _____ The two dog's food dish is full of bugs.

4. _____ Damians walls are covered with Post-it Notes.

5. _____ My one brothers' dream is to climb Mount Everest.

6. _____ Uncle Bobs' boat sank in Lake Erie.

7. _____ They broke into their friend's room and left a present.

8. _____ Can you see the childrens' department from here?

9. _____ The many customers complaints have been reviewed.

10. _____ Are you going to Eddies' birthday party?

B. Correct the apostrophe errors in Practice 4A by rewriting each incorrect sentence.

PRACTICE 5: Completing Add apostrophes to the possessive nouns in the following paragraph.

Last year we spent Mothers Day at the Rollerama with my little sister. We decided that our familys time together was important, so we promised each other we would stay together all day. Beths passion is to roller-skate. Dads passion is not to roller-skate. I was somewhere in the middle, and Mom was just enjoying the days activities. The roller rinks entrance fee was waived that day, and all the other prices were discounted. My sisters friends were there, and I was embarrassed to be there. But I have to admit that I had fun.

PRACTICE 6: Writing Your Own Create possessive nouns from the following phrases, and write a sentence of your own for each one.

1. the program of the children

_____

2. the dress code of the school

_____

3. the lunch break of the workers

_____

4. the cookies of the grandmother

_____

5. the problems of Susanna

_____

COMMON APOSTROPHE ERRORS

Two common errors occur with apostrophes. The following guidelines will help you avoid these errors.

No Apostrophe with Possessive Pronouns

Do not use an apostrophe with a possessive pronoun.

Possessive pronouns already show ownership, so they do not need an apostrophe.

Incorrect	Correct
his'	his
her's or hers'	hers
it's or its'	its
your's or yours'	yours
our's or ours'	ours
their's or theirs'	theirs

No Apostrophe to Form the Plural

Do not use an apostrophe to form a plural word.

This error occurs most often with plural words ending in *-s*. An apostrophe indicates possession or contraction; it does *not* indicate the plural. Therefore, a plural word never takes an apostrophe unless it is possessive.

NOT The **bike's** are in the garage.
Correct: The **bikes** are in the garage.

NOT He bought a new pair of **shoe's** yesterday.
Correct: He bought a new pair of **shoes** yesterday.

NOT I saw eight hockey **game's** this season.
Correct: I saw eight hockey **games** this season.

Reviewing Apostrophe Errors

List three possessive pronouns.

_____

Why don't possessive pronouns take apostrophes?

_____

What is wrong with the apostrophe in each of the following sentences?

The last float in the parade is ours'.

_____

There must be 100 floats' in the parade.

_____

PRACTICE 7: Identifying and Correcting

A. Put an X next to the sentence if an apostrophe is missing or used incorrectly.

1. _____ That new car is her's.

2. _____ I lost my handouts, so I had to borrow theirs.

3. _____ There were four nails' in my front tire.

4. _____ This is my paper, but can I see your's?

5. _____ Jackson ordered pizza's for our meeting.

6. _____ Office Depot has computer's on sale.

7. _____ Do you have his telephone number?

8. _____ These book's are going to the basement.

9. _____ You can sit at any of the tables in this room.

10. _____ When they ran out of their soft drinks, I offered to share our's.

B. Correct the apostrophe errors in Practice 7A by rewriting each incorrect sentence.

PRACTICE 8: Completing Correct the apostrophe errors in the following paragraph.

After breakfast, Sam walked around the cabin. Bug's had come in through the hole in the screen door, and Sam squashed some of them with his' bare hand's. The cabin was especially quiet, so he began looking through the cabinet's in the kitchen. He was hungry, but he didn't want to bother any of the other campers'. He found a jar of grape jelly that was labeled "Homemade by Marci," and he tasted it.

He also found some homemade biscuit's that he knew were her's too, but he didn't think she'd mind if he ate them. When he'd just about filled his' stomach, Marci walked into the room. She smiled at him and gave him two napkin's to wipe the jelly off of his face.

PRACTICE 9: Writing Your Own Write a sentence of your own for each of the following possessive pronouns.

1. hers _____

2. its _____

3. his _____

4. yours _____

5. theirs _____

CHAPTER REVIEW

Reviewing Apostrophes

Not only does spelling and punctuation count in the Apply section, but correct spacing does as well, which makes this exercise a bit tricky.

To review this material before you complete the Review Practices, watch the **Apostrophes** video at **MyWritingLab.com** one more time. This time, keep the video open as you complete the rest of the practices in this chapter. For best results, do the **MyWritingLab** exercises online as well as the Chapter Review practices in the book.

REVIEW PRACTICE 1: Identifying Underline the words missing apostrophes or the words in which apostrophes are used incorrectly in each of the following sentences.

1. Terrys piano needs to be tuned.

2. The library's hour's change every six month's.

3. Some of the actor's werent familiar with their lines.

4. Im going to the mall to buy pant's like your's.

5. My geranium's havent bloomed yet.

6. Its impossible to see those planet's without a telescope.

7. Shes going to Magic Mountain for the day.

8. The waters too cold for swimming right now.

9. My principals wife is one of my aunts friend's.

10. I shouldnt have told you about that new house of their's.

Practicing Apostrophes

Now complete the **Recall** activity for **Apostrophes** at **MyWritingLab.com.**
Remember to read the answers carefully because many of them look similar.

REVIEW PRACTICE 2: Correcting Correct the apostrophe errors in Review
Practice 1 by rewriting the sentences.

Practicing Apostrophes

Next, complete the **Apply** activity for **Apostrophes** at
MyWritingLab.com. If you're stuck, go to the lower right-hand corner
and open up the video again, or you can click on the hint button.

REVIEW PRACTICE 3: Writing Your Own Write your own paragraph about your
favorite birthday celebration in your life so far. Use at least six apostrophes
correctly.

Practicing Apostrophes

For more practice, complete the **Write** activity for **Apostrophes** at
MyWritingLab.com. Pay close attention to which sentences might
contain apostrophe errors as you revise the paragraph.

EDITING THE STUDENT WRITING

Return to the student paragraph at the beginning of this chapter, and do the following activities.

Individual Activity   Did you find the 12 apostrophes in this passage? Next, place an X above the eight words that are missing apostrophes. Place a second underline under the four plural nouns that use apostrophes incorrectly.

Collaborative Activity   With a partner, check to make sure you have found the same errors in the paragraph. Then, working together, use what you have learned in this chapter to correct these errors. Rewrite the paragraph with your corrections.

EDITING YOUR OWN WRITING

Exchange paragraphs from Review Practice 3 with a classmate, and do the following:

1. Circle any misplaced or missing apostrophes.

2. Indicate whether they mark possession (P) or contraction (C).

Then return the paper to its writer, and use the information in this chapter to correct any apostrophe errors in your own paragraph. Record your errors on the Error Log in Appendix 1.

Quotation Marks

The following paragraph, written by a student, contains correct and incorrect quotation marks. Read the paragraph, and underline the 4 sets of quotation marks.

Listening to music is my favorite way to relax. The only instrument that I can play is my stereo, but I like to play it nice and loud. I really enjoy alternative rock bands, such as Blink 182. I listen to the band's CD "Cheshire Cat" almost every single day. Touchdown Boy is my favorite song, even though my mother hates the lyrics. She always screams, Turn that music down!" But all of my friends like the music too. In fact, I didn't realize that Blink 182 had so many fans. I went to a concert last month and saw about 20 people from my school standing in the audience. I've heard people say, Classical music is the best," but I believe that all music is an expression. It's both an expression of the artist and an expression of the person or people listening to it. With that in mind, I'd say that alternative rock expresses my personality best.

Quotation marks are punctuation marks that work together in pairs. Their most common use is to indicate someone's exact words. They are also used to mark the title of a short piece of writing, such as a short story or a poem.

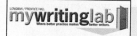

Understanding Quotation Marks

To understand more about this form of punctuation, go to **MyWritingLab.com,** and view the video on **Quotation Marks.** Then, return to this chapter, which will go into more detail about these punctuation marks and give you opportunities to practice them. Finally, you will apply your understanding of quotation marks to your own writing.

DIRECT QUOTATIONS

Use quotation marks to indicate a **direct quotation**—someone's exact words. Here are some examples that show the three basic forms of a direct quotation.

Direct Quotation: "This is a great song," said the teenager.

In this example, the quoted words come first.

Direct Quotation: The teenager said, "This is a great song."

In the example above, the quoted words come after the speaker is named.

Direct Quotation: "This," the teenager said, "is a great song."

In this example, the quoted words are interrupted, and the speaker is named in the middle. This form emphasizes the first few words.

INDIRECT QUOTATIONS

If you just talk about someone's words, you do not need quotation marks. Indirect quotations usually include the word *that,* as in *said that.* In questions, the wording is often *asked if.* Look at these examples of **indirect quotations**.

Direct Quotation: "I'm joining a rock band," said Rick.

These are Rick's exact words, so you must use quotation marks.

Indirect Quotation: Rick **said that** he is going to join a rock band.

This sentence explains what Rick said but does not use Rick's exact words. So quotation marks should not be used.

Direct Quotation:	"There will be a jazz concert next weekend," said Donna.
Indirect Quotation:	Donna **said that** there will be a jazz concert next weekend.
Direct Quotation:	"Could you sing at my wedding?" Jordan asked.
Indirect Quotation:	Jordan **asked if** I could sing at her wedding.

Reviewing Quotation Marks with Quotations

How do you show that you are repeating someone's exact words?

_____

What is an indirect quotation?

_____

PRACTICE 1: Identifying and Correcting

A. Put an X next to the sentence if quotation marks are missing or used incorrectly.

1. _____ "Run! yelled the first base coach.

2. _____ Ricardo said, The apple pie "tastes delicious."

3. _____ "Going to the movies," she said, "is my favorite pastime."

4. _____ Angela asked if "we could help her with her car."

5. _____ Jackie replied, "Of course, you are invited.

6. _____ "Is this the best you could do?" I asked.

7. _____ "Give me one reason," he said, why I should believe you."

8. _____ Nicole said "that she wanted to see Big Ben."

9. _____ "Can I get you something to drink? the hostess asked.

10. _____ "Don't forget," she said, "that we have a test tomorrow."

B. Correct the quotation mark errors in Practice 1A by rewriting each incorrect sentence.

PRACTICE 2: Completing Add quotation marks to the following paragraph.

Kevin had the day off, so he called Marty and asked, Do you want to play golf today? Well, I don't know, said Marty. What do you mean? asked Kevin. Marty explained, I promised my girlfriend we'd go to the beach. The beach? Kevin said. Well, it's our six-month anniversary, Marty said. You don't count months for anniversaries, Kevin responded, because anniversaries mark only years. Marty didn't follow his logic. The word is related to the word *annual,* which means yearly, Kevin continued, so you don't owe her anything until you have dated for one year. Marty thought for a minute and then replied, I think you should be the one to explain that to my girlfriend. No thanks, Kevin replied. I'd have better luck finding someone else to golf with!

PRACTICE 3: Writing Your Own Write a sentence of your own for each of the following items.

1. a question Rochelle asked

_____

2. a statement spoken by a police officer

_____

3. an exclamation spoken by Randy

_____

4. an indirect question that Tabitha asked

_____

5. a statement spoken by the plumber

_____

CAPITALIZING AND USING OTHER PUNCTUATION MARKS WITH QUOTATION MARKS

When you are quoting someone's complete sentences, begin with a capital letter and use appropriate end punctuation—a period, a question mark, or an exclamation point. You do not need to capitalize the first word of a quotation if it is only part of a sentence. Here are some examples.

Capitalize the first letter of the first word being quoted, and put a period at the end of the sentence if it is a statement. Separate the spoken words from the rest of the sentence with a comma.

"This is a very good band," he said.

She said, "Turn up the stereo."

If the quotation ends with a question mark or an exclamation point, use that punctuation instead of a comma or a period.

He yelled, "Stop that car!"

"Why are you leaving?" she asked.

In a quotation that is interrupted, capitalize the first word being quoted, but do not capitalize words in the middle of the sentence. Use a comma both before and after the interruption. End with a period if it is a statement.

"Yes," said the guitar player, "we will give you a concert."

You do not need to capitalize the first word of a quotation that is only part of a sentence.

My mom told me to relax and "have faith."

Hint: Look at the examples again. Notice that periods and commas always go inside the quotation marks.

NOT	"No", he said, "this isn't the way to Woodstock".
CORRECT	"No," he said, "this isn't the way to Woodstock."

Reviewing Capitalization and Punctuation with Quotation Marks

When you quote someone's exact words, why should you begin with a capital letter?

_____

Where do commas go in relation to quotation marks? Where do periods go?

_____

PRACTICE 4: Identifying and Correcting

A. Put an X next to the sentence if it contains capitalization or punctuation errors.

1. _____ "Give up", he said as he tackled his opponent.

2. _____ Rudolfo complained, "There's no more turkey in the refrigerator."

3. _____ "Walk me to my car, she said, "so I can talk to you."

4. _____ The tree trimmer asked, "How long has that tree been infected?"

5. _____ "Have you seen," I asked, "That new horror movie?"

6. _____ "If you leave," she told him, don't come back."

7. _____ My neighbor asked, "can we borrow your wheelbarrow?"

8. _____ Landon said, "My fraternity is having a big fund-raiser."

9. _____ Michael greeted his guests and said, "welcome to my home."

10. _____ "This," she said, "is my favorite part of the game."

B. Correct the errors in Practice 4A by rewriting each incorrect sentence.

PRACTICE 5: Completing Add quotation marks and other necessary punctuation to the following paragraph.

I took my tomcat to a local pet groomer and asked her, How much would it cost to get this cat bathed? Well, does he have fleas? she asked. Not that I know of, I replied. Then that will make it cheaper, she said, because he won't need to be dipped. Dipped? I asked. Yes, she explained, we have a flea dip that is really effective on cats, but it's more expensive. Well, I think he only needs a normal bath, I said. Actually, she said, he's pretty clean already. I think he just needs a good brushing. OK, I said, how much would that cost? She stroked my cat's back and answered, I'll do it for $20.

PRACTICE 6: Writing Your Own Write a sentence of your own for each of the following direct quotations.

1. "Get off the bus!"

_____

2. "Maureen is coming over for dinner."

_____

3. "Are you sure we have ice cream?"

_____

4. "Hand me that book."

_____

5. "You need a new tennis racket."

_____

QUOTATION MARKS AROUND TITLES

Put quotation marks around the titles of short works that are parts of larger works. The titles of longer works are put in italics (or underlined).

Quotation Marks	Italics/Underlining
"The Wild Swans" (short story)	_Hans Andersen's Fairy Tales_ (book)
"Mud Master" (poem)	_The Collected Poems of Wallace Stevens_ (book)
"There's Your Trouble" (song)	_Home_ (CD)
"Losing Weight the Easy Way" (magazine article)	_Parenting_ (magazine)
"Power Bills on the Rise" (newspaper article)	_Orange County Register_ (newspaper)
"The Inferno" (episode of a TV show)	_Third Watch_ (TV series)

Reviewing Quotation Marks with Titles

When do you put quotation marks around a title?

_____

When do you italicize (or underline) a title?

_____

PRACTICE 7: Identifying and Correcting

A. Put an X next to the sentences in which the titles are punctuated incorrectly.

1. _____ "Beloved" is my favorite novel by Toni Morrison.

2. _____ When I hear the Beach Boys sing "Surfin' USA," it makes me want to go to the beach.

3. _____ I read some good gardening advice in Making Roses Your Friends in *American Gardener Magazine*.

4. _____ The "Denver Herald" ran an article on the recent snowstorm.

5. _____ I can't wait to watch "American Idol" tonight.

6. _____ *Success Is Counted Sweetest* is a popular poem by Emily Dickinson.

7. _____ "The Weakest Link" is having the "Celebrity Episode" next Thursday night.

8. _____ "Brown-Eyed Girl" is the theme song for our charity event.

9. _____ Xavier read a great article in "Newsweek" about the recent election.

10. _____ My literature class studied Hawthorne's short story "Young Goodman Brown" this quarter.

B. Correct the quotation mark errors in Practice 7A by rewriting each incorrect sentence.

PRACTICE 8: Completing
Place quotation marks around the titles of short works, and underline the titles of long works in the following paragraph.

Marjorie Clemens is a popular celebrity agent in Hollywood. She spotted the band Four Up when it was playing in a small hometown talent show. The group sang Hangin' with My Girl, and Marjorie knew it would be a hit. She put Four Up in contact with Arista Records, who released the album Just Four Fun only a few months later. Soon all of the teen magazines, such as Bop and Teen Dream, were printing articles about Four Up. The guys were stunned by their overnight success as they read articles titled Four Up Not Coming

Down and Americans Want These Guys Four Keeps. Three years later, a journalist named Walt Gentry worked with them on a book he titled One, Two, Three, Four Up: Counting on Our Fans. But just when the group had become a household name, the lead singer, Eric Bassy, left for a solo career. Music fans all over America were in tears as they read Four Up Is One Down across the front page of the newspapers.

PRACTICE 9: Writing Your Own Write a sentence of your own for each of the following titles. Make up a title if you can't think of one.

1. a short story _____

2. a song title _____

3. a newspaper article _____

4. a poem _____

5. a magazine article _____

CHAPTER REVIEW

Many of the Recall answers for this topic look similar so you will need to read them carefully.

Reviewing Quotation Marks

To review this material before you complete the Review Practices, watch the **Quotation Marks** video at **MyWritingLab.com** one more time. This time, keep the video open as you complete the rest of the practices in this chapter. For best results, do the **MyWritingLab** exercises online as well as the Chapter Review practices in the book.

REVIEW PRACTICE 1: Identifying Mark an X above each place where punctuation is missing or used incorrectly.

1. Seth is watching his favorite video, I said.

2. Austin asked Can I use your shower?

3. Arlene titled her essay The Truth About Being Twenty.

4. When we arrived at the hotel, the valet asked if "we wanted him to park the car."

5. Zane memorized Roethke's poem My Papa's Waltz for his English class.

6. When Mother Teresa died, the *New York Times* ran an article with the headline Saint Taken Home.

7. When you get back she said let's go out to dinner.

8. Edgar said that "we could meet at his house."

9. We sang Happy Birthday to Fran in class today.

10. I read an article in *Tennis Weekly* titled How Venus Williams Stays in the Game.

 **Practicing Quotation Marks**

Now complete the **Recall** activity for **Quotation Marks** at **MyWritingLab.com.** If you're having a difficult time with a question, open up the video in the lower right-hand corner for some help.

REVIEW PRACTICE 2: Correcting Correct the quotation marks and other punctuation errors in Review Practice 1 by rewriting each of the sentences.

 **Practicing Quotation Marks**

Next, complete the **Apply** activity for **Quotation Marks** at **MyWritingLab.com.** Pay close attention to the directions and only click only on what you're asked to.

REVIEW PRACTICE 3: Writing Your Own In paragraph form, record a conversation from your day. What did you talk about? What was the point of this conversation? What were your exact words?

Practicing Quotation Marks

For more practice, complete the **Write** activity for **Quotation Marks** at **MyWritingLab.com.** Make sure to pay close attention to the use of quotation marks.

EDITING THE STUDENT WRITING

Return to the student paragraph at the beginning of this chapter, and do the following activities.

Individual Activity   Did you find the four sets of quotation marks in the paragraph? Now underline twice the six quotation mark errors, including the missing quotation marks, in the paragraph.

Collaborative Activity   With a partner, check to make sure you have found the same six quotation mark errors. Then, working together, use what you have learned in this chapter to correct these errors.

EDITING YOUR OWN WRITING

Exchange paragraphs from Review Practice 3 with a classmate, and do the following:

1. Circle any incorrect or missing quotation marks.

2. Underline any faulty punctuation.

3. Put an X over any incorrect use of italics/underlining.

Then return the paper to its writer, and use the information in this chapter to correct any errors with quotation marks and italics/underlining in your own paragraph. Record your errors on the Error Log in Appendix 1.

Other Punctuation Marks

READING FOR OTHER PUNCTUATION MARKS

The following paragraph, written by a student, contains correct and incorrect punctuation. Read the paragraph, and underline the 14 semicolons, colons, dashes, and parentheses.

My family used to have the same routine from Christmas Eve to Christmas Day. This ritual started sometime when I was young (maybe around the time I was 10 or 11). On Christmas Eve: my sister, my brother, and I would get to open one present from under the tree. We were allowed to choose it: we had to get approval before we could actually open it; just in case it was an expensive gift. We loved getting a taste of Christmas before the day arrived. That night, we would set out a plate of cookies for Santa and some carrots for Rudolph—which we later learned was for Dad and Sparky the dog. We were supposed to go to bed early—after all, Santa doesn't come when children are awake. But I usually decided to do my spring cleaning early and cleaned my room until I was too tired to keep my eyes open. Then (like clockwork) my little brother would wake us up at 3:30 a.m., excited to begin the day. This was the best part of the day: waking up our parents, opening our gifts, and enjoying the morning with the family. My mom would make homemade doughnuts; the best around; before we would all go back to bed for a nap. Later that evening, we would eat a wonderful dinner and just celebrate the holiday and our family; I miss those days.

This chapter explains the uses of the **semicolon**, **colon**, **dash**, and **parentheses**. We'll look at these punctuation marks one by one.

Understanding Other Punctuation Marks

To learn more about other punctuation marks, go to **MyWritingLab.com**, and view the video on **Semicolons, Colons, Dashes, and Parentheses.** Then, return to this chapter, which will go into more detail about these marks and give you opportunities to practice them. Finally, you will apply your understanding of semicolons, colons, dashes, and parentheses to your own writing.

SEMICOLONS

Semicolons are used to separate equal parts of a sentence. They are also used to avoid confusion when listing items in a series.

1. Use a semicolon to separate two closely related independent clauses.

    An independent clause is a group of words with a subject and a verb that can stand alone as a sentence. You might use a semicolon instead of a coordinating conjunction (*and, but, for, nor, or, so, yet*) or a period. Any one of the three options would be correct.

	Independent	Independent
Semicolon:	Carter wants to buy a new truck**; he** took one for a test drive yesterday.	
Conjunction:	Carter wants to buy a new truck**, so** he took one for a test drive yesterday.	
Period:	Carter wants to buy a new truck**. He** took one for a test drive yesterday.	

2. Use a semicolon to join two independent clauses that are connected by such words as *however, therefore, furthermore, moreover, for example*, or *consequently*. Put a comma after the connecting word.

	Independent	Independent
Semicolon:	Studying for exams is hard work**; however,** getting good grades is important.	
Semicolon:	You promised to help me paint the house**; therefore,** I expect you to be here.	
Semicolon:	She had a weakness for sweets**; for example,** she couldn't resist chocolate candy.	

3. Use a semicolon to separate items in a series when any of the items contain commas.

NOT   To avoid leaving anyone out, we invited all of our friends from high school, college, and work, my mother's bridge club, and my father's tennis buddies.

Correct: To avoid leaving anyone out, we invited all of our friends from high school, college, and work; my mother's bridge club; and my father's tennis buddies.

Reviewing Semicolons

How are semicolons used between two independent clauses?

_____

How are semicolons used with items in a series?

_____

PRACTICE 1: Identifying and Correcting

A. Put an X next to the sentence if it contains errors with semicolons.

1. _____ My house caught fire; I lost all of my pictures from elementary school.

2. _____ We have saved more than $3,000, therefore; it is time that we took a nice vacation.

3. _____ We need to leave right now the movie; starts in five minutes.

4. Jonathan is our strongest runner; he should be the first man in our relay team.

5. _____ Mr. Cheng raises corn; wheat; and oranges on his farm.

6. _____ Deena works at Stairway to Beauty; she cuts hair and does nails.

7. _____ Our toilet overflowed and flooded our carpet, consequently, our insurance premium was raised.

8. _____ The sale items include the furniture, appliances, and bedding; some of the ceiling fans, and the patio furniture.

9. _____ I vacuumed the carpets, but; I didn't polish the hardwood floors.

10. _____ We have two orange cats in our neighborhood, however, I think one of them belongs to Mrs. Ayala.

B. Correct the punctuation errors in Practice 1A by rewriting each incorrect sentence.

PRACTICE 2: Completing Add semicolons to the following paragraph.

This summer, my friend Laura had to have knee surgery. She's a very active person she dances and plays volleyball constantly. She has had to sit still for two weeks now, which is almost impossible for her. She is one of those people who can't quit moving she's always in constant motion. If she's not dancing around while she's talking to you, she's sitting in an odd position she's extremely limber. I don't know how much longer she has to stay off her knee I hope it's not long. I think she'll go crazy soon I can already see her dancing in her mind.

PRACTICE 3: Writing Your Own Write a sentence of your own for each of the following types.

1. two closely related independent clauses joined with a semicolon

_____

2. two independent clauses joined by the word "nonetheless"

_____

3. a list that has items that include commas

_____

4. two independent clauses joined by the word "however"

_____

5. two independent clauses joined by the words "for example"

_____

COLONS

Colons introduce a list or idea that follows them.

1. The main use of the colon is to introduce a list or thought. Here are some examples:

   Colon: Bring the following items with you to the beach: a swimsuit, a towel, sun block, and sunglasses.

Colon: The mall opened several new stores: Gap, Bath and Beauty, Victoria's Secret, and Old Navy.

Colon: The answer is clear: take the trip.

The most common error with colons is using one where it isn't needed.

2. Do not use a colon after the words *such as* or *including*. A complete sentence must come before a colon.

NOT   Use only primary colors, **such as:** blue, yellow, and red.

Correct: Use only primary colors, **such as** blue, yellow, and red.

NOT   They traveled to many places this summer, **including:** New Mexico and Arizona.

Correct: They traveled to many places this summer, **including** New Mexico and Arizona.

3. In addition, you should not use a colon after a verb or after a preposition. Remember that a complete sentence must come before a colon.

NOT   The best forms of cardiovascular exercise **are:** tennis and aerobics.

Correct: The best forms of cardiovascular exercise **are** tennis and aerobics.

NOT   Put the clothes **in:** the closet, the dresser, or the armoire.

Correct: Put the clothes **in** the closet, the dresser, or the armoire.

Reviewing Colons

What is the main use of a colon?

_____

Why should you not use a colon after such words as is or of?

_____

PRACTICE 4: Identifying and Correcting

A. Put an X next to the sentence if it contains colon errors.

1. _____ We need to bring these things with us, as well as: the sodas, the chips, and the hot dogs.

2. _____ Nathan has: three goals, graduate from college, get accepted by Harvard Law School, and meet Judge Ito.

3. _____ My father always told me to: take pride in myself, believe in my abilities, and trust my instincts.

4. _____ Computers are good for many things: they speed communication, they organize finances, and they format important documents.

5. _____ I learned a great deal in this class: how to proofread, how to check spelling, and how to use colons.

6. _____ My best friends are: Shawna, Kayla, and Margie.

7. _____ I knew she was lying when she: started playing with her hair, wouldn't look me in the eyes, and tried to change the subject.

8. _____ If you forget everything else, remember the following things: be patient, try your best, and forgive yourself.

9. _____ Darren left four things: on the nightstand—his wallet, his glasses, his passport, and his keys.

10. _____ On our vacation, we are going to: Disneyland, Lake Tahoe, and Mount Rushmore.

B. Correct the colon errors in Practice 4A by rewriting each incorrect sentence.

PRACTICE 5: Completing Add colons to the following letter.

Dear Howard,

    Here are our choices for dinner tonight barbecue the steak in the freezer, heat the leftover lasagna in the fridge, or order a pizza. If you decide on barbecue, I'll need you to do a few things sweep off the back porch, refill the propane tank at the hardware store, and go to the market for barbecue sauce. There are only three brands of barbecue sauce I like. They are Hunts, El Paso, and O'Malley's. Thank you so much for this help. If you decide on pizza, make sure you tell them to add my favorite veggies mushrooms, bell peppers, and olives. If you have any questions, please call me at work. I should be home for dinner.

Thanks again,
Vera

PRACTICE 6: Writing Your Own Write a sentence of your own for each of the following directions, using colons correctly. Remember that a complete sentence must come before a colon.

1. three reasons to eat fast food

   _____

2. three colors in your bedroom

   _____

3. three things on a to-do list

   _____

4. three sports cars you would like to drive

   _____

5. three reasons to own a computer

   _____

DASHES AND PARENTHESES

Dashes and parentheses set ideas off from the rest of their sentence.

Dashes

Dashes emphasize ideas.

1. Use dashes to emphasize or draw attention to a point.

   Dash: Nancy pinpointed her biggest source of stress—her husband.

   In this example, the beginning of the sentence introduces an idea, and the dash then sets off the answer.

   Dash: Faithfulness and honesty—these are the keys to a lasting relationship.

   In this example, the key words are set off at the beginning and the explanation follows. Beginning this way adds some suspense to the sentence.

   Dashes: Patrick gave me a very nice birthday gift—a crystal vase—and I was quite impressed.

   The dashes divide this sentence into three distinct parts, which makes the reader pause and think about each part.

Parentheses

Whereas dashes set off material that the writer wants to emphasize, **parentheses** do just the opposite. They are always used in pairs.

2. Use parentheses to set off information that is interesting or helpful but not necessary for understanding the sentence.

> **Parentheses:**   My second cousin **(who owns an auto parts store)** is coming to visit.

> **Parentheses:**   The best coffee in town **(if you don't mind waiting in line)** is at a coffeehouse called Common Grounds.

3. Parentheses are also used to mark a person's life span and to number items in a sentence. They are always used in pairs. Here are some examples:

> **Parentheses:**   Charles Dickens **(1812–1870)** wrote the long novel *Bleak House.*

> **Parentheses:**   I have three important errands today: **(1)** pick up the dry cleaning, **(2)** mail the bills, and **(3)** order the flowers.

Reviewing Dashes and Parentheses

What is the difference between dashes and parentheses?

_____

_____

When do you use dashes?

_____

_____

When do you use parentheses?

_____

_____

PRACTICE 7: Identifying and Correcting

A. Put an X next to the sentence if it contains errors with dashes or parentheses.

1. _____ I wanted to buy this jacket but (I didn't have enough money).

2. _____ Mandy who plays tennis with my brother is going to Yale next year.

3. _____ There is only one solution—take more time off work.

4. _____ Greta made a good point—and I agree—Bill should not be in charge of that department.

5. _____ Charles Divine lived (from 1919 to 1988).

6. _____ (Courage and respect) these are two things I look for in a man.

7. _____ We gave Janner a television—a big-screen TV—so that he could enjoy the Super Bowl.

8. _____ The highest priorities are 1 the customer complaints, 2 the late bills, and 3 this month's invoices.

9. _____ I could sum up all of my problems with two words (money management).

10. _____ Movies and music—two things every American teen is interested in.

B. Correct the punctuation errors in Practice 7A by rewriting each incorrect sentence.

PRACTICE 8: Completing Add dashes or parentheses around the underlined words in the following paragraph.

When Dad found Skipper <u>or rather, Skipper found Dad,</u> it was a hot summer day in my southern Kentucky hometown. For most of his life, Dad had never cared for pets, but the sight of that skinny, flea-infested puppy seemed to open his heart. <u>Filthy and smelly</u> that's how I described Skipper when I first saw him. Skipper was curled up in the corner of an abandoned warehouse <u>the old Carter's Machinery building</u> that Dad's company was preparing to tear down. Dad carried Skipper to his truck and drove him to the neighborhood vet <u>who usually treated large farm animals.</u> The vet gave Dad something for the fleas <u>Bug-Out Flea Dip</u> and some vitamins to add to his food. He told Dad that Skipper was lucky to be found. If he'd been on the streets much longer, he would have surely picked up some kind of an infection <u>and most likely would have died.</u> After a couple of weeks in our home, Skipper began to look healthy again. It took several flea baths <u>at least four</u> to get rid of the fleas, but Skipper didn't mind. As soon as Skipper was back on his feet, Dad began taking him to work with him. In no time, there was only one word to describe them   inseparable.

PRACTICE 9: Writing Your Own Write a sentence of your own for each of the following types.

1. a sentence that uses dashes to set off key words at the end

   _____

2. a sentence that uses dashes to set off key words at the beginning

   _____

3. a sentence that uses dashes to divide the sentence into three parts

   _____

4. a list of three things using parentheses around the numbers

   _____

5. a sentence that places the years of someone's life in parentheses

   _____

CHAPTER REVIEW

Many of the answers in this topic are based on style choices, which is an advanced skill.

Reviewing Other Punctuation Marks

To review this material before you complete the Review Practices, watch the **Semicolons, Colons, Dashes, and Parentheses** video at **MyWritingLab.com** one more time. This time, keep the video open as you complete the rest of the practices in this chapter. For best results, do the **MyWritingLab** exercises online as well as the Chapter Review practices in the book.

REVIEW PRACTICE 1: Identifying Underline the semicolons, colons, dashes, and parentheses used incorrectly or missing in the following sentences.

1. Sinclair—Lewis 1885–1951—was an American author who won the Nobel Prize in 1930.

2. There are only three things I will do when I'm on vacation; check my e-mail, buy groceries, and read the paper.

3. She was crying for an hour today: however, she wouldn't tell us why.

4. Devon was wearing pants in my favorite color today (teal blue).

5. Pablo: who never forgets anything: locked his keys in the car.

6. Cookies and cupcakes: are my biggest weakness.

7. (This chair comes in four colors) navy, black, brown, or beige.

8. My two-year-old is a very good climber (today I found him on the refrigerator)!

9. We have to meet Mark, Julie, and Craig: walk to the park: and set up the volleyball net.

10. This class requires that we—1, read two novels, 2, write five essays, and 3, do eight hours of community service.

Practicing Other Punctuation Marks

Now complete the **Recall** activity for **Semicolons, Colons, Dashes, and Parentheses** at **MyWritingLab.com.** Remember to read the answers carefully because many of them look similar.

REVIEW PRACTICE 2: Correcting Correct the errors in Review Practice 1 by rewriting the sentences.

Practicing Other Punctuation Marks

Next, complete the **Apply** activity for **Semicolons, Colons, Dashes, and Parentheses** at **MyWritingLab.com.** If you're stuck, you can go to the lower right-hand corner and open up the video again, or you can click on the hint button.

REVIEW PRACTICE 3: Writing Your Own Write your own paragraph explaining to someone how to do something you do well.

Practicing Other Punctuation Marks

For more practice, complete the **Write** activity for **Semicolons, Colons, Dashes, and Parentheses** at **MyWritingLab.com.** Make sure to pay close attention to which sentences might contain these types of errors as you revise the paragraph.

EDITING THE STUDENT WRITING

Return to the student paragraph at the beginning of this chapter, and do the following activities.

Individual Activity   After you identify the 14 semicolons, colons, dashes, and parentheses, place a second underline beneath the 10 punctuation errors in the paragraph.

Collaborative Activity   With a partner, check to see if you found the same punctuation errors. Then, working together, use what you learned in this chapter to correct these errors. Rewrite the paragraph with your corrections.

EDITING YOUR OWN WRITING

Exchange paragraphs from Review Practice 3 with a classmate, and do the following:

1. Circle any incorrect or missing semicolons.

2. Circle any incorrect or missing colons.

3. Circle any incorrect or missing dashes.

4. Circle any incorrect or missing parentheses.

Then return the paper to its writer, and use the information in this chapter to correct any punctuation errors in your own paragraph. Record your errors on the Error Log in Appendix 1.

UNIT QUIZZES

Here are some exercises that test your understanding of all the material in this unit: End Punctuation, Commas, Apostrophes, Quotation Marks, Semicolons, Colons, Dashes, and Parentheses.

Unit Quiz 1 Identifying

Underline the punctuation errors in the following sentences.

1. I wonder if I left the lights on?

2. "Where's my credit card" yelled the woman in the store!

3. The gardener mowed the grass; raked the leaves; and pruned the hedges this afternoon.

4. We studied all night long; but we still missed several questions on the exam.

5. There are five yellow house's on my block.

6. Are you ready yet.

7. The magnets on my refrigerator door are from: London, Paris, and Venice.

8. I can't believe they wo'nt take personal checks here.

9. When he was a little boy; he ran around in his front yard naked.

10. My great-grandfather, Sylvester Martin—1870–1950—founded this hardware store.

11. Are you going to be here for a few more minutes!

12. Please turn off (the television) before you leave the room.

13. "If you can't find me, Paul said, I'm probably in the library."

14. I went to the post office; which is near my office; and mailed those letters.

15. At 5:00 p.m., we need to pick up Sharon, Camilla, and Tony, drive to the restaurant, and reserve a table for six.

16. The best desserts to bring are: lemon cream pie, chocolate brownies, or peach cobbler.

17. Shell be here in about 10 minutes.

18. Gary is riding his bike today because (his car ran out of gas).

19. This weekend I plan to—1—visit my sister,—2—make cookies for Eddie, and—3—finish this needlepoint.

20. "Did you drive or fly to Boston" asked Sheryl?

Unit Quiz 2 Correcting

Correct the punctuation errors in Unit Quiz 1 by rewriting each sentence.

Unit Quiz 3 Identifying

Underline the punctuation errors in the following paragraph.

> In July, we bought our very first house? There was only one word to describe it (finally). My wife and I have three small children so it was about time for this move. We had a house-warming party on August 1, and we asked all of our friends to come see the new place. About 30 people said they would stop by, so we bought lots of: hamburgers, hot dogs, and sodas. When people started to arrive; they immediately told us how beautiful the house was. "You guys have really done a great job, they said." One of our friends—who works with my wife—was especially impressed that we did all of the landscaping ourselves. We really enjoyed visiting and showing off our new house, the party was over before we knew it. It was'nt until everyone had left that I saw what a mess they had made. There were spills on the carpet and glasses of punch left in every room. Napkins and trash had been dropped in the strangest places. "Wow" I exclaimed! "I think our house has been officially warmed!"

Unit Quiz 4 Correcting

Correct the punctuation errors in Unit Quiz 3 by rewriting the paragraph.

UNIT WRITING ASSIGNMENTS

1. How do you unwind? When you have a particularly stressful day, what do you do to relax? Do you read a book, listen to music, watch television, or do something else? Write about the steps you take to get rid of stress.

2. There are some natural differences between men and women, but most often we hear about the stereotypes. The reality is that women are *not*

born to be better cooks or housekeepers than men, and men are *not* the only ones capable of repairing cars. What are some of the gender stereotypes you have personally proved wrong? For example, are you a female who has a talent for math but an aversion to needlepoint? Are you a male who doesn't mind ironing his own shirts but who cannot change the oil in his car? Describe one of your talents, interests, or dislikes that contradicts the stereotypes for your gender.

3. If you won an all-expenses-paid vacation anywhere in the world, where would you go? If you knew that whatever you wanted to do at your vacation spot would be absolutely free, what would you do? What would you like to see if you only had the chance? Write about this vacation place and the activities you would find there. Use as many details as possible.

7

Mechanics

The mechanical aspects of a sentence are much like the mechanical features of a car, an appliance, or a clock. They are some of the smallest—yet most important—details in a sentence. In writing, the term "mechanics" refers to capitalization, abbreviations, and numbers. We usually take these items for granted, but when they are used incorrectly, a sentence—just like a mechanical appliance with a weak spring—starts to break down.

Following a few simple guidelines will help you keep your sentences running smoothly and efficiently. They are explained in two chapters:

Chapter 21: Capitalization
Chapter 22: Abbreviations and Numbers

Capitalization

The following paragraph contains correct and incorrect capitalization. Read the paragraph, and underline the 27 capital letters.

I have always been small—not just short, but small. When we lived in new jersey, mom used to have to pick me up and put me on the school bus. I was too small to manage what appeared to be a mountain of a step. Because I was so small, others naturally made false judgments about my age and my intellect. On my first day at Willis High School, I knew no one. I had just finished my english literature class and was fumbling with *the complete works of william shakespeare* at my locker trying to remember the combination when a very polite young man came up to me. His name was richard marquez, and he asked me if I was lost. "No," I said, "But thank you." Obviously he didn't believe me because he then told me that the junior high school was just South of the high school—and he was serious! This was my d-day, the day I recognized just how others saw me, and it was devastating. I guess somewhere in the back of my mind I always assumed people took me seriously, even though they often thought I was five years younger than I looked. I learned a valuable lesson on that day. But I have since learned another valuable lesson about my size—people often underestimate me, and that gives me an advantage.

Because every sentence begins with a capital letter, **capitalization** is the best place to start discussing the mechanics of good writing. Capital letters signal where sentences begin. They also call attention to certain kinds of words, making sentences easier to read and understand.

Understanding Capitalization

For more information about this topic, go to **MyWritingLab.com,** and watch the video on **Capitalization.** Then, return to this chapter, which will go into more detail about capitalization rules and give you opportunities to practice them. Finally, you will apply your understanding of capitalization to your own writing.

Correct capitalization coupled with correct punctuation adds up to good, clear writing. Here are some guidelines to help you capitalize correctly.

1. Capitalize the first word of every sentence, including the first word of a quotation that forms a sentence.

> **We** are vacationing in Hawaii.
> "**We** are vacationing in Hawaii," he said.
> **He** said, "We are vacationing in Hawaii."

Do not capitalize the second part of a quotation that is split.

> "**We** are vacationing," he said, "in Hawaii."

2. Capitalize all proper nouns. Do not capitalize common nouns.

Common Nouns	Proper Nouns
person	George Washington
state	Texas
building	Eiffel Tower
river	Columbia River
airplane	*Spruce Goose*

Here are some examples of proper nouns.

People:	Cindy, Marilyn Monroe, Jack Nicholson
Groups:	Russians, New Yorkers, Cherokees, Canadians, Vietnamese
Languages:	Latin, Gaelic, German
Religions, Religious Books, Holy Days:	Taoism, Baptist, Upanishads, Bible, Lent, Good Friday, Chanukah

Organizations:	American Kennel Club, Independent Party, American Association of University Women, National Council of Teachers of English
Places:	Yosemite National Park, New Orleans, Orange County, Bunker Hill, Sunset Boulevard, Highway 99, London Bridge, Tampa International Airport
Institutions, Agencies, Businesses:	North High School, Harvard University, UCLA Harbor Hospital, Pacific Bell
Brand Names, Ships, Aircraft:	Adidas, Dr Pepper, *Spirit of St. Louis*

3. Capitalize titles used with people's names or in place of their names.

Mr. Judson L. Montgomery, **Ms.** Christy Waldo, **Dr.** Crystal Reeves
Aunt Janet, Grandpa Bill, Cousin Margaret, Sis, Nana

Do not capitalize words that identify family relationships.

NOT	I talked with **my** Grandfather last month.
Correct:	I talked with **my** grandfather last month.
Correct:	I talked with Grandfather last month.

4. Capitalize the titles of creative works.

Books:	*The Stand*
Short Stories:	"Barn Burning"
Plays:	*Tea Party*
Poems:	"Icarus"
Articles:	"Ah, Happiness"
Magazines:	*Life*
Songs:	"Come Together"
Albums or CDs:	*Abbey Road*
Films:	*Gladiator*
TV Series:	*King of the Hill*
Works of Art:	*The Woman in the Red Hat*
Computer Programs:	Endnotes

Do not capitalize *a, an, the,* or short prepositions unless they are the first or last word in a title.

5. Capitalize days of the week, months, holidays, and special events.

   Monday, September, Mother's Day, the Fourth of July, Ramadan, Halloween

   Do not capitalize the names of seasons: summer, fall, winter, spring.

6. Capitalize the names of historical events, periods, and documents.

   D-Day, the Battle of Wounded Knee, the Age of Enlightenment, the War of the Roses, the Seventies, the Bill of Rights

7. Capitalize specific course titles and the names of language courses.

   Sociology 401, Physics 300, French 202, Economic History

   Do not capitalize a course or subject you are referring to in a general way unless the course is a language.

   my math course, my English course, my German course, my economics course

8. Capitalize references to regions of the country, but not words that merely indicate direction.

   If you travel west from the Midwest, you will end up in the West.

9. Capitalize the opening of a letter and the first word of the closing.

   Dear Dr. Rogers, Dear Sir,
   Fondest regards, Sincerely

   Notice that a comma comes after the opening and closing.

Reviewing Capitalization

Why is capitalization important in your writing?

_____

_____

What is the difference between a proper noun and a common noun?

_____

_____

PRACTICE 1: Identifying and Correcting

A. Put an X next to the sentence if any of the underlined words are capitalized incorrectly.

1. _____ Uncle John used to live in <u>Cairo</u>, Egypt, before he moved to Flower <u>street</u> in Willis, Texas.

2. _____ After graduating from <u>Permian High School</u>, I attended college at <u>South Coast University</u>.

3. _____ <u>when</u> I was 13 years old, my dog ran away.

4. _____ The letter from <u>father</u> began, "<u>dear</u> son."

5. _____ "We should leave," she said, "<u>Before</u> the rain starts."

6. _____ Sandra shopped at <u>Kmart</u> for some <u>Martha Stewart</u> bathroom accessories, some <u>Coca-Cola</u>, and a Dixie Chicks CD.

7. _____ For <u>christmas</u>, I got season tickets to the <u>red sox</u> games.

8. _____ I bought <u>aunt</u> Eustice a Liz Claiborne outfit.

9. _____ In <u>anthropology</u> 400, we are studying the <u>paleolithic age</u>.

10. _____ "Go <u>west</u>, young man," is a famous saying.

B. Correct the capitalization errors in Practice 1A by rewriting each incorrect sentence.

PRACTICE 2: Completing Fill in each blank in the following sentences with a word that makes sense, and capitalize when necessary.

1. Before _____ left the country, he made sure he had his _____ watch and hearing aid.

2. When we lived in _____, we saw the _____.

3. Jane's _____, George, used to work for the _____.

4. In _____ 405, we are studying the _____ Period.

5. According to my _____ instructor, _____ was famous for his efforts.

6. People from _____ think their state is the best.

7. Travel _____ on _____ to reach.

8. This _____, we will celebrate.

9. "Everybody needs a few basic necessities," he said, "_____."

10. I belong to the _____, which helps needy families every _____.

PRACTICE 3: Writing Your Own Write 5 sentences of your own that cover all nine of the capitalization rules.

1. _____

2. _____

3. _____

4. _____

5. _____

CHAPTER REVIEW

Reviewing Capitalization

Remember that you lose points for every incorrect answer (as well as when you take hints) in the Grammar Apply exercises.

To review this material before you complete the Review Practices, watch the **Capitalization** video at **MyWritingLab.com** one more time. This time, keep the video open as you complete the rest of the practices in this chapter. For best results, do the **MyWritingLab** exercises online as well as the Chapter Review practices in the book.

REVIEW PRACTICE 1: Identifying Underline the capitalization errors in the following sentences.

1. I would love a dress like the one marilyn monroe wore when she sang "diamonds are a girl's best friend."

2. The letter began, "dear Mary," and then said, "You must turn North on bombay street."

3. Kim took pictures of the empire state building.

4. My Mother always makes me chocolate chip cookies when I'm feeling blue.

5. We have been learning about taoism in chinese politics 403.

6. latin may be considered a Dead Language, but it is still beneficial to english majors.

7. Aunt betty is a member of MADD, mothers against drunk driving.

8. We had dinner with senator Williams to celebrate mardi gras.

9. When *the x-files* came out, more people were convinced that the Government was covering up the existence of alien beings.

10. The death of thousands of native americans along the trail of tears was a terrible waste of human life.

Practicing Capitalization

Now complete the **Recall** activity for **Capitalization** at **MyWritingLab.com**. If you're having a difficult time with a question, open up the video in the lower right-hand corner for some help.

REVIEW PRACTICE 2: Correcting Correct the capitalization errors from Review Practice 1 by rewriting each incorrect sentence.

Practicing Capitalization

Next, complete the **Apply** activity for **Capitalization** at **MyWritingLab.com**. Pay close attention to the directions and only click on what you're asked to.

REVIEW PRACTICE 3: Writing Your Own Write a paragraph about a state, famous person, or course you find particularly interesting.

Practicing Capitalization

For more practice, complete the **Write** activity for **Capitalization** at **MyWritingLab.com**. Make sure to pay close attention to any capitalization errors.

EDITING THE STUDENT WRITING

Return to the student paragraph at the beginning of this chapter, and do the following activities.

Individual Activity   After locating all the capital letters, underline twice the 14 words that are capitalized incorrectly in the paragraph.

Collaborative Activity   With a partner, check to see if you have found the same 14 capitalization errors. Then, working together, use what you have learned in this chapter to correct the errors. Rewrite the paragraph with your corrections.

EDITING YOUR OWN WRITING

Exchange paragraphs from Review Practice 3 with a classmate, and do the following:

1. Circle any capital letters that don't follow the capitalization rules.

2. Write the rule number next to the error for the writer to refer to.

Then return the paper to its writer, and use the information in this chapter to correct any capitalization errors in your own paragraph. Record your errors on the Error Log in Appendix 1.

Abbreviations and Numbers

READING FOR ABBREVIATIONS AND NUMBERS

The following student paragraph contains correct and incorrect abbreviations and numbers. Read the paragraph, and underline the eight abbreviations and numbers.

When I graduated from high school, I thought I was prepared for college. What I discovered was that this was not so. But I think this is as much my fault as it was my school's. I knew 3 years ago I wanted to work for the Central Intelligence Agency or the FBI in Wash, D.C. And even though I did what was required of me in high school, I never learned how to study because my grades were decent enough without having to worry about it. Now I'm at a univ, and I wish I had better study skills to help me manage my time better here. I'll never get my Master of Arts degree at the rate I'm going. People in my high school were aware that many students were barely trying but making decent grades, yet they never really taught us to be prepared for crash-course study skills lessons. Of course, it's difficult for teachers to keep an eye on four thousand students. To have learned these skills would have made my life one hundred % easier.

Like capitalization, abbreviations and numbers are also mechanical features of writing that help us communicate what we want to say. Following the rules that govern their use will make your writing as precise as possible.

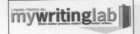

Understanding

To expand your understanding of this topic, go to **MyWritingLab.com**, and view the video on **Abbreviations and Numbers.** Then, return to this chapter, which will go into more detail about abbreviations and give you opportunities to practice them. Finally, you will apply your understanding of abbreviations to your own writing.

ABBREVIATIONS

Abbreviations help us move communication along. They follow a set of rules when used in writing.

1. Abbreviate titles before proper names.

    Mr. Jason Best, **Mrs.** Baker, **Ms.** Susan Elias, **Dr.** George Carlton, **Rev.** Sid Peterson, **Gov.** Arnold Schwarzenegger, **Sgt.** Milton Santos

    Abbreviate religious, governmental, and military titles when used with an entire name. Do not abbreviate them when used only with a last name.

    NOT   We support **Gov.** Wilson.
    Correct: We support **Governor** Wilson.
    Correct: We thought that **Gov.** Lionel Wilson would be supported.

    Professor is not usually abbreviated: **Professor** Angela Perez will be teaching again this year.

2. Abbreviate academic degrees.

    B.S. (Bachelor of Science)
    A.A. (Associate of Arts)
    E.M.T. (Emergency Medical Technician)

3. Use the following abbreviations with numbers.

    A.M. *or* **a.m.** (ante meridiem)
    P.M. *or* **p.m.** (post meridiem)
    B.C. *and* **A.D.**

4. Abbreviate *United States* only when it is used as an adjective.

    NOT   The **U.S.** is a capitalist society.
    Correct: The **United States** is a capitalist society.
    Correct: The **U.S.** president will address the people today.

5. Abbreviate only the names of well-known government agencies, businesses, and educational institutions by using their initials without periods.

CIA (Central Intelligence Agency)
DMV (Department of Motor Vehicles)
AMA (American Medical Association)
USC (University of Southern California)
KCEOC (Kern County Economic Opportunity Corporation)

6. Abbreviate state names when addressing mail or writing out the postal address. Otherwise, spell out the names of states.

Christy moved to 504 Frontier Street, New York, **NY** 10011.
Christy moved to New York, **New York.**

Reviewing Abbreviations

When you write, are you free to abbreviate any words you want?

_____

PRACTICE 1: Identifying and Correcting

A. Put an X next to the sentence if the underlined word is incorrect.

1. _____ <u>Mr.</u> Hewett helped settle the crowd down.

2. _____ My family migrated to the <u>U.S.</u> in the early 1800s.

3. _____ <u>Rev.</u> Thomas performed the marriage ceremony.

4. _____ <u>Washington</u> is a wonderful state for a vacation.

5. _____ Your new address is 121 Bennington Avenue, Iowa City, <u>Iowa</u> 52241.

6. _____ When I woke up, the alarm clock read 3:30 <u>ante meridiem.</u>

7. _____ <u>Prof.</u> Angus will be the guest speaker at the ceremony.

8. _____ This company reports all earnings to avoid an audit by the <u>I.R.S.</u>

9. _____ I plan to get my <u>Associate of Arts</u> degree at a community college before attending a four-year university.

10. _____ The <u>United States</u> Supreme Court will rule today.

B. Correct the errors you identified in Practice 1A by rewriting each incorrect sentence.

PRACTICE 2: Completing Fill in each blank in the following sentences with either an abbreviation or a word that makes sense.

1. _____ Lang will be taking over this class for the rest of the quarter.

2. Karl decided to attend college at _____.

3. In four years, you could have your _____ in English, history, or philosophy.

4. _____ Williams is head of the mission from our church.

5. It is a myth that everything is bigger in the state of _____ than anywhere else.

6. The _____ is a somewhat controversial organization.

7. The U.S. _____ is strong this year.

8. The letter was addressed to 1011 Sunny Boulevard, Los Angeles, _____.

9. We moved from Spain to the _____ more than five years ago.

10. Jason was going over 75 _____ when the police officer pulled him over.

PRACTICE 3: Writing Your Own Write a sentence of your own for each of the following abbreviations.

1. Gov. _____

2. a.m. _____

3. CBS _____

4. CA _____

5. U.S. _____

NUMBERS

Most writers ask the same question about using **numbers:** When should a number be spelled out, and when is it all right to use numerals? The following simple rules will help you make this decision.

1. Spell out numbers from *zero* to *nine*. Use figures for numbers 10 and higher.

   I own **two** houses.

   My sister has **11** dogs and **15** cats living on her ranch.

   Do not mix spelled-out numbers and figures in a sentence if they refer to the same types of items. Use numerals for all numbers in that case.

NOT	I have **three** reports, **11** files, and **two** memorandums to finish today.
Correct:	I have **3** reports, **11** files, and **2** memorandums to finish today.

2. For very large numbers, use a combination of figures and words.

   The company's profits this fiscal year were **$21 million.**

   His cabin in the mountains cost **$1.1 million.**

3. Always spell out a number that begins a sentence. If this becomes awkward, reword the sentence.

   Twenty-five apples fell from the tree.

   A total of 25 apples fell from the tree.

4. Use figures for dates, addresses, zip codes, telephone numbers, identification numbers, and time.

   On July **22, 1998,** we relocated to **2504** Box Drive, Bryan, TX **77805.**

   Scott's old telephone number was **(661) 555-3405.**

   My Social Security number is 101-112-1314.

   The alarm went off at **4:30** a.m.

5. Use figures for fractions, decimals, and percentages.

   Mix ½ cup of butter and **2** tablespoons of vanilla in a saucepan.

   His GPA is **3.8.**

   Only **10** percent of the people polled were in favor of the measure.

   Notice that *percent* is written out and is all one word.

6. Use figures for exact measurements, including amounts of money. Use a dollar sign for amounts over $1.

   The backyard is **20** feet by **22** feet.

   She paid **$10.99** for her shorts—**99 cents** more than I paid.

7. Use figures for the parts of a book.

   Chapter **9**   page **119**   Exercise **7**   questions **2** and **8**

   Notice that *Chapter* and *Exercise* are capitalized.

Reviewing Numbers

What is the general rule for spelling out numbers as opposed to using numerals?

_____

PRACTICE 4: Identifying and Correcting

A. Put an X next to the sentence if the underlined number is in the incorrect form.

1. _____ We caught 3 fish for supper.

2. _____ Clear off an area measuring twenty feet by thirty feet.

3. _____ Approximately 2.9 percent of his sentences were compound-complex.

4. _____ 9 people perished in the flood.

5. _____ Please read Chapter Two for the discussion next week.

6. _____ I was born on December 22, 1978.

7. _____ Thirty people showed up for the surprise party.

8. _____ The address is two, three, nine Woodrow Avenue.

9. _____ Only five percent of the people exposed actually got sick.

10. _____ They paid over two thousand dollars for their new carpet.

B. Correct the errors in Practice 4A by rewriting each incorrect sentence.

PRACTICE 5: Completing Fill in each blank in the following sentences with a number or figure that makes sense.

1. _____ new recruits joined the army today.

2. My telephone number is _____.

3. I have _____ brothers and sisters and _____ cousins.

4. The construction on this building to bring it up to code will cost _____ million.

5. In the future, my GPA will be _____.

6. Over _____ percent of the incoming freshmen are from out of state.

7. I woke up at _____ today.

8. The dorm room measures _____ feet by _____ feet.

9. Did you complete Exercises _____ and _____?

10. This new CD cost _____.

PRACTICE 6: Writing Your Own Write 5 sentences of your own that cover all seven of the number rules.

1. _____

2. _____

3. _____

4. _____

5. _____

CHAPTER REVIEW

Reviewing

Not only does spelling count in the Apply exercises, but correct punctuation does as well.

To review this material before you complete the Review Practices, watch the **Abbreviations and Numbers** video at **MyWritingLab.com** one more time. This time, keep the video open as you complete the rest of the practices in this chapter. For best results, do the **MyWritingLab** exercises online as well as the Chapter Review practices in the book.

REVIEW PRACTICE 1: Identifying Underline the abbreviation and number errors in each of the following sentences. Some sentences contain more than one error.

1. There are only 5 new houses being built with a ten-by-twelve entryway.

2. I couldn't imagine living anywhere but the U.S.

3. Over three hundred thousand claims were handled this month.

4. Sen. Wood earned his Bachelor of Science degree at the same university that my dad attended.

5. 4 contestants claimed to have the winning number.

6. The new telephone number is three, nine, eight, four, four, five, four.

7. Benjamin fled the country to avoid the Internal Revenue Service.

8. The recipe on page one hundred twenty calls for one-eighth cup of chili powder.

9. Ramon rides his motorbike forty miles to work each day.

10. The best Cajun food comes from LA.

Practicing

Now complete the **Recall** activity for **Abbreviations and Numbers** at **MyWritingLab.com.** Remember to read the answers carefully because many of them look similar.

REVIEW PRACTICE 2: Correcting Correct the abbreviation and number errors in Review Practice 1 by rewriting each incorrect sentence.

Practicing

Next, complete the **Apply** activity for **Abbreviations and Numbers** at **MyWritingLab.com.** If you're stuck, go to the lower right-hand corner and open up the video again, or you can click on the hint button.

REVIEW PRACTICE 3: Writing Your Own Write a paragraph explaining what you would change and what you would keep the same about your academic background in preparation for college.

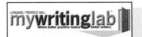

Practicing

For more practice, complete the **Write** activity for **Abbreviations and Numbers** at **MyWritingLab.com.** Make sure to pay close attention to abbreviation and number errors as you revise the paragraph.

EDITING THE STUDENT WRITING

Return to the student paragraph at the beginning of this chapter, and do the following activities.

Individual Activity   After identifying the eight abbreviations and numbers, put a second underline below the seven errors in the paragraph.

Collaborative Activity   Check with a partner to see if you found all the errors in the paragraph. Then, working together, use what you have learned in this chapter to correct these errors. Rewrite the paragraph with your corrections.

EDITING YOUR OWN WRITING

Exchange paragraphs from Review Practice 3 with another student, and do the following:

1. Underline all abbreviations and numbers.

2. Circle any abbreviations and numbers that are not in their correct form.

Then return the paper to its writer, and use the information in this chapter to correct any abbreviation and number errors in your own paragraph. Record your errors on the Error Log in Appendix 1.

UNIT QUIZZES

Here are some exercises that test your understanding of all the material in this unit: Capitalization, Abbreviations, and Numbers.

Unit Quiz 1 Identifying

Underline the capitalization, abbreviation, and number errors in each of the following sentences. Some sentences contain more than one error.

1. "hey, you," the boy shouted, "Throw me the ball."

2. When Kimmie was eight, she moved from the midwest to the south.

3. Rev. Dunn wrote many satirical sermons.

4. You can purchase a duplicate title for your car at the Department of Motor Vehicles.

5. While visiting Alaska, we sampled 9 different types of fish.

6. Since I gave up television for Lent, I decided to occupy myself with J.R.R. tolkien's *lord of the rings* trilogy.

7. I have always wanted to work for the Central Intelligence Agency.

8. Last spring, Barney bought his Mother a family bible for mother's day.

9. The politician spent over two million dollars on her campaign.

10. Around three thirty this afternoon, you will need to add two and a half cups of stewed tomatoes to the soup simmering on the stove.

11. This picture of my Dog ralph is hilarious.

12. Last night, I got ahead in my Sociology class by reading Chapters Twenty through Twenty-Five.

13. The new playground will measure one hundred feet by one hundred and fifty feet.

14. After the dallas cowboys game, grandpa Roland asked for his slippers and his english tea.

15. I am currently pursuing my Master of Arts degree in psychology.

16. He signed the letter, "your secret admirer."

17. 250 people were hired for the job.

18. The U.S. offers many trade opportunities to other nations.

19. In history 401, we are studying the war of 1812.

20. The state of NV was the first to legalize gambling.

Unit Quiz 2 Correcting

Correct the errors in Unit Quiz 1 by rewriting each incorrect sentence.

Unit Quiz 3 Identifying

Underline the capitalization, abbreviation, and number errors in the following paragraph.

In the Spring of 2003, I was out of the U.S. trying to get some much needed relaxation away from phones, work, and television. I was staying in the french countryside at uncle Mike's small villa. Unfortunately, I was unavoidably detained and could not mail my taxes in on time. Once I realized the problem, I drove North to the nearest town to call the Internal Revenue Service. But it was a holiday, and the post office was closed. I had to make the same trip the following day at 4:00 post meridiem. My french 307 class was apparently a waste of time because the lady on the other side of the counter, Missus Ideaux, who was wearing clothes from the nineteen-fifties, and I could not communicate. I followed the advice in Chapter one of my psychology text (*getting along in life*) when I counted to 3, took a deep breath, and tried once again to explain that I needed a phone. I finally reached someone at the IRS who told me that I owed over one million dollars. "1 million dollars!" I screamed. "Are you sure you have the right Social Security number?" I asked. "It's four, five, eight, two, one, seven, nine, three, eight." "Ah, yes," returned the voice on the other end. "Here is your record. You're a student getting an Associate of Arts degree. I'll make a note in your file, but you'll have to pay a three percent penalty fee and fill out some paperwork when you return to the United States." I said that was fine and hung up the phone. But before I could leave, Missus Ideaux asked for ten dollars for the phone call, which I gladly paid. Boy, was I glad to get back to my home in OR, where there is a phone in every room.

Unit Test 4 Correcting

Correct the errors in Unit Quiz 3 by rewriting the paragraph.

UNIT WRITING ASSIGNMENTS

1. Most of us know people who go about life in dramatically different ways, such as parents disciplining their children or friends handling relationships. Compare two people you know who have different approaches to the same task. Explain how each goes about the task and why.

2. You have been asked to write a short article for your local newspaper about the best fast-food restaurants in town. Which restaurants are they, and why are they the best? You might want to consider the atmosphere, the service, the price, and the food.

3. When we are children, play is an important part of our day. But as we get older, responsibilities soon take up most of our spare time, and our "play" changes. Now that you are an adult, what do you do for playtime? How has this changed from childhood, if at all? Why? What were the benefits of play as a child? As an adult?

Choosing the Right Word

Choosing the right word is like choosing the right snack to satisfy your appetite. If you don't select the food you are craving, your hunger does not go away. In like manner, if you do not choose the right words to say what is on your mind, your readers will not be satisfied and will not understand your message.

Choosing the right word depends on your message, your purpose, and your audience. It also involves recognizing misused, nonstandard, and misspelled words. We deal with the following topics in Unit 8:

Standard and Nonstandard English

The following student paragraph contains standard and nonstandard English. Read the paragraph, and underline the 17 instances of nonstandard English or slang.

Unfortunately, I now only speak one language. I say "now" because I use to speak Spanish until I was three, but I have lost all memory of the language. In a way, however, the statement that I only speak one language is false, because I kinda speak two languages—a form of English I use with adults and a form of English I use with my friends. And believe me, one is definitely different than the other. When I speak to my friends, I go, "Dude, I went to a phat party last night. Carly was chillin' with a hottie named Dan. Man, she was a dog." Of course, I ain't gonna say this to my grandma. I would say, "I went to a great party last night. A girl named Carly spent time with a good-looking guy named Dan, but she wasn't very attractive." Irregardless of the situation, it be real disrespectful, in some ways, to talk to adults in slang being that they don't understand, but it's also not proper. But I wouldn't talk in proper English all the time to my friends because we'd eventually never communicate. I'd be left behind somewheres in the conversation. So I do believe that language is important, and I do believe I speak two languages. They just both happen to be English.

Choosing the right words for what you want to say is an important part of effective communication. This chapter will help you find the right words and phrases for the audience you are trying to reach.

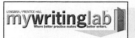 ## Understanding Standard and Nonstandard English

To expand your understanding of this topic, go to **MyWritingLab.com,** and view the video on **Standard and Nonstandard English.** Then, return to this chapter, which will go into more detail about levels of English and give you opportunities to practice them. Finally, you will apply your understanding of standard and nonstandard English to your own writing.

Student Comment:
"I like **MyWritingLab** with *Mosaics* because I learn best by doing and hearing. In this way, I obtain and remember information a lot better."

STANDARD AND NONSTANDARD ENGLISH

Most of the English language falls into one of two categories—either *standard* or *nonstandard*. **Standard English** is the language of college, business, and the media. It is used by reporters on television, by newspapers, in most magazines, and on Web sites created by schools, government agencies, businesses, and organizations. Standard English is always grammatically correct and free of slang.

Nonstandard English does not follow all the rules of grammar and often includes slang. Nonstandard English is not necessarily wrong, but it is more appropriate in some settings (with friends and family) than others. It is not appropriate in college or business writing. To understand the difference between standard and nonstandard English, compare the following paragraphs.

Nonstandard English

I just got a new pad and went to the grocery store to stock the fridge with some grub. Since I only had 40 bucks, I knew I oughta play it cool and just stick to the list: milk, eggs, cereal, soda, bread, peanut butter, and jelly. Irregardless of my good intentions, I sorta lost it in the frozen food section. By the time I got outta there, I must of picked up one of each kind of food—pizza, corn dogs, burritos, pies, and apple turnovers. And somewheres underneath all that stuff were the bread and the eggs. I was real embarrassed when I go to check out cuz I didn't have enough money and I had to put some of the stuff back. At that moment, I realized I was a long ways from home.

Standard English

I just got a new apartment and went to the grocery store to stock the refrigerator with some food. Since I had only $40, I knew I had to stick to my list: milk, eggs, cereal, soda, bread, peanut butter, and jelly. Regardless of my good intentions, I made too many choices in the frozen food section. By the time I got out of that aisle, I must have picked up one of each kind of food—pizza, corn dogs, burritos, pies, and apple turnovers. Somewhere underneath all that food were the bread and the eggs. I was really embarrassed when I went to check out because I didn't have enough money and I had to put some of the items back. At that moment, I realized I was a long way from home.

In the rest of this chapter, you will learn how to recognize and correct ungrammatical English and how to avoid slang in your writing.

Reviewing Standard and Nonstandard English

Where do you hear standard English in your daily life?

_____

What is nonstandard English?

_____

Give two examples of nonstandard English.

_____   _____

NONSTANDARD ENGLISH

Nonstandard English is ungrammatical. It does not follow the rules of standard English required in college writing. The academic and business worlds expect you to be able to recognize and avoid nonstandard English. This is not always easy because some nonstandard terms are used so often in speech that many people think they are acceptable in writing. The following list might help you choose the correct words in your own writing.

ain't

NOT	He **ain't** leaving until tomorrow.
CORRECT	He **isn't** leaving until tomorrow.

anywheres

NOT	Susie can't find her glasses **anywheres**.
CORRECT	Susie can't find her glasses **anywhere**.

be

NOT	I **be** really good at art.
CORRECT	I **am** really good at art.

(For additional help with *be*, see Chapter 7, "Verb Tense.")

being as, being that

NOT	Jamal will not be joining the study group tonight, **being as** his car broke down.
CORRECT	Jamal will not be joining the study group tonight, **because** his car broke down.

coulda/could of, shoulda/should of

NOT	She **could of** made the sauce with cream instead of milk.
CORRECT	She **could have** made the sauce with cream instead of milk.

different than

NOT	This sandwich is no **different than** that sandwich.
CORRECT	This sandwich is no **different from** that sandwich.

drug

NOT	I **drug** the rug across the floor.
CORRECT	I **dragged** the rug across the floor.

enthused

NOT	Jim was **enthused** about his GPA.
CORRECT	Jim was **enthusiastic** about his GPA.

everywheres

NOT	My little sister follows me **everywheres**.
CORRECT	My little sister follows me **everywhere**.

goes

NOT	Then Nancy **goes,** I'm taking the bus.
CORRECT	Then Nancy **says,** "I'm taking the bus."
CORRECT	Then Nancy **said** that she was taking the bus.

hisself

NOT	Evan made **hisself** sick on peanut butter.
CORRECT	Evan made **himself** sick on peanut butter.

in regards to

NOT	I got your memo **in regards to** the changes.
CORRECT	I got your memo **in regard to** the changes.

irregardless

NOT   **Irregardless** of your healthy lifestyle, you still need to lower your cholesterol.

CORRECT **Regardless** of your healthy lifestyle, you still need to lower your cholesterol.

kinda/kind of, sorta/sort of

NOT   This tastes **kinda** sweet, **sorta** like cherries.

CORRECT This tastes **rather** sweet, **much** like cherries.

most

NOT   **Most** everyone is going.

CORRECT **Almost** everyone is going.

must of

NOT   I **must of** left my backpack in the park.

CORRECT I **must have** left my backpack in the park.

off of

NOT   Michael skated **off of** the ramp.

CORRECT Michael skated **off** the ramp.

oughta

NOT   Sometimes you **oughta** say please and thank you.

CORRECT Sometimes you **ought to** say please and thank you.

real

NOT   She was **real** glad to see us.

CORRECT She was **really** glad to see us.

somewheres

NOT   His books are **somewheres** in that dirty room.

CORRECT His books are **somewhere** in that dirty room.

suppose to

NOT   They were **suppose to** meet us here.

CORRECT They were **supposed to** meet us here.

theirselves

NOT   The children hid **theirselves** throughout the house.

CORRECT The children hid **themselves** throughout the house.

use to

NOT	I **use to** work while listening to music.
CORRECT	I **used to** work while listening to music.

ways

NOT	We are lost and a long **ways** from home.
CORRECT	We are lost and a long **way** from home.

where . . . at

NOT	**Where** is the remote control **at?**
CORRECT	**Where** is the remote control?

Reviewing Nonstandard English

What is one reason using nonstandard English in written work is easy to do?

_____

Give four examples of nonstandard English; then correct them.

_____   _____

_____   _____

_____   _____

_____   _____

PRACTICE 1: Identifying and Correcting

A. Underline the ungrammatical words or phrases in each of the following sentences.

1. Mom was real mad when I left the milk out.

2. They made theirselves a promise to spend more time together.

3. We have wandered a long ways from the path.

4. Your wallet could be anywheres in the backyard.

5. The plant have only two blooms.

6. Irregardless of how much time you spent on your paper, it still needs revision.

7. Somewheres out there is the perfect car for me.

8. Where is the phone at?

9. You could of taken the freeway instead of the back roads.

10. The receptionist must of written down the wrong phone number.

B. Correct the standard English errors in Practice 1A by rewriting each incorrect sentence.

PRACTICE 2: Completing Fill in each blank in the following sentences with standard English using the list at the beginning of this chapter.

1. The girl's behavior is very different _____ the boy's.

2. With his teeth, the puppy _____ his toy across the living room.

3. Then William _____ that he would do the job.

4. They received the letter in _____ to the board meeting.

5. He fell _____ the sidewalk and sprained his ankle.

6. My little sister didn't realize that she wasn't _____ to eat the mud pies.

7. The cake _____ ready yet.

8. I _____ very fond of seafood.

9. That smells _____ bad, _____ like garbage.

10. The dog has buried my keys _____ in the backyard.

PRACTICE 3: Writing Your Own Write a sentence of your own for each of the following words and phrases.

1. should have _____

2. in regard to _____

3. ought to _____

4. must have _____

5. dragged _____

SLANG

Another example of nonstandard English is **slang,** popular words and expressions that come and go, much like the latest fashions. For example, in the 1950s, someone might call his or her special someone *my steady*. In the 1970s, you might hear a boyfriend or girlfriend described as *foxy*, and in the 1980s, *stud* was a popular slang term for males. Today, your significant other might be your *man* or *homegirl*.

These expressions are slang because they are part of the spoken language that changes from generation to generation and from place to place. As you might suspect, slang communicates to a limited audience who share common interests and experiences. Some slang words, such as *cool* and *neat*, have become part of our language, but most slang is temporary. What's in today may be out tomorrow, so the best advice is to avoid slang in your writing.

Reviewing Slang

What is slang?

_____

Give two examples of slang terms that were popular but aren't any longer.

_____   _____

Give two examples of slang terms that you and your friends use today.

_____   _____

PRACTICE 4: Identifying and Correcting

A. Underline the slang words or phrases in the following sentences.

1. These CDs are da bomb.

2. Everyone knows Jason is a player.

3. She's down with the plan.

4. You have to get your groove on at the party.

5. Me and my dawgs are going to the show.

6. Keep it real.

7. I got your back.

8. I dig your new ride.

9. Give it to me straight.

10. What's crackin'?

B. Correct the slang errors in Practice 4A by rewriting each sentence.

PRACTICE 5: Completing Translate each of the following slang expressions into standard English.

1. go with the flow _____

2. as if _____

3. get outta here _____

4. pump it up _____

5. fries your brain _____

6. homies _____

7. five-finger discount _____

8. keep it on the DL _____

9. give him props _____

10. give big ups _____

PRACTICE 6: Writing Your Own List five slang words or expressions, and use them in sentences of your own.

1. _____

2. _____

3. _____

4. _____

5. _____

CHAPTER REVIEW

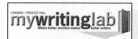 **Reviewing Standard and Nonstandard English**

This topic is especially helpful to students whose first language is not English since it includes instruction on clichés, slang, and nonstandard English.

To review this material before you complete the Review Practices, watch the **Standard and Nonstandard English** video at **MyWritingLab.com** one more time. This time, keep the video open as you complete the rest of the practices in this chapter. For best results, do the **MyWritingLab** exercises online as well as the Chapter Review practices in the book.

REVIEW PRACTICE 1: Identifying Underline any nonstandard English and slang in the following sentences.

1. We're really rolling now.

2. She must of forgotten that we were going to have lunch today.

3. The monkeys at the zoo acted real hyper when they saw us.

4. That's jacked.

5. You don't understand, man.

6. Somewheres out there is the girl for you.

7. These are my peeps.

8. Where's the sugar at?

9. Say what?

10. This ain't the best idea.

 **Practicing Standard and Nonstandard English**

Now complete the **Recall** activity for **Standard and Nonstandard English** at **MyWritingLab.com.** Remember to read the answers carefully because many of them look similar.

REVIEW PRACTICE 2: Correcting Correct the nonstandard English and slang in Review Practice 1 by rewriting each sentence.

 **Practicing Standard and Nonstandard English**

Next, complete the **Apply** activity for **Standard and Nonstandard English** at **MyWritingLab.com.** If you're stuck, you can go to the lower right-hand corner and open up the video again, or you can click on the hint button.

REVIEW PRACTICE 3: Writing Your Own Write a paragraph on a community problem. What are the details? What is the problem? What solution do you propose?

 **Practicing Standard and Nonstandard English**

For more practice, complete the **Write** activity for **Standard and Nonstandard English** at **MyWritingLab.com.** Make sure to pay close attention to the use of standard and nonstandard English as you revise the paragraph.

EDITING THE STUDENT WRITING

Return to the student paragraph at the beginning of this chapter, and do the following activities.

Individual Activity   Did you find the 17 nonstandard and slang expressions in the selection?

Collaborative Activity   With a partner, compare the errors you both found in the paragraph. Then, working together, use what you have learned in this chapter to correct these errors. Rewrite the paragraph with your corrections. Don't change any words in quotations.

EDITING YOUR OWN WRITING

Exchange paragraphs from Review Practice 3 with a classmate, and do the following:

1. Underline any ungrammatical language.

2. Circle any slang.

Then return the paper to its writer, and use the information in this chapter to correct any nonstandard or slang expressions in your own paragraph. Record your errors on the Error Log in Appendix 1.

Easily Confused Words

READING FOR EASILY CONFUSED WORDS

The following paragraph contains correct and incorrect usage of easily confused words. Read the paragraph, and underline the 21 words that may be confused.

The technological age has arrived, and people who don't learn what technology has too offer will soon be left behind. The biggest way technology has effected everyone's is threw the Internet. The Internet has brought the world to every person's doorstep. If a person in Hong Kong wants to find out the whether at Catalina Island, he or she could go find the information on the Web. If a person wants to buy a house, chose a college, or even find a husband or wife, than a click of the mouse is all it takes. Pretty soon, all people will know were their kids are, can check on the house from work, or can turn on there heat in the car from inside the house. Its really quiet amazing. People who are frightened bad by technology need to learn to understand it because it's hear too stay. And soon it will be a part of every aspect of our lives.

Some words are easily confused. They may look alike, sound alike, or have similar meanings, but they all play different roles in the English language.

Understanding Easily Confused Words

To find out more about this topic, go to **MyWritingLab.com,** and view the video called **Easily Confused Words.** Then, return to this chapter, which will go into more detail about word choice and give you opportunities to practice it. Finally, you will apply your understanding of word choice to your own writing.

EASILY CONFUSED WORDS, PART I

a/an: Use *a* before words that begin with a consonant. Use *an* before words that begin with a vowel (*a, e, i, o, u*).

> **a** letter, **a** cookie, **a** fax
>
> **an** answer, **an** eon, **an** animal

accept/except: *Accept* means "receive." *Except* means "other than."

> I **accept** your apology.
>
> I found all the marbles **except** the black one.

advice/advise: *Advice* means "helpful information." *Advise* means "give advice or help."

> His **advice** is sound.
>
> He **advises** me on financial matters.

affect/effect: *Affect* (verb) means "influence." *Effect* means "bring about" (verb) or "a result" (noun).

> This decision will **affect** the final outcome.
>
> The new law will **effect** important reforms.
>
> The **effect** was caused by changes in weather patterns.

already/all ready: *Already* means "in the past." *All ready* means "completely prepared."

> Sarah has **already** received her shots.
>
> They were **all ready** to leave when the car broke down.

among/between: Use *among* when referring to three or more people or things. Use *between* when referring to only two people or things.

> The doctors discussed the diagnoses **among** themselves.
>
> She lives **between** those two houses.

bad/badly: *Bad* means "not good." *Badly* means "not well."

That rash on your arm looks **bad.**

He performed **badly** on his driving test.

He felt **bad** about the ruined sweater.

beside/besides: *Beside* means "next to." *Besides* means "in addition (to)."

I sat **beside** a large oak tree.

Besides smelling bad, the sneakers were covered with mud.

brake/break: *Brake* means "stop" or "the parts that stop a moving vehicle." *Break* means "shatter, come apart" or "a rest between work periods."

She put her foot on the **brake** as soon as she saw the dog.

I saw the vase **break** when it hit the floor.

I like my job, but I look forward to my lunch **break.**

breath/breathe: *Breath* means "air." *Breathe* means "taking in air."

Take a deep **breath** and count to 10.

If you **breathe** too quickly, you could hyperventilate.

choose/chose: *Choose* means "select." *Chose* is the past tense of *choose.*

You **choose** the restaurant.

He **chose** to go with his friends.

Reviewing Words That Are Easily Confused, Part I

Do you understand the differences in the sets of words in Part I of the list?

_____

Have you ever confused any of these words? If so, which ones?

_____

PRACTICE 1: Identifying and Correcting

A. Put an X next to the sentence if the underlined word is incorrect.

1. _____ <u>Among</u> the two of us, we can cook a great meal.

2. _____ I <u>already</u> gave to that charity.

3. _____ The <u>affect</u> was subtle.

4. _____ Sometimes the air we <u>breath</u> is not healthy.

5. _____ The dog food is <u>beside</u> the dog's bowl.

6. _____ She was so nervous that she sang <u>bad</u>.

7. _____ You should listen to your mother's <u>advice</u>.

8. _____ Please don't <u>brake</u> my heart.

9. _____ <u>A</u> ant just crawled up my pant leg.

10. _____ Yesterday you <u>choose</u> the red one, but now you want the blue one.

B. Correct the word errors in Practice 1A by rewriting each incorrect sentence.

PRACTICE 2: Completing Fill in each blank in the following sentences with a correct word that makes sense from Part I of the list of easily confused words.

1. Anna did _____ your invitation to lunch.

2. _____ dictionary is a good reference tool.

3. The loan officer has _____ left for the day.

4. _____ those two students sits my mother.

5. Why did Martin _____ to move to Ohio!

6. My accountant gives me good _____ regarding stocks.

7. That dog has turned _____, so don't pet him.

8. His yawning _____ the rest of us.

9. Mints will sweeten your _____.

10. _____ for balancing the checkbook and going to the grocery store, I don't have any plans for today.

PRACTICE 3: Writing Your Own Use each of the following pairs of words correctly in a sentence of your own.

1. choose/chose _____

2. breath/breathe _____

3. bad/badly _____

    4. beside/besides _____

    5. advice/advise _____

EASILY CONFUSED WORDS, PART II

coarse/course: *Coarse* refers to something that is rough. *Course* refers to a class, a process, or a part of a meal.

> This cornmeal is **coarse.**
>
> My future **course** is clear.
>
> The meals in this restaurant have many **courses.**

desert/dessert: *Desert* refers to dry, sandy land or means "abandon." *Dessert* refers to the last course of a meal.

> The **desert** has many strange animals.
>
> He **deserted** the army.
>
> The strawberry shortcake **dessert** was the best I ever had.

Hint: You can remember that *dessert* has two *s*'s if you think of *strawberry shortcake*.

does/dose: *Does* means "performs." *Dose* refers to a specific portion of medicine.

> He **does** the yard work, and I do the housework.
>
> A large **dose** of cranberry juice will clear up that infection.

fewer/less: *Fewer* refers to things that can be counted. *Less* refers to things that cannot be counted.

> Now that I am older, I have **fewer** really good friends.
>
> I have **less** time for play now that I am in college.

good/well: *Good* modifies nouns. *Well* modifies verbs, adjectives, and adverbs. *Well* also refers to a state of health.

> Jane is a **good** instructor.
>
> She did **well** on the state exam.
>
> My goldfish is swimming sideways; he must not feel **well.**

hear/here: *Hear* refers to the act of listening. *Here* means "in this place."

> The child didn't speak until he was 4 because he couldn't **hear** well.
>
> **Here** are the Easter eggs from last year—yuck!

it's/its: *It's* is the contraction for *it is* or *it has*. *Its* is a possessive pronoun.

It's the best solution.

The water buffalo flicked **its** tail at the flies.

knew/new: *Knew* is the past tense of *know*. *New* means "recent."

He **knew** about the **new** television set.

know/no: *Know* means "understand." *No* means "not any" or is the opposite of *yes*.

No, I didn't **know** that you had lived overseas.

lay/lie: *Lay* means "set down." (Its principal parts are *lay, laid, laid*.) *Lie* means "recline." (Its principal parts are *lie, lay, lain*.)

She **lays** material out before cutting it.

He **laid** down the heavy firewood.

My mom **lies** on the couch to watch her soaps.

They **lay** under the stars.

(For additional help with *lie* and *lay*, see Chapter 10, "Regular and Irregular Verbs.")

loose/lose: *Loose* means "free" or "unattached." *Lose* means "misplace" or "not win."

Ben knocked his tooth **loose.**

I'm fighting hard not to **lose** this game.

passed/past: *Passed* is the past tense of *pass*. *Past* refers to an earlier time or means "beyond."

Brittany **passed** us in her car, but she didn't see us.

We can learn about ourselves from the **past.**

Suddenly, a bird swooped **past** me.

Reviewing Words That Are Easily Confused, Part II

Do you understand the differences in the sets of words in Part II of the list?

_____

Have you ever confused any of these words? If so, which ones?

_____

PRACTICE 4: Identifying and Correcting

A. Put an X next to the sentence if the underlined word is incorrect.

1. _____ Be careful because your pants are really <u>lose</u> and might fall off.

2. _____ <u>Its</u> time for you to make your entrance.

3. _____ The <u>dessert</u> can be a beautiful place if you know where to look.

4. _____ The <u>knew</u> uniforms are still in their boxes.

5. _____ The <u>does</u> she took was too strong.

6. _____ Her language was <u>coarse</u> and uncalled for.

7. _____ Speak louder since I can't <u>hear</u> you.

8. _____ There is <u>fewer</u> water in your cup than in mine.

9. _____ Ben's presentation in class went <u>good</u>.

10. _____ Since Tabitha just moved here, she doesn't <u>know</u> anybody.

B. Correct the word errors in Practice 4A by rewriting each incorrect sentence.

PRACTICE 5: Completing Fill in each blank in the following sentences with a correct word that makes sense from Part II of the list of easily confused words.

1. The maximum _____ is 2 tablespoons.

2. They are taking a _____ together.

3. We could _____ the class laughing all the way down the hall.

4. _____ wines go well with fruit and cheeses.

5. The _____ time you spend editing, the more mistakes you're likely to make.

6. Candice doesn't want to go to the party because she doesn't _____ how to dance.

7. Leroy always _____ a blanket down for the baby.

8. _____ perhaps the funniest thing I've seen all day.

9. This cap is too _____ for this jar.

10. I love to _____ in the sun and read a good novel.

PRACTICE 6: Writing Your Own Use each of the following pairs of words in a sentence of your own.

1. know/no _____

2. passed/past _____

3. fewer/less _____

4. good/well _____

5. it's/its _____

EASILY CONFUSED WORDS, PART III

principal/principle: *Principal* means "main, most important," "a school official," or "a sum of money." A *principle* is a rule. (Think of *principle* and *rule*—both end in *-le*.)

> My **principal** reason for attending college is to get a good job.
>
> Our **principal** was strict but kind.
>
> Sometimes it's hard to live by one's **principles.**

quiet/quite: *Quiet* means "without noise." *Quite* means "very."

> We have to be **quiet** so we don't disturb the others.
>
> I found the book **quite** fascinating.

raise/rise: *Raise* means "increase" or "lift up." *Rise* means "get up from a sitting or reclining position."

> Do not **raise** the lid on the stew; it's simmering.
>
> As the temperature **rises,** so does everyone's temper.

set/sit: *Set* means "put down." *Sit* means "take a seated position."

> You can **set** those anywhere you like.
>
> Bailey can **sit** and watch TV for hours.

(For additional help with *sit* and *set*, see Chapter 10, "Regular and Irregular Verbs.")

than/then: *Than* is used in making comparisons. *Then* means "next."

> I am older **than** my aunt.
>
> Allen smelled the daisies, and **then** he sneezed.

their/there/they're: *Their* is possessive. *There* indicates location. *They're* is the contraction of *they are.*

> **Their** coats are in the entryway.
> We went **there** first.
> **They're** all happy for you.

threw/through: *Threw*, the past tense of *throw*, means "tossed." *Through* means "finished" or "passing from one point to another."

> The quarterback **threw** the ball.
> Are you **through** with studying?
> The mouse ate **through** the cupboard wall.

to/too/two: *To* means "toward" or is used with a verb. *Too* means "also" or "very." *Two* is a number.

> Diane always goes **to** the reunion **to** catch up on the gossip.
> The coffee was **too** strong.
> We have **two** children.

wear/were/where: *Wear* means "have on one's body." *Were* is the past tense of *be*. *Where* refers to a place.

> You can **wear** casual clothes but not shorts or jeans.
> **Where were** those candles?

weather/whether: *Weather* refers to outdoor conditions. *Whether* expresses possibility.

> **Whether** you believe it or not, you can trust the **weather** to stay sunny.

who's/whose: *Who's* is a contraction of *who is* or *who has*. *Whose* is a possessive pronoun.

> **Who's** going to determine **whose** display is the best?

your/you're: *Your* means "belonging to you." *You're* is the contraction of *you are.*

> **Your** actions will tell others if **you're** a loyal friend or not.

Reviewing Words That Are Easily Confused, Part III

Do you understand the differences in the sets of words in Part III of this list?

_____

Have you ever confused any of these words? If so, which ones?

_____

PRACTICE 7: Identifying and Correcting

A. Put an X next to the sentence if the underlined word is incorrect.

1. _____ I was <u>quiet</u> upset when I got to the station and couldn't find my train.

2. _____ Few of us are able to live strictly by our <u>principals</u>.

3. _____ That was <u>to</u> much information to digest at once.

4. _____ Allow the dough to <u>raise</u> for one hour.

5. _____ <u>Their</u> asking a lot of questions that I cannot answer.

6. _____ <u>Whose</u> giving Sheila a ride to the airport?

7. _____ Make sure the children <u>wear</u> their coats.

8. _____ The snake slithered underneath the bed, and <u>than</u> I ran screaming out the door.

9. _____ <u>Your</u> hair is snagged on a tree branch.

10. _____ I'm never going to make it <u>threw</u> this traffic on time.

B. Correct the word errors in Practice 7A by rewriting each incorrect sentence.

PRACTICE 8: Completing
Fill in each blank in the following sentences with a correct word that makes sense from Part III of the list of easily confused words.

1. _____ shoes are untied.

2. You must be _____ in this hospital ward.

3. If you _____ those books on that table, they are going to fall.

4. The students have prepared _____ orals in advance.

5. _____ watch is this?

6. _____ the hood of the car very carefully.

7. Benjamin always eats what she cooks for him, _____ he likes it or not.

8. There are _____ letters in the mailbox for Palmer.

9. The reporter listened intently, and _____ she took out her pen and notebook.

10. What was Gregory thinking when he _____ that rock at the beehive?

PRACTICE 9: Writing Your Own Use each of the following sets of words in a sentence of your own.

1. quiet/quite _____

2. their/there/they're _____

3. threw/through _____

4. than/then _____

5. raise/rise _____

CHAPTER REVIEW

Remember that spelling is calculated in your score in the Apply exercises.

Reviewing Easily Confused Words

To review this material before you complete the Review Practices, watch the **Easily Confused Words** video at **MyWritingLab.com** one more time. This time, keep the video open as you complete the rest of the practices in this chapter. For best results, do the **MyWritingLab** exercises online as well as the Chapter Review practices in the book.

REVIEW PRACTICE 1: Identifying Underline the words used incorrectly in each of the following sentences.

1. It is to hot in here to pay attention.

2. Jacinta choose to tour Europe for a year before attending college.

3. My mom cannot except the fact that I am an adult.

4. It looks like its going to be another long day.

5. Peter will be getting a rise next month.

6. The kids new they could talk us into agreeing.

7. What will be the affect if we mix these two chemicals?

8. You must be absolutely quite, or else we are going to get caught.

9. Whose going to call the fire department?

10. Owen dropped his desert down the front of his shirt.

 **Practicing Easily Confused Words**

Now complete the **Recall** activity for **Easily Confused Words** at **MyWritingLab.com.** If you're having a difficult time with a question, open up the video in the lower right-hand corner for some help.

REVIEW PRACTICE 2: Correcting Correct the words used incorrectly in Review Practice 1 by rewriting each incorrect sentence.

 **Practicing Easily Confused Words**

Next, complete the **Apply** activity for **Easily Confused Words** at **MyWritingLab.com.** Pay close attention to the directions and click only on what you're asked to.

REVIEW PRACTICE 3: Writing Your Own Write a paragraph about a recent decision you had to make, explaining what the problem was and why you made the decision you did. Try to use some of the easily confused words from this chapter.

 **Practicing Easily Confused Words**

For more practice, complete the **Write** activity for **Easily Confused Words** at **MyWritingLab.com.** Pay close attention to the use of any easily confused words.

EDITING THE STUDENT WRITING

Return to the student paragraph at the beginning of this chapter, and do the following activities.

Individual Activity   After you identify the 21 words that are easily confused, add a second underline below the 13 words used incorrectly in the paragraph.

Collaborative Activity   Team up with a partner, and check to see if you have found the same 13 errors. Then, working together, use what you have learned in this chapter to correct these errors. Rewrite the paragraph with your corrections.

EDITING YOUR OWN WRITING

Exchange paragraphs from Review Practice 3 with a classmate, and do the following:

1. Circle any words used incorrectly.

2. Write the correct form of the word above the error.

Then return the paper to its writer, and use the information in this chapter to correct any confused words in your own paragraph. Record your errors on the Error Log in Appendix 1.

Spelling

Following is a paragraph written by a student. Read the paragraph, and underline the 11 misspelled words. Do not count words that are misspelled intentionally.

I'm an average speller. Just like everybody else, I usualy confuse "effect" with "affect" or "accept" with "except," have difficulty remembering if an ending should be "-ant" or "-ent," or have difficulty remembering those weird words (like "weird") that don't follow the "i before e except after c" rule. But for the most part, I tend to get by with my spelling—until I'm asked to spell in public. When someone asks me to spell a word, even the simplest word like "of," my brain freezes. (I once spelled "of" ove!) But this problem becomes most embarassing when I'm called to the chalkboard to write. My heart starts to pound. My palms get sweaty. I try counting to 10. I try taking deep breathes. I have even tryed to quickly go over the spelling rules in my mind as I approach the board. But it doesn't matter weather I no the spelling rules or not. My spelling knowledge vanishes somewhere between my desk and the board. Now, I consider myself a fairly intelligent person. My achievments are many. Yet I always look foolish in these moments, no matter how brilliant my ideas. But happyly—or perhaps sadly—I have learned that I'm not alone. Many others suffer from the same phobia. My nieghbor calls it "fear of public spelling." Perhaps we should join forces and start a support group, because until someone figures out a way to rewire or recondition the brain, I don't know how to overcome this problem. I know what spelling errors say about me: "You're lazy," "You can't write," "Your anxiety got the better of you." Even though these statements aren't true, I still hate the messages. But I'm no quiter. I'll continue that long walk to the front of the class whenever I hear, "Sabrina, could you come to the board and . . ."

If you think back over your education, you will realize that teachers believe spelling is important. There is a good reason they feel this way: Spelling errors send negative messages. Misspellings seem to leap out at readers, creating serious doubts about the writer's abilities in general. Because you will not always have access to spell-checkers—and because spell-checkers do not catch all spelling errors—improving your spelling skills is important.

Student Comment:
"Everything's repeated in **MyWritingLab,** and I need that 'cause my memory is short."

Understanding Spelling

To improve your understanding of this topic, go to **MyWritingLab.com,** and view the video on **Spelling.** Then, return to this chapter, which will go into more detail about spelling rules and give you opportunities to practice them. Finally, you will apply your understanding of these rules to your own writing.

SPELLING HINTS

The spelling rules in this chapter will help you become a better speller. But first, here are some practical hints that will also help you improve your spelling.

1. Start a personal spelling list of your own. Use the list of commonly misspelled words on pages 337–341 as your starting point.
2. Study the lists of easily confused words in Chapter 24.
3. Avoid all nonstandard expressions (see Chapter 23).
4. Use a dictionary when you run across words you don't know.
5. Run the spell-check program if you are writing on a computer. Keep in mind, however, that spell-check cannot tell if you have incorrectly used one word in place of another (such as *to, too,* or *two*).

> **Reviewing Hints for Becoming a Better Speller**
>
> *Name two things you can do immediately to become a better speller.*
>
> _____
>
> *Why can't you depend on a spell-check program to find every misspelled word?*
>
> _____

PRACTICE 1: Identifying and Correcting

A. Underline the misspelled words in each of the following sentences. Refer to the spelling list in this chapter as necessary.

1. There are undoubtably more people living in the United States now than ever before.

2. Ouch! I bit my tonge.

3. The cotton candy made my tooth ach.

4. Because Alyssa is allergic to wasps, we called the ambulence immediately.

5. Many soldeirs who fought in the war died from disease.

6. The original masterpiece was lost.

7. Beverly was jealus of Evan's new Mustang convertible.

8. If you drink and drive, you will lose your lisence.

9. The Louisiana bayous are a dangcrous placc for the inexperienced.

10. Even though Febrary is a cold month, it is filled with warmth on Valentine's Day. (February)

B. Correct the spelling errors in Practice 1A by rewriting each incorrect sentence.

PRACTICE 2: Completing Fill in each blank in each of the following sentences with hints that help with spelling.

1. Use a _____ to look up words you don't know.

2. You can always use the _____ on your computer, but you should remember that it cannot correct confused words, only misspelled words.

3. Start a _____ to help you remember words you commonly misspell.

4. Study the lists of _____ in Chapter _____.

5. Try to avoid all _____ English.

PRACTICE 3: Writing Your Own

A. Choose the correctly spelled word in each pair, and write a sentence of your own for it. Refer to the spelling list in this chapter as necessary. Sentences will vary.

1. banana/bannana

   _____

2. volunter/volunteer

   _____

3. desision/decision

   _____

4. oposit/opposite

   _____

5. recommend/recomend

   _____

B. Write five words that you often misspell, and use each in a sentence of your own. Underline these words.

1. _____

2. _____

3. _____

4. _____

5. _____

SPELLING RULES

Four basic spelling rules can help you avoid many misspellings. It pays to spend a little time learning them now.

1. **Words that end in -e:** When adding a suffix beginning with a vowel (*a, e, i, o, u*), drop the final *-e*.

ache + -ing	=	aching
challenge + -ed	=	challenged
value + -able	=	valuable

   When adding a suffix beginning with a consonant, keep the final *-e*.

aware + -ness	=	awareness
improve + -ment	=	improvement
leisure + -ly	=	leisurely

2. **Words with *ie* and *ei*:** Put *i* before *e* except after *c* or when sounded like *ay* as in *neighbor* and *weigh*.

c + *ei*	(no *c*) + *ie*	Exceptions
receive	anxiety	science
receipt	niece	foreign
deceive	convenience	leisure
neighbor	fiery	height

3. **Words that end in -y:** When adding a suffix to a word that ends in a consonant plus *-y*, change the *y* to *i*.

silly + er	=	sillier
cry + ed	=	cried
shy + er	=	shier

4. **Words that double the final consonant:** When adding a suffix starting with a vowel to a one-syllable word, double the final consonant.

big + -est	=	biggest
quit + -er	=	quitter
bet + -ing	=	betting

   With words of more than one syllable, double the final consonant if (1) the final syllable is stressed and (2) the word ends in a single vowel plus a single consonant.

beget + ing	=	begetting
permit + ing	=	permitting
uncap + ed	=	uncapped

The word *travel* has more than one syllable. Should you double the final consonant? No, you should not, because the stress is on the *first* syllable (*tra´ vel*). The word ends in a vowel and a consonant, but that is not enough. Both parts of the rule must be met.

Reviewing Four Basic Spelling Rules

What is the rule for adding a suffix to words ending in -e (such as date + -ing)?

_____

_____

_____

What is the rule for spelling ie and ei words (such as receive, neighbor, *and* friend)?

_____

_____

_____

When do you change -y to -i before a suffix (such as sunny + -est)?

_____

_____

_____

When do you double the final consonant of a word before adding a suffix (such as cut, begin, *or* travel + -ing)?

_____

_____

_____

PRACTICE 4: Identifying and Correcting

A. Underline the misspelled words in each of the following sentences.

1. Upon reaching the door, I hesitated when I heard the strange noise.

2. My father accompanyed me on my first date.

3. The lieutenant ordered us to peel potatoes.

4. Before they agreed to buy the house, they asked that the cieling be repaired.

5. The mountain climbers faced many difficulties.

6. The oceanographer is mapping out the ocean floor.

7. The elaboratness of the room was overwhelming.

8. Now that Veronica has been accepted at Yale, she is happyer.

9. Let the dog smell your hand before you begin peting him.

10. I had problems unwraping the plastic from the CD.

B. Correct the spelling errors in Practice 4A by rewriting each incorrect sentence.

PRACTICE 5: Completing Complete each of the following spelling rules.

1. When adding a suffix beginning with a vowel to a word that ends in -e, _____.

2. Put -i before -e except after _____ or when sounded like _____ as in _____.

3. When adding a suffix starting with a _____ to a one-syllable word, _____ the final consonant.

4. When adding a suffix to a word the ends in a consonant plus y, change the _____ to _____.

5. With words of more than one syllable, _____ the final consonant if (1) the final syllable is _____ and (2) the word ends in a single _____ plus a single _____.

PRACTICE 6: Writing Your Own

A. Choose the correctly spelled word in each pair, and write a sentence of your own for it. Refer to the spelling list in this chapter as necessary.

1. believing/believeing

   _____

2. audience/audience

   _____

3. tried/treid

_____

4. seting/setting

_____

5. weigh/wiegh

_____

B. Write five words that you often misspell, and use them each in a sentence of your own.

1. _____

2. _____

3. _____

4. _____

5. _____

MOST COMMONLY MISSPELLED WORDS

Use the following list of commonly misspelled words to check your spelling when you write.

abbreviate	address	appropriate
absence	adequate	approximate
accelerate	advertisement	architect
accessible	afraid	arithmetic
accidentally	aggravate	artificial
accommodate	aisle	assassin
accompany	although	athletic
accomplish	aluminum	attach
accumulate	amateur	audience
accurate	ambulance	authority
ache	ancient	autumn
achievement	anonymous	auxiliary
acknowledgment	anxiety	avenue
acre	anxious	awkward
actual	appreciate	baggage

balloon	certificate	courteous
banana	challenge	cozy
bankrupt	champion	criticize
banquet	character	curiosity
beautiful	chief	curious
beggar	children	curriculum
beginning	chimney	cylinder
behavior	coffee	dairy
benefited	collar	dangerous
bicycle	college	dealt
biscuit	column	deceive
bought	commit	decision
boundary	committee	definition
brilliant	communicate	delicious
brought	community	descend
buoyant	comparison	describe
bureau	competent	description
burglar	competition	deteriorate
business	complexion	determine
cabbage	conceive	development
cafeteria	concession	dictionary
calendar	concrete	difficulty
campaign	condemn	diploma
canoe	conference	disappear
canyon	congratulate	disastrous
captain	conscience	discipline
career	consensus	disease
carriage	continuous	dissatisfied
cashier	convenience	divisional
catastrophe	cooperate	dormitory
caterpillar	corporation	economy
ceiling	correspond	efficiency
cemetery	cough	eighth
census	counterfeit	elaborate
certain	courageous	electricity

eligible	forfeit	immortal
embarrass	fortunate	impossible
emphasize	forty	incidentally
employee	freight	incredible
encourage	friend	independence
enormous	fundamental	indispensable
enough	gauge	individual
enthusiastic	genius	inferior
envelope	genuine	infinite
environment	geography	influential
equipment	gnaw	initial
equivalent	government	initiation
especially	graduation	innocence
essential	grammar	installation
establish	grief	intelligence
exaggerate	grocery	interfere
excellent	gruesome	interrupt
exceptionally	guarantee	invitation
excessive	guess	irrelevant
exhaust	guidance	irrigate
exhilarating	handkerchief	issue
existence	handsome	jealous
explanation	haphazard	jewelry
extinct	happiness	journalism
extraordinary	harass	judgment
familiar	height	kindergarten
famous	hesitate	knife
fascinate	hoping	knowledge
fashion	humorous	knuckles
fatigue	hygiene	laboratory
faucet	hymn	laborious
February	icicle	language
fiery	illustrate	laugh
financial	imaginary	laundry
foreign	immediately	league

legible	monotonous	persuade
legislature	mortgage	physician
leisure	mysterious	pitcher
length	necessary	pneumonia
library	neighborhood	politician
license	niece	possess
lieutenant	nineteen	prairie
lightning	ninety	precede
likable	noticeable	precious
liquid	nuisance	preferred
listen	obedience	prejudice
literature	obstacle	previous
machinery	occasion	privilege
magazine	occurred	procedure
magnificent	official	proceed
majority	omission	pronounce
manufacture	omitted	psychology
marriage	opportunity	publicly
material	opponent	questionnaire
mathematics	opposite	quotient
maximum	original	realize
mayor	outrageous	receipt
meant	pamphlet	recipe
medicine	paragraph	recommend
message	parallel	reign
mileage	parentheses	religious
miniature	partial	representative
minimum	particular	reservoir
minute	pastime	responsibility
mirror	patience	restaurant
miscellaneous	peculiar	rhyme
mischievous	permanent	rhythm
miserable	persistent	salary
misspell	personnel	satisfactory

scarcity	surprise	valuable
scenery	syllable	various
schedule	symptom	vegetable
science	technique	vehicle
scissors	temperature	vicinity
secretary	temporary	villain
seize	terrible	visible
separate	theater	volunteer
significant	thief	weather
similar	thorough	Wednesday
skiing	tobacco	weigh
soldier	tomorrow	weird
souvenir	tongue	whose
sovereign	tournament	width
spaghetti	tragedy	worst
squirrel	truly	wreckage
statue	unanimous	writing
stomach	undoubtedly	yacht
strength	unique	yearn
subtle	university	yield
succeed	usable	zealous
success	usually	zoology
sufficient	vacuum	

Reviewing Commonly Misspelled Words

Why is spelling important in your writing?

_____

Start a personal spelling log of your most commonly misspelled words.

_____   _____   _____

_____   _____   _____

_____   _____   _____

_____   _____   _____

PRACTICE 7: Identifying and Correcting

A. Underline the misspelled words in each of the following sentences.

1. Driving is a privelege, not a right.

2. Special scisors are made for left-handed people.

3. Though the twins are not identical, they are similar-looking.

4. My knowledge is lacking in this area.

5. Dean recommends the Chinese restaurant on Blossom Avenue.

6. The doctor had to reschedle my appointment.

7. Real sucess isn't gained through money.

8. I accidentally ran over my bicycle with my car.

9. Yes, Martha is familar with linear math.

10. Alisha's stomache hurts.

B. Correct the spelling errors in Practice 7A by rewriting each incorrect sentence.

PRACTICE 8: Completing Fill in each blank in the following sentences with a word that makes sense from the spelling list in this chapter.

1. The _____ was caught at the airport.

2. The _____ stars look like diamonds.

3. My _____ is bothering me.

4. His new house is rather _____.

5. The show *Who's Line Is It, Anyway?* always makes people _____.

6. I filled out the _____ even though it was very long.

7. Take a picture of that _____.

8. Cassidy met her future husband in _____.

9. Don't worry; your mismatched socks aren't _____.

10. For a doctor, your writing is quite _____.

PRACTICE 9: Writing Your Own

A. Choose the correctly spelled word in each pair, and write a sentence for each one. Refer to the spelling list in this chapter as necessary.

1. appreciate/apprecate

_____

2. laundry/landry

_____

3. mariage/marriage

_____

4. excellent/excelent

_____

5. oposite/opposite

_____

B. Choose five words from the spelling list in this chapter that you often mis-spell, and use each in a sentence of your own. Underline these words.

1. _____

2. _____

3. _____

4. _____

5. _____

CHAPTER REVIEW

The **Spelling** video focuses primarily on suffix rules. So keeping *Mosaics* open to the other spelling rules while you work in **MyWritingLab** will be beneficial.

Reviewing Spelling

To review this material before you complete the Review Practices, watch the **Spelling** video at **MyWritingLab.com** one more time. This time, keep the video open as you complete the rest of the practices in this chapter. For best results, do the **MyWritingLab** exercises online as well as the Chapter Review practices in the book.

REVIEW PRACTICE 1: Identifying Underline the misspelled words in each of the following sentences. Refer to the spelling list in this chapter as necessary.

1. There is a terrable flu going around.

2. My kitten's curosity landed him in the toilet.

3. Who says chocolate isn't an essintial food group?

4. That smells delicous.

5. The show will air tommorrow.

6. Catapillars may be cute, but they wreak havoc in my garden.

7. I may be an amature baseball player today, but I plan to play professional ball in a few years.

8. The bread nife is in the third drawer.

9. She has all the symtoms of someone in love.

10. That perfume is just sutle enough.

Practicing Spelling

Now complete the **Recall** activity for **Spelling** at **MyWritingLab.com**. Remember to read the answers carefully because many of them look similar.

REVIEW PRACTICE 2: Correcting Correct the spelling errors in Review Practice 1 by rewriting each sentence.

Practicing Spelling

Next, complete the **Apply** activity for **Spelling** at **MyWritingLab.com**. If you're stuck, you can go to the lower right-hand corner and open up the video again, or you can click on the hint button.

REVIEW PRACTICE 3: Writing Your Own Write a paragraph explaining what you think spelling errors say about a person.

Practicing Spelling

For more practice, complete the **Write** activity for **Spelling** at **MyWritingLab.com.** Pay close attention to the spelling of each word as you revise the paragraph.

EDITING THE STUDENT WRITING

Return to the student paragraph at the beginning of this chapter, and do the following activities.

Individual Activity Did you find the 11 spelling errors in the paragraph?

Collaborative Activity Team up with a partner to see if you found the same errors. Then, working together, use what you have learned in this chapter to correct these errors. Rewrite the paragraph with your corrections.

EDITING YOUR OWN WRITING

Exchange paragraphs from Review Practice 3 with a classmate, and do the following:

1. Underline any misspelled words.

Then return the paper to its writer, and use the information in this chapter to correct any misspellings in your own paragraph. Record your errors on the Spelling Log in Appendix 2.

UNIT QUIZZES

Here are some exercises that test your understanding of all the material in this unit: Standard/Nonstandard English, Easily Confused Words, and Spelling.

Unit Quiz 1 Identifying

Underline the words used incorrectly in each of the following sentences.

1. Everywheres I look, I see smiling, happy faces.

2. Today, Carol will chose a major.

3. These physics problems are frying my brain.

4. Surely Tom exaggerrated the story.

5. He ain't going to like your plan.

6. Its been a very long and exhausting day.

7. It's been a eon since I've seen you.

8. Being that it is so hot outside, let's go ice-skating.

9. Carlie has a vast awarness of herself.

10. The package was unwraped when Scott bought it.

11. We're going to rock the house tonight.

12. The fake blood and gore looked grusome in the moonlight.

13. That is to much information for me to process at the moment.

14. Mac was very enthused about winning the door prize.

15. Jan's new boyfriend is a hottie.

16. The little girl cryed for her lost kitten.

17. In the dessert, the temperature drops dramatically at night.

18. With her fair skin, she oughta wear sunscreen.

19. Don't touch that pan—it's firy hot.

20. Everyone can fit in the truck accept the dog.

Unit Quiz 2 Correcting

Correct the errors in Unit Quiz 1 by rewriting each incorrect sentence.

Unit Quiz 3 Identifying

Underline the words used incorrectly in the following paragraph.

Being that my brother got a chemistry set for his birthday one summer, I figureed it was time to take up science. Scott, my brother, played with the set a couple of times, and than he forgot about it, so I five-fingered it. I remember waiting for the weekend to come, for the nights when everyone was asleep and no one could censure me and the experiments could begin. The secrecy of those nighttime rituals made me feel sorta like an ancient goddess performing sacred rites while the world slept and the moon shone threw my window. I was quiet lax when it came to the rules—who needed instructions? Needless to say, there were a few accidents in my labortory. But the joy of discovery and the thrill of creating were addictive. I never set out to actually create anything specific. The lure was the adventure itself. Now I get the same thrill from journal writing. I can mix new ingredients, feelings, and ideas and see were they take me. I can explore any crazy notion that comes into my head because they're is no censorship: I am the audeince. Occasionally, my writing becomes flammable, and if I survive the flame, I'm left with illumination. Sometimes I wait for the night to come, and when everybody is asleep and the moonlight from the window casts a glow on my computer, I write. Again I am a goddess, only this time the chemical reaction happens within my heart, my mind, my psyche, my soul. My new discovery is myself. I be the creator and the created.

Unit Quiz 4 Correcting

Correct the errors in Unit Quiz 3 by rewriting the paragraph.

UNIT WRITING ASSIGNMENTS

1. Are you aware of listening to the languages spoken around you? Are the languages different? What can you tell from people's tone of voice even when you don't speak the language? Think of a time you went to an amusement park or a public place where you heard many different

languages. What were your observations? What were the differences among the speakers? What were the similarities?

2. You have just taken the Pepsi challenge. What brand of soda—Pepsi or Coca-Cola—did you choose? Prepare an article for your college newspaper comparing the two sodas and arguing why one soda is better than the other.

3. At one time or another, we have all been let down by our computer's spell-check, and yet many of us continue to use only the computer's tools to find words used incorrectly in our papers. Why is relying only on spell-check not a good editing habit? Can spell-check catch every word used incorrectly? Why or why not? Should an author use other methods along with the computer? If so, what methods?

Appendix 1: Error Log

List any grammar, punctuation, and mechanics errors you make in your writing on the following chart. Then, to the right of this label, record (1) the actual error from your writing, (2) the rule for correcting this error, and (3) your correction.

Error		
	Example	I went to the new seafood restaurant and I ordered the shrimp.
Comma	**Rule**	Always use a comma before *and, but, for, nor, or, so,* and *yet* when joining two independent clauses.
	Correction	I went to the new seafood restaurant, and I ordered the shrimp.
Error	Example	
	Rule	
	Correction	
Error	Example	
	Rule	
	Correction	
Error	Example	
	Rule	
	Correction	
Error	Example	
	Rule	
	Correction	
Error	Example	
	Rule	
	Correction	
Error	Example	
	Rule	
	Correction	
Error	Example	
	Rule	
	Correction	

Appendix 2: Spelling Log

On this chart, record any words you misspell, and write the correct spelling in the space next to the misspelled word. In the right column, write a note to yourself to help you remember the correct spelling. (See the first line for an example.) Refer to this chart as often as necessary to avoid misspelling the same words again.

Misspelled Word	Correct Spelling	Definition/Notes
there	their	there = place; their = pronoun; they're = "they are"

INDEX